Special Affects

Special Affects

Cinema, Animation and the Translation of Consumer Culture

Eric S. Jenkins

EDINBURGH
University Press

© Eric S. Jenkins, 2014

Edinburgh University Press Ltd
The Tun – Holyrood Road
12(2f) Jackson's Entry
Edinburgh EH8 8PJ
www.euppublishing.com

Typeset in Monotype Ehrhardt by
Servis Filmsetting Ltd, Stockport, Cheshire,
and printed and bound in Great Britain by
CPI Group (UK) Ltd, Croydon CR0 4YY

A CIP record for this book is available from the British Library

ISBN 978 0 7486 9547 8 (hardback)
ISBN 978 0 7486 9548 5 (webready PDF)

The right of Eric S. Jenkins to be identified as Author of this work has been asserted in
accordance with the Copyright, Designs and Patents Act 1988, and the Copyright and
Related Rights Regulations 2003 (SI No. 2498).

Contents

Acknowledgements

Any project of this magnitude is never completed alone. Finishing *Special Affects* depended on so many people, whether they spent time reading the manuscript and commenting, or simply provided emotional and physical support. The project began as my dissertation at the University of Georgia and evolved greatly over the past five years with the help and support of many. I would thus like to thank the following people: my PhD advisor Kevin DeLuca, Davi Thornton, Josue Cisneros, Peter Zhang, Nicole Starkoleski, Allison Dunn, Mary Buehler, Chip Miller, Kevin Marinelli, Barbara Biesecker, Ronald Greene, Jamie Landau and my dissertation committee, including Celeste Condit, Roger Stahl, James Hamilton and Thomas Lessl. My apologies for not listing specifically the innumerable others whose conversations also aided my thinking. I know the world is a better place because of these people. Much love and my eternal gratitude.

Portions of Chapters 5 and 6 were previously published in 'Seeing Life in Disney's Mutual-Affection Images', *Quarterly Review of Film and Video*. Vol. 30. 2013. Pp. 421–34. Taylor & Francis Ltd, http://www.tandf.co.uk/journals.

List of Illustrations

CHAPTER 1

Introduction

A consumer boom seems to accompany the emergence of every new communication medium, as the alterations of perceptual capacities transform into habits that subsequently become the source of economic value. Consider how cinema accompanied the growth of the Roaring Twenties, just as television helped fuel the postwar expansion of the 1950s and 1960s. More recently, the Internet spurred the dot-com bubble of the 1990s, one whose short life still resonates today in the proliferation of mobile, networked media.[1] Indeed, digital media remains one of the few briskly expanding and continuously evolving areas of the consumer economy, even in the midst of a seemingly never-ending recession and its repeated belt-tightening. Furthermore, commentators frequently connect media to consumerist ideology, especially that old standby ideograph, the American Dream.[2] Cinema, television and the Internet alike are penned and pinned as prime representatives of either the continued reality of, or the misleading illusion called, the American Dream.

Today, the air seems tinged with a pessimism about consumerism that contrasts with the bountiful optimism of earlier periods. More and more people feel that the American Dream lies in ruins, with some recognising how consumerism pulls the levers behind environmental extirpation and societal oppression. Yet nevertheless, media consumption grows apace, perhaps because our proliferating, always-at-hand media devices mask this stark reality or, at the least, provide us with some measure of escapist joy when the aching sadness innervated by the avalanche of bad news proves too much to bear. We should ask, then, how did media and consumerism become such accomplices? How can we explain this linkage between media and consumerism? When did their association begin and why do the two seem so inextricably interconnected today?

Scholars, those whose modes of long, reflective thinking potentially render them the best equipped for making sense of these connections, have recently offered two concepts for understanding our ongoing sociocultural changes – affect and the cyborg (or, alternatively, the posthuman or virtual body). Affect is all the rage, with critical scholars proclaiming an affective turn that shifts the focus from the emphasis on language, ideology and subjectivity to one centred on experience, on embodiment, on the intensities of sensation and the flows of energy that leap from body to body and that provide the texture and tone of lived experience.[3] Affect has already been hinted at in the preceding paragraph, with its emphasis on feelings, senses, something in the air, aches, joys and sorrow. Prior to the affective turn, scholars tended to dismiss or despise such affects, seeing them as a cover for the pernicious ideological content.[4] For instance, Theodor Adorno critiques consumer culture, through an extension of Marx's notion of commodity fetishism, for proffering 'false' or 'pseudo' pleasures because these pleasures revolve more around exchange than use value.[5] Today, instead, scholars stress the import of affect, especially since consumerism seems dependent upon generating pleasurable affections. In Nigel Thrift's words, '[E]conomies must be engaging: they must generate or scoop up affects and then aggregate and amplify them in order to produce value, and that must involve producing various mechanisms of fascination.'[6]

One might wonder if this was not always the case, but, for many scholars, the affective turn is perfectly suited for analysing the future in which we live, especially the contemporary sociocultural changes some describe as the rise of an 'affect economy' and 'control society'.[7] In an affect economy, corporations seek to direct and capture affective value.[8] The affect economy relies upon extracting surplus value from the consumer's sensual and perceptual labour, turning affect into manipulable and renewable resources. By modulating flows of affect, the culture industries produce economic value by generating affections that entice consumers to attend repeatedly to commodities.[9] Today, many surging sectors of the economy – including health care, flight attendants, the service industry, tourism, entertainment and sex working – all sell affective experiences. This surge represents a mutation of capitalism that Gilles Deleuze describes as the shift from disciplinary society to control society, away from concentration in factories and mass production into a focus on the experience of consumption. As Deleuze remarks, what capitalism today 'seeks to sell is services, and what it seeks to buy, activities. It's a capitalism no longer directed toward production but toward products, that is, towards sales or markets.'[10]

Digital media play a central role in these sociocultural changes and the accompanying affective turn, as computer-based media have become a primary and growing sector of the consumer economy. Consider the plethora of websites, blogs, games, apps, social media, gambling and pornography that all trade in, funnel or direct affect. These contributions to the affect economy stem from the ways that digital media alter bodily experience. By constituting new ways for bodies to interface and interact with media, digital technologies create greater access to and diversity in the types of affective experiences available. As bodies become differently distributed and engaged across digital networks and platforms, different modes for generating affect emerge. Paying attention to affect necessarily requires analysis of bodies, and given the proliferating ways that digital media interface with bodies, scholars have developed a number of terms for conceptualising our newly distributed bodies, including the dividual, desiring-machines, assemblages, cyborgs, virtual bodies and the posthuman.[11]

Affect and the cyborg, then, seem well equipped as concepts for looking forward, for making sense of the vast sociocultural changes of the present and the near future. Yet, as Marshall McLuhan demonstrates in his analysis of the transition from literate to electronic media, the emergence of new media often exposes sociocultural grounds previously invisible or taken for granted by revealing hidden aspects of the contemporary media ecology.[12] Thus these concepts also afford a look back in the hopes that analysing older media anew, through fresh perspectives, may inform us not only about the past from which we came but also about the future into which we are headed. *Special Affects* does precisely this – retelling a major moment in media history through the concepts of affect and virtual bodies, which we will call *modes*. I approach the emergence of Disney's full-length feature animation in the 1930s and early 1940s as a translation of media interface, a translation that constitutes a new mode designed to generate affect primarily through image modulation. Despite Disney's emergence before the digital computer, we can see their efforts as enabling new modes, whose engagement innervates special affects. Such an approach understands Disney's images as interfaces, its viewers as cyborgs, and the coming-together of these images and viewers as modes, a concept with profound connections to digital media since most devices today allow users the option to switch between modes that modify the processing of inputs and outputs.

Many historians of communication media note how cultures often greet new media with feelings of astonishment, wonder, amazement, marvel, awe, shock and disbelief.[13] Such affections frequently raise metaphysical questions about the status of reality, life, space, time, community, meaning and identity. Indeed, such responses may be one of the 'messages' of media, in McLuhan's sense, messages that send people scrambling for metaphors to encapsulate their affective experiences. I call these affections *special* because, whereas new media may access older affections, such as the cinema's pleasures of a well-woven narrative also potentially evoked by literature or of captivating acting found in theatre, they also frequently innervate new affections, ones only made possible by the new distribution of bodies (the new modes) that emerge.

The book begins by tracing the historical occurrence of these special affections, what we will call *sparks*, employing them as a launching point for retelling the emergence of full-length feature Disney animation. Specifically, *Special Affects* outlines the astonishment of seeing lifelike movement accompanying early cinema, the marvel of seeing the transforming graphic line accompanying early animation, the fantastic feeling from seeing things with human eyes that seem to exist only in the imagination accompanying classical cinema, and, most centrally, the wonder of sensing animated characters as alive that accompanies Disney's first full-length feature movies. I argue that Disney's 'wondrous' affect explains the widespread popularity and vehement criticism of Disney alike, as various players struggle to 'make sense' of their felt perceptual, cognitive and sensory alterations. In other words, these new modes and special affections explain why certain practices of consumer culture emerge and how they are greeted with ideological rhetoric.

The analysis presented here reveals, as its major conclusion, a unique contribution of Disney animation to consumer culture, with two secondary implications. First, Disney's contribution to consumer culture illustrates why there exists a fundamental connection between our two accomplices – media and consumerism – well beyond the simple fact that media devices and products constitute a burgeoning commodity market themselves. Instead, media enable new modes and affections that make perceivable new (virtual) consumer bodies, whose existence becomes translated into the practice of the culture industries as well as into ideological rhetoric coloured simultaneously by a great attraction and great distress. Such a viewpoint, then, precludes conflating the impact of various media on consumer culture – as has been done in much critical scholarship on the topic – calling attention instead to the differences in embodied, affective experience that result in different rhetorical and economic translations as well. Second, the analysis in *Special Affects* offers insights not only into media history but also into the present digital remediation of cinema and animation alike, uncovering, by tracing the translations from medium to medium, what is repeated and what is different about the newly emergent image-interfaces, modes and affections.[14]

Although the bulk of this book focuses on media history, this insight into digital cinema and animation represents another major contribution of the work, one that closely parallels Lev Manovich's *The Language of New Media*. Manovich uses live-action cinema as a contrasting example to unearth what is different about computer-based media. As he states, 'The theory and history of cinema serves as the key conceptual lens through which I look at new media.'[15] Especially in the final chapter, *Special Affects* similarly employs the history and theory of animation as a lens for understanding how digital remediation is altering animation and cinema, and, concomitantly, contemporary consumer culture. Manovich concludes that there is a strong affinity between digital cinema and animation, since both entail constructing images frame by frame and both contain such capacities as modularity, variability and manipulability. He concludes (emphasis original), '*Digital cinema is a particular case of animation that uses live-action footage as one of its many elements . . . Born from animation, cinema pushed animation to its periphery, only in the end to become a particular case of animation.*'[16]

In fact, animation offers an ideal case for comparison to digital remediation today and for the retelling of media history through the lenses of affect and modes for a few reasons. First, as Manovich notes, 'The opposition between the styles of animation and cinema defined the culture of the moving image in the twentieth century,'[17] yet the vast majority of scholarship has focused on live-action cinema, either treating animation as a subgenre, ignoring it completely, or downplaying the differences. Even Manovich, who concludes on such a strong note about the importance of animation today, primarily employs live-action cinema as his contrasting example in the search for what truly makes digital media 'new'.[18] Today, such relegation of animation deserves correction because 'animation as an art, an approach, an aesthetic and an application', as Paul Wells states, 'is the omnipresent pictorial form of the modern era.'[19] From games to smart phones to web sites to desktops, on computer, phone, television and cinema screens, in our homes and on the side of our buildings, in digital and physical spaces, animation has become the dominant language of digital media and Disney remains a prominent player. Wells, along with a handful of other scholars, has thankfully begun to correct for the lack of attention to animation as a distinct medium, yet even their work rarely approaches animation through the theoretical perspective of affect and modes; nor does much of this work seek to outline the unique contributions of animation to consumer culture.[20]

Second, animation provides an ideal subject to retell a part of media history because of animation's deep connections to affect. Animation has a dual meaning of life and motion similar to affect, since affect describes both a body's relations of movement and rest, and a felt vitality, a life force or intensity. Animation and affect alike entail the sensations of movement and life. In addition, many commentators have noted the affective intensity of animation; animation often innervated sparks of affection, especially Disney's movies during the 1930s and 1940s. Viewers reportedly cried, laughed, gasped, stirred, cowered and exhaled in response to *Snow White*, *Pinocchio*, *Fantasia* and *Dumbo*. Although such sparks are often noted, especially at the time of their first experience, most scholarship tends to overlook them, perhaps because affects pass so quickly, or because they seem trivial, or because the sociocultural events that unfold after such affects are generated provides much more concrete, prevalent and bountiful material for analysis. Given animation's import in relation to digital media and affect alike, allow me to develop further the concepts of affect and modes through which this book proceeds, also detailing some of the historical methodology before previewing the chapters that follow.

On Affect

Let us begin by further elaborating the affective turn, before outlining the concept of modes, which represents the major theoretical contribution of *Special Affects*. The affective turn draws upon many different traditions, including phenomenology, psychoanalysis, cognitive psychology, queer theory and critical emotion studies.[21] As developed here, affect is conceived in a way that is closest to Deleuze, who reads Baruch Spinoza to describe affect as a pre-conscious intensity, resulting from a body's capacity to affect and be affected.[22] Deleuze and Spinoza distinguish between affect and affections.[23] Affections designate the impingement of one body on another, the being affected by an encounter – such as the sun affecting my skin or the fear evoked by seeing a bear while hiking. Affects, on the other hand, are the passages from one state to another, the continuous variations in duration, the increasing or diminishing of one's power to act. Affects are not the warmth or the fear but the passage from one state to another, from the joy of the warm sun to the fear of the bear. Affect names the flows of sensed intensity, the changes or transitions experienced in encounter. Affection names the intensities themselves, such as interest, excitement, joy, shock, surprise, shame, distress, anger and terror.[24]

In order to emphasise the priority of affect, most scholars describe affect as pre-subjective, pre-conscious and pre-personal, coming before the intentional acts of perception and cognition. This means pre-cognitive in the temporal sense; the affect and affection come before the conscious processing of them. Recent developments in neuroscience have shown an approximately half-second delay between the reception of a stimulus and the consciousness of that reception, seeming to confirm that affect both precedes and works through different channels from the brain's conscious processing.[25] As such, most scholars distinguish affect from emotion. Emotion is a conscious response to affect, its personalisation and signification. In movies, we see affect in the moment of shock registered in close-up split seconds before the person gathers herself, interprets and responds. Emotion is one possible response of the conscious subject; the surprised (affect) person might become scared (emotion). Brian Massumi, one of the best interpreters of Deleuze, puts it thus: 'An emotion is a subjective content, the sociolinguistic fixing of the quality of an experience . . . It is intensity owned and recognised.'[26] By pre-subjective, scholars mean that affection only occurs in the encounter and affect only results from the transitions from encounter to encounter. That is, affect reverberates or transfers between bodies, as our capacities to affect and be affected communicate reciprocally, forming a force field not possessed by any*one* but only generated in the partaking, in participating.[27] Affect is thus not the property or possession of the subject but arises in between, in the intervals connecting bodies, connecting subjects and objects, often forming a shared flesh or texture to experience, such as the sorrow we might feel in the 'air' that I depicted in the opening paragraph.

Affect continues persistently throughout lived experience, often as the vague feeling of simply being alive. Yet in particularly sharp moments, affection is felt like a shock, a prick, or what Roland Barthes calls a *punctum* in the context of photography.[28] *Special Affects* traces some of these moments, these *sparks*, developing a general concept applicable across mediated experience. Sparks represent a metaphor of energy, with denotations that include the discharge of electricity, something that activates or stimulates, and a trace of life and vitality. Sparks thus should remind the reader of the two definitions of animation – life and movement – and should be seen, once again, as an affection that results from an encounter and is thus not the property of the subject. In fact, in these sparks or moments of intense affect, there is often a de-subjectifying effect, a sense that one has become lost or displaced, a feeling Barthes describes as going through a black hole – attracting and distressing at the same time, sucked into a void and pulled apart. These affections may be experienced by the person but the affect itself, the transition or variation, seems to come from elsewhere, our selves seem split or unmoored, confronted with some energy or force we cannot explain and which may even contradict what we know or believe, such as when a critical scholar finds themselves affected with wonder by a Disney movie despite detesting Disney's contributions to, say, capitalist hegemony and white, male, heterosexual supremacy.

Sparks occur when the outside becomes infolded inside, splitting affective, neural and perceptual pathways differently from how it occurs in accustomed and habituated modes of perception. As Gregory Seigworth explains,

> To be affected (as the baby is by a song) or to affect (as the singer is to baby) . . . is to participate in this act of folding, outside-in and inside-out . . . In part, affect – from the standpoint of its infolding – is deposited as the condensation (of force acting upon a body) of a contextual excess that arises during the folding of relations between bodies.[29]

Infolding is something always occurring in experience, but in particularly sharp moments we can envision that the infolding creates creases that rub receptive surfaces together, producing friction and the brief, intense release of energy – a spark.

Similar to Barthes's depiction of the *punctum* in his discussion of photography, a spark pierces, wounds, pricks.[30] For Barthes, the punctum stems from sensitive points in a photograph that break the *studium*, with the *studium* designating the mode of looking at a photo's represented subject matter.[31] The concept of sparks helps to extend and generalise the *punctum* beyond the medium of photography. We can similarly understand sparks as a rupture or punctuation in the typical mode of perceiving, which innervates a sense of wonder, astonishment, shock, marvel or awe and often leads perceivers to ponder metaphysical questions. The *spark* represents the rupturing of perceptual mode, the experience of being transported from one mode to another modal spatio-temporality. In one of Barthes's *punctums*, for instance, a detail shoots out and takes us on an adventure; in another, the photo evokes consideration of human mortality. In my account, all sparks transport the person from the space–time of one perceptual mode to another realm. Of course, the person does not actually move in real space–time but the spark innervates an affective transition, like the 'temporal hallucination' Barthes describes.[32] For instance, the classical Hollywood mode folds the subject between the viewer and the spectator position (the camera position), enabling the viewer to witness the events *as* the spectator, *as if* they were present, without the risk of inserting their actual bodies into the scene. Disney's mode – what we will call *animistic mimesis* – allows subjects to fold themselves between affections sensing the characters as alive and their conscious knowledge that they are not, producing the tickle or tingling sensation many describe as wondrous.

I extend the concept of the spark to film and animation, and generalise it to cultures at large. In other words, sparks can be idiosyncratic but cultures also widely experience such sharp affections as amazement, astonishment, the fantastic or wonder with the emergence of new media and their modes of perception, precisely because affects are pre-subjective. Media history reveals that many people experience similar sparks with the emergence of new media, even if the experience varies and some individuals do not ever feel the affection. Indeed, many people felt Barthes's *punctum* of death for over a century before Barthes senses it in some photographs.[33] Furthermore, developing a general concept of the spark that applies across media meshes with contemporary media theory that recognises the mutual influence and interaction of media, particularly in the age of the massive convergence of media corporations and the widespread remediation of all media into the digital format.[34] Animation exemplifies why the strict boundaries between media are evaporating. Animation is a distinctly hybrid medium, employing drawing, photography, film and sound recording while borrowing from literature, movies, painting, theatre and dance. Just as photography did for Barthes, multi-media such as animation can also spark intense affections.

Affect's ephemerality, variations and punctuated nature make it difficult to describe and analyse. Thus I will give the affective sparks under examination here somewhat arbitrary labels for clarification purposes. We will focus on such sparks as marvel, astonishment, the fantastic and wonder, terms that were frequently used to describe the intense sensations of watching early animation, early live-action film, classical Hollywood movies and classical Disney features. The labels are somewhat arbitrary because these terms are nearly synonymous; in fact, each designates a variety of what Spinoza describes as wonder, which he defines as the perception of 'something special that we have never seen before . . . in so far as it alone engages the mind'.[35] These sparks are admixtures of the affections Sylvan Tomkins outlines, such as excitement, joy, surprise, sadness and shock, innervated through particular perceptual or receptive experiences, *so the descriptions of the experience should take precedence over the labels employed.*[36] Although the labels are somewhat arbitrary, I draw the terminology from the historical record, pulling the terms astonishment, amazement, the fantastic and wonder from the published responses to the reception of new media and their modes. These terms are attempts to 'make sense' of – to translate into personalised emotion – the affective experience and it is those affections of wonder and astonishment, amazement and the fantastic that, according to my thesis, contain the germ of the great attraction and distress that followed in the wake of cinema and Disney's emergence alike.

In sum, I contend that Disney's (and classical Hollywood's) major, unique contributions to consumer culture stem from the various ways these special affects have been mined and translated. Illustrating this history of mining and translating affect demonstrates a fundamental connection between media and consumerism, a major conclusion of *Special Affects*. As media enable new foldings, those foldings produce affections that can be a renewable source of value in an affect economy. As such, media and their modes can be envisioned as sparkplugs that enable the firing of the engines of (consumer) desire.

Undeniably, Disney has played a significant role as a component and promoter of modern consumerism, selling gobs of commodities, revered by a plethora of devoted consumers, and embodying the precepts of most contemporary culture industries. Released in 1937, Disney's first full-length animated feature, *Snow White*, broke all the box-office records of the time, sparking a major merchandising boom, and its video sales and rereleases have accrued billions in profit.[37] By 1966, over 240 million people had seen a Disney movie and another 80 million had purchased Disney merchandise.[38] Disneyland and Disneyworld attract millions of yearly visitors and revived the struggling American amusement park, reshaping it into the modern theme park whose principles now inform much of the consumer landscape, from shopping malls to mega-churches, from Times Square in New York City to the Strip in Las Vegas.[39] Today, the Disney Company is widely considered the progenitor and pinnacle of the post-Fordist, synergistic corporation. Disney controls the largest radio network in the United States, serving 3,400 stations, three music studios, the television companies ABC and ESPN, five motion picture studios, Hollywood Records, book publishers, sports teams, magazines and cruise lines, and licenses over 200 Disney flagship stores worldwide, as well as selling the rights to merchandise its name and images on countless products, including toys, fashion, watches, art and home goods.[40]

Disney's connection to consumerism is often encapsulated in the metaphor of the American Dream. Consumerist ideology finds a potent guise in such American Dream narratives. The narratives promise that American society allows anyone to climb the social ladder, so the inequalities and injustices of capitalism are portrayed as mere accidents of fate or character, not systemic flaws. Similar to Marx's commodity fetish, since it erases the social relations of production, the American Dream provides a second fetish, a distorted image of the society whereby we represent and think ourselves.[41] It is no surprise, then, that the American Dream metaphor emerged, along with Disney, during the early twentieth century.[42] Its first usage coincides with one of America's consumer booms, beginning in the 1920s, when many features of consumer culture evident today, such as suburban homes, cars and media like cinema and animation, took root and spread. Modern industrialism provided an abundant bounty of never-before-seen wishes; dreams had seemingly become reality. To many, such commodified wonders offered proof of the reality of the American Dream. Many Disney movies follow a similar American Dream template, in which a character pursues and achieves their dream. As animation scholar Paul Wells remarks,

> The dominant presence of the Disney canon . . . has inhibited any potential reading of animation from the United States as anything but a medium which endorses and promotes ideological certainty in the guise of utopian populism and the rhetorical promise of 'the Dream'.[43]

These connections to consumer culture and consumerist ideology mark Disney as yet another, albeit significant, contributor to the general trends of modern and postmodern capitalism, a trend often traced to Hollywood cinema. Scholars have thoroughly demonstrated how cinema became a major proponent of consumerism and a significant prod to consumption, contributing to the fashion cycles, merchandising practices and fetishism necessary to fuel consumerism. Indeed, cinema's influence on consumer culture is practically a tenet of studies of contemporary capitalism. From a certain angle, such analysis seems correct; both animation and live-action cinema contribute to the production of imagistic commodities that fuel corporate branding practices, circulate across multiple media, and accrue profit from the perceptual labour of attentive consumers, thereby contributing to an 'affect' economy. From this top-down perspective, Disney, like live-action Hollywood, proffers fare drenched in sentimental emotions that represent corporate interests by promoting consumerism while denuding critical consciousness.

Yet from the perspective taken in *Special Affects*, affect precedes all of this —representation, emotion, consciousness, interest. Affect undergirds and motivates the states of activity and passivity from which consciously emoting and interpreting subjects mould their understandings of self and existence. Without significant, felt affections, there would be no motivation for investments in certain subjectivities, representations, and interests. Without innervating interest, excitement, joy and wonder, Disney could neither entice consumption nor spread an ideology of consumerism. As Lawrence Grossberg states, 'Affect identifies the strength of the investment which anchors people in particular experiences, practices, identities, meanings and pleasures . . . It is the affective investment which enables ideological relations to be internalized and, consequently, naturalized.'[44]

Focusing on affect, then, directs us to the movements of emergence, to the becomings of experience, which constitute the 'origin' of ideological representation. Affect is immanent to experience and thus a fundamental ground of emergence, ideological and otherwise.[45] Beginning with a focus on affective experience entails understanding ideology as its result, as the capturing or translation of affective experience.[46] Ideology is not imposed but is the conscious response to and translation of affective experience.

If affect undergirds ideology, affect theory precludes reducing Disney animation to the general trends of consumer culture by directing attention to the inexhaustible differences in embodied experience. Affect theory denies that similar perceptual processes and affections result from such different media as animation and live-action cinema. Ideological analyses suggesting that the impacts of live-action cinema and animation on consumer practice and consumerist ideology are largely similar conflate these media and modes, eliminating the differences in the ways that bodies sense, feel and, most importantly, *interface* with the images and sounds from the films. Such a conflation does little, then, to tell us why Disney animation or live-action cinema attracts attention by ignoring the various affections experienced in engagement with these different modes. For instance, viewers repeatedly associate Disney with feelings described as wondrous and childlike, whereas these attributions are less common with live-action Hollywood movies.[47] Conflating live-action Hollywood and Disney animation must erase these experiential differences in favour of finding ideological and social sameness in Disney and Hollywood's contributions to consumer capitalism.

Instead, I contend that, as different modes emerge and different affections become experienced, new consumers and their commodities become perceivable. In other words, as people engage these modes, infolding differently, they produce new habits. Seigworth explains the connection between affection and habit: 'Take, for example, a body that encounters a pleasurable or joyful affection. The tendency is to wish for or actively seek its occurrence again (and again): habit . . . Within habit, the folding process . . . becomes something that is imagined and anticipated.'[48] Such habits, in turn, become translated by the culture industries into understandings of consumers; new consumers become perceivable. As we will see in Chapter 3, cinema makes perceivable a lifestyle consumer that seeks commodities for display. As an affective experience, animation does not offer a mode of human display; it seems unlikely that people watch Mickey in order to learn how to use clothing or other commodities to stand out or fit in. Rather than being socially oriented, animation's special pleasures stem from a self-affection we will call *wonder*, which is more closely connected to Marx's notion of commodity fetishism (as further developed in Chapter 6). As such, these habits become translated into an understanding of the consumer as daydreamer, one who experiences affection directly through image-objects. Hence the culture industries rush to provide commodities for self-affection, like toys, instead of those for social display, like fashion and cinema's other tie-ins.

In sum, rather than just another in a long line of promoters of a homogenised consumer ideology, *Special Affects* contends that there exists a unique economic and ideological impact of Disney animation, tracing how Disney's full-length features developed a mode that makes new consumers perceivable and becomes differently translated into consumerist ideology (as typically expressed in American Dream narratives). Cinema and animation helped make new consumers and their commodities perceivable, contributing to the creation of modes conducive to modern consumerism and effecting different translations of the American Dream. Although they make different consumers perceivable and therefore spur the production of different commodities, both cinema's lifestyle consumer and Disney's daydreaming consumer demonstrate the fundamental connection between media and consumerism. By making new modes available, media create the potential for new affections, affections that, when habituated, result in newly perceivable consumers, newly articulable commodities, and new translations of consumerist ideology. In short, there is a fundamental connection between media and consumerism because media enable new modes of affection, and affection underwrites both the desire to consume and the translation of those desires into consumerist ideology.

On Modes

Here I hope to contribute to affect theory by further developing the concept of modes, before illustrating it by example throughout *Special Affects*. Affection is the impingement of a body upon another, the sensation of intensity or force produced from a folding. As such, affect calls attention to the relation between bodies (in our case, the medium and viewer, interfaced via images), which is, in Deleuzian parlance, attention to the virtual. This conceptualisation of the virtual comes from the initial theorising of Henri Bergson and is quite distinct from one that conceives the virtual as simulations on a computer screen.[49] Instead, Bergson defines the virtual as the reality of relations, stating, 'Besides *things*, there are *relations*.'[50] The term 'virtual' designates the series of relations accompanying all actualisations. Relations create a field of potential within which things take place, so the virtual can also be described as the real potential coexisting with all actualisations. Movements (including perceptions, affections and cognitions) become actual by drawing from this field of relations and potential. The virtual has, therefore, always been with us, further warranting the application of the concept of virtual bodies (modes) to older media like Disney animation.

Let us take the simple example of walking across a room. The walking takes place in a field of relations – including the positions of the walls and other objects, as well as the relations of arms to legs to torso and to these other objects. With each actual step, this field changes and feeds back into the virtual, creating new potentials by altering the field of relations. As such, the virtual accompanies all actualisation, including the movements of perception and language, not just physical movement. In writing and speaking, each actual word alters the relations of the whole, creating new potential trajectories for the words to follow. In perceiving movies, for instance, relations between the work, location and viewer create a field of potential (what can be seen, what cannot) from which the present perception is actualised. We will describe the virtual potentials of media as -abilities, following Walter Benjamin, like the *reproducibility* of cinema or the *transformability* of animation outlined in Chapter 4. Modes constitute a relationship between a medium's -abilities and the capacities of the perceiver, providing an orientation to these virtual fields from which affections become actualised.

As this description indicates, the virtual is opposed not to the 'real', as it is frequently in popular rhetoric, but to the actual, with the two terms existing in a 'circuit'.[51] The virtual is fully real – the reality of the past and future in the present actualisation, the real relations constituted by past actualisations, and the real potential enabled by the future's openness. Each movement of perception, affection and cognition actualises from a virtual field, yet each actualisation reconstitutes and reshapes this field of potential. Each step reorganises the relations in the room and alters the potential next move, which in turn actualises from this renewed field. Thus the virtual is empirically real, if not quite ever material. In Massumi's words, the virtual is the *'felt reality of a relation'*.[52] In Deleuze's, *'The virtual is fully real in so far as it is virtual . . .* The reality of the virtual consists of the differential elements and relations along with the singular points that correspond to them. The reality of the virtual is structure.'[53]

This structure of a relation is a *mode*, a concept that is central for Spinoza and Deleuze alike. Modes are a manner of relating, the operations productive of an assemblage or desiring-machine, how one body plugs into or interfaces with another to produce affections. As such, modes are the flip-side of affects, the orientations or manners necessary for certain perceptions to flow forth and thus for certain affects to be sparked. One of the finest scholars of affect, Sara Ahmed, has noted the connection between particular affects and perceptual and cognitive orientations.[54] Fear is the affective expression of an orientation that runs away or hides from an object, just as disgust recoils from an object: 'Emotions are relational: they involve (re)actions or relations of "towardness" or "awayness" in relation to such objects. The bear becomes the object in both senses: we have a contact with an object, and an orientation towards that object.'[55] Modes are particular manners of these orientations, ways of generating particular affections like disgust or fear or wonder. It is only by engaging a mode that a particular form can trigger specific affections for a person. In other words, modes link subjects to objects. To take the example of Disney movies, modes link the viewer to the images and sounds, providing the perceptual orientation or manner through which experience proceeds. Modes are a virtual orientation between bodies, with affections being the actualisations of these virtual fields, the intensities that flow forth from the engagement of the mode. Thus modes go hand in hand with studies of affect, providing the flip-side (the virtual or relational side) of the actualised affections. As Deleuze writes,

> The affections . . . are the modes themselves. The modes are the affections of substance or of its attributes. At a second level, the affections designate that which happens to the mode, the modifications of the mode, the effects of other modes on it.[56]

Modes offer a concept of bodies as virtual, as a series of relations, both to its own parts and to other bodies. Bodies – and by bodies I mean any *thing* – are complex and composite relations, and modes are the orientations of those relations. As Deleuze remarks, 'Every reader of Spinoza knows that for him bodies and minds are not substances or subject, but modes.'[57] To apply this idea to media, media extend different human faculties, as McLuhan maintains, and modes constitute a manner for relating or orienting these extensions to one another. Modes are an orientation for the *folding* of bodies into a distributed body, a folding that produces a *crease* – a line along which new neural and affective pathways may run. Because of the crease, cognitive, perceptual and affective surfaces may rub against one another differently, producing friction and at times a spark. Such a perspective envisions all bodies as virtual, as relational, as situated in the world, further justifying approaching older media like Disney through newer concepts like the virtual, affect and modes. As Deleuze describes at length:

[T]hese relations and capacities . . . select, in the world or in Nature, that which corresponds to the thing; that is, they select what affects or is affected by the thing, what moves it or is moved by it. For example, given an animal, what is this animal unaffected by in the infinite world? What does it react to positively or negatively? What are its nutriments and poisons? What does it 'take' in its world? Every point has its counterpoints: the plant and the rain, the spider and the fly. So an animal, a thing, is never separable from its relations with the world . . . The speed or slowness of metabolisms, perceptions, actions, and reactions link together to constitute a particular individual in the world . . . [E]thology studies the compositions of relations or capacities between different things . . . How do individuals enter into composition with one another . . . ? How can a being take another being into its world . . . ?[58]

How, then, can we outline or map a mode? Here, Deleuze offers some initial guidance, drawing on Spinoza's call for ethology. Basically, ethology isolates the virtual capacities of bodies, tracing how these capacities enter into series of modal relations. Specifically, Spinoza isolates two series of relations Deleuze calls the mode's longitude and latitude. The longitude represents the relations of speed and slowness or motion and rest between parts of the individual body. The latitude represents the relations of capacities or affectability between different bodies (like a movie's form and the viewer). Diagramming a mode entails performing an ethology depicting the capacities of individual bodies and then outlining the structure of their relation, illustrating how the capacities of one body become linked to the capacities of another. Mapping a mode, therefore, does not attempt to describe the bodies – what have been typically conceived as subjects and objects – separately but instead focuses on the manner of their coming-together. Modes link subjects and objects, in our case, perceptions and forms, constituting a distributed, virtual body. Studying modes calls attention not to distinct subjects and objects but to the relations or procedures for interfacing between perceiver and perceived.

I will describe the medium's capacities as virtual -abilities, drawing on a conceptualisation of Benjamin's, read through Jacques Derrida. As Derrida's repeated critique of the metaphysics of presence makes abundantly clear, media cannot be seen as a presence or substance responsible for the origin of subjects or their affections. Instead, media enable or disable possibilities, creating virtual fields of potential that condition but do not determine emergence. Derrida will discuss these potentialities with terms that end in -ability, such as the iterability of language, language's ability to be repeated in another time and place.[59] Iterability designates the structurally necessary potential for repetition, of new iterations, not the actual iterations themselves. The -ability remains whether the discourse ever becomes repeated, just as the potential for particular forms of mediation remain whether people actually engage them (for instance, montage was enabled by film long before it emerged historically).

This conceptualisation of -abilities constitutes one of the most prominent affinities between Benjamin and Derrida.[60] Examples of -abilities from Benjamin include citability, communicability, translatability, recognisability, legibility and, in his 'Work of Art' essay, reproducibility. -Abilities are starkly different from an ability possessed by a subject, such as a person's ability to draw Mickey. An -ability is defined by the dash, the gap, the absence marking the economy of a relationship. As with iterability, -abilities describe a structural necessity – a potentiality or virtuality – rather than an empirical, existent substance. Media thus shape modes by enabling or disabling certain capacities; the -abilities of media influence the mode, shaping the emergent virtual bodies.

Depicting media as virtual -abiltiies avoids technological determinism by understanding media as shaping the potential actualisation of affection and image-form but not determining them. The virtual is real, it exists, but its existence does not require actualisation; the iterability of language and the reproducibility of photography remain even if no one ever repeats this sentence or prints more copies from the negative. Instead, the virtuality of media creates the potential for certain actualisations, a potential that persists and has force whether ever actualised. A virtual medium, in Samuel Weber's words, 'cannot be *measured* by the possibility of self-fulfillment but by its constitutive alterability'.[61] In other words, the -abilities of media shape the affections and images by constituting a virtual field of potential alterations or modulations.

Yet it is only by putting the capacities of the medium into relation with the capacities of the viewer that any actualisations or determinations emerge, and, as we will see, numerous cinematic and animatic modes differently relate the viewer and medium, in ways that produce different actualisations of form and intensities of affection. We will describe these capacities of the viewer as *folds*. The concept of folds, which Deleuze traces to Michel Foucault, addresses the separation of inside and outside in Western philosophy.[62] Western philosophy typically conceives of an interior individual that engages the outside world from this inside location. Foucault and Deleuze challenge this idea of the subject as inside and indivisible, whole, *individual*. Instead, they recognise subjectivity as a production necessarily thrown into or located amidst the world, with the supposed boundaries between inside and outside being porous and shifting. That is, the subject is produced by the world, infolding or internalising it, but they also externalise or unfold, affecting the world around them. Folds thus designate the capacities of the subject to affect (unfold) and be affected (infold). The virtual potentials of media are outside forces, and these forces enter into a modal relationship with subjective forces: that is, with the person's ability to affect (as well as be affected). Human bodies affect the medium through their forces of perception at the same time that the medium affects the viewer through its -abilities, like cinema's reproducibility of time. Folding therefore helps explain the reciprocal and resonant constitution of subjectivity, with insides and outsides mutually imbricated or blended. Folding represents a perfect metaphor for such a view, since folding something causes the inside and outside to shift places and change positions. As Deleuze concludes, 'These folds are eminently variable, and moreover have different rhythms whose variations constitute irreducible modes of subjectivation.'[63]

Modes relate the -abilities of media to the folds of viewers, producing varying splits or fusions in perception, affection and cognition that innervate special affects. Of course, modes and their relations of infolding and unfolding occur long before media. However, it is my contention that media, by relating differently to human faculties of folding, produce the special affects under investigation here. In a mode, media enable the splitting or fusing of the viewer's folds, producing a rupture in their perceptual, cognitive and affective infoldings that produces sparks. As Deleuze describes, 'It is as if the relations of the outside folded back to create a doubling, allow a relation to oneself to emerge, and constitute an inside which is hollowed out and develops its own unique dimension.'[64] In other words, the outside (communication media) is folded back, creating a doubling or splitting of oneself (of one's infolding capacities). Such a splitting or fusing, especially when newly experienced, can create creases in perceptual, affective and cognitive foldings. Once split or fused, new affective, perceptual and cognitive folds come into contact, producing friction as they rub against one another. This friction, when sharply felt, becomes a spark.

The relations of -abilities and folds constituting a mode result in an 'economy'.[65] An economy is a structure of difference, a system of exchange resultant from the opposition of two forces: 'Economy is a metaphor of energy – where two opposed forces playing against each other constitute the so-called identity of a phenomenon.'[66] An economy is not a dichotomy, a structure whose pairs are conceived as mutually exclusive oppositions, or a dialectic, where the two blend into a synthesis. An economy issues forth from the energy produced via two opposing tendencies or trajectories, like the magnetic field produced by the force of the earth's poles. Economies are tensive structures in which the presence of contrasting forces creates an absent relationship. Modes operate through such economies; an economic relation between forces or capacities drives a mode's operation.

Such economies constitute the limits – the poles – within which the movements of form and perception oscillate. In other words, both the form and the viewer must operate between these poles, never reaching either limit, or the relation becomes severed or altered into another mode. With Disney's animistic mimesis, for instance, an economy of *semblance* and *play* directs the differences and deferrals, what audiences see and do not see, *as well as* what the form includes and does not include. Mickey must both look like a mouse and not. It is the tension, the oscillation between semblance and play that enables the folding of animistic mimesis between sensing the character as alive and knowing they are not. The mimetic semblances enable the sensation of life while the play – the animistic transformations of character – reminds us of their artifice. This folding potentially sparks that wondrous Disney tingle, drawing from the energy produced by the contrast between the forces of semblance and play, the forces of affective sensation and conscious knowledge. The forces are flows of attention, affect and desire, meaning that these forces are economic in the more restrictive sense as well: that is, part of the consumer economy. Disney's economic success requires tapping into two opposing forces, a consumer desire for more realistic animation and yet an established audience enjoying the playfulness of the animated image. Thus Disney was motivated to develop animation that enhanced semblances to life but never came too close, employing the transformability and transferability of animation as a way to modulate this operating economy.

Since they operate through an economy, modes can be depicted, from the point of view of the subject, as a metaphor; for the viewer, modes entail a *perceiving as* similar to metaphor, linking sense and image, subjects and objects, by providing a manner for their interfacing.[67] Modes are bodies understood as manners, in duration, in becoming, as the interfacing processes for perceiving and conceiving. Modes, like metaphors, orient a perspective and entail a *perceiving as*, perceiving one focus through the frame of another. For instance, Disney's animistic mimesis entails, for the viewer, *perceiving animated images as living beings*. Viewers do not typically express this metaphor and only remain subconsciously aware of their modal orientation. However, expressing these modes as metaphors serves a clarifying function for us, helping elucidate the economic structure from the viewer's point of view, which, again, only constitutes one side of the modal relationship or virtual body.

This clarification is essential because we should not understand modes as either the person or the form but instead as the two combined in an assemblage or desiring-machine. Throughout *Special Affects*, I attempt to use the mode as the subject of the sentence, bestowing on the mode the agency rather than, alternatively, the medium or viewer. Modes, not particular viewers, become perceivable and hence translatable into socio-cultural forms related to consumerism. While giving the mode agency, however, I will often refer to both production techniques and viewer's reception to demonstrate the shared modes. This is because modes are liminal or in between, a relational multiplicity between speaker-text and text-audience directed more by forces of potential rather than substance or being. This liminality, the interfacing of textual form and consumer participation, precludes locating the origin of the mode in any producer, audience or text and instead views them as emergent, collective phenomena. All these agents play a crucial role in the completion, repetition and circulation of a mode. In short, modes are relational structures, not the province of a single producer, audience or situation. Hence modes, like affect, can be conceived of as pre-subjective and pre-personal. The modes exist virtually, relationally, as a potential orientation, before any particular person engages them.

Humanists should not fret over the concept of modes, however, because humans do retain some agency as a partner in a relationship. Modes require the perceiver's participation; audiences must interface via the mode to perceive in a particular manner. Nothing guarantees adherence to a mode; someone might watch a Disney movie and never feel life. Mediated forms may cue a mode, but modes also require audience participation to take the cues and perceive according to the mode's metaphor. In other words, there is a reciprocal, interactive coupling of actualised forms and affections via the virtual mode. Modes constitute the orientation that must be taken up in order for a particular form to trigger a specific affect, yet the form does not guarantee these affects because the mode itself must be engaged. This engagement is not guaranteed because such bodies, such desiring-machines, are always breaking down in actualisation, as Deleuze and Guattari maintain.

This theorisation of modes developed here has the advantage of enhancing affect theory by correcting for its tendency to overshoot into a corporeal determinism by portraying affect as an automatic reflex uninfluenced by perception, cognition and culture. In my take, perception, cognition and affection form a feedback loop, influencing one another, even if not reducible to the other and even if affect precedes cognition. In fact, Deleuze insists that the idea or image holds 'logical and chronological' primacy over affect.[68] In other words, there must be some kind of bodily perception prior to the experience of affect. To take an example famous in the emotion literature, one must first see a bear before one feels fear.[69] Such perceptions depend upon cognitive and perceptual orientations – modes. That is, only by being oriented toward the world in a certain manner can we perceive and be affected by other objects or beings in a certain way. For instance, hiking through the woods, I am oriented to perceive bears as wild and unpredictable, and thereby primed to be affected by them with fear, evoking a fight-or-flight response. The same bear, in a different mode, can be received quite differently, with starkly different affects. Oriented to a circus or zoo, the same bear might instead evoke feelings of amusement or awe. As Ahmed concludes,

> So fear is not in the child, let alone in the bear, but is a matter of how child and bear come into contact. This contact is shaped by past histories of contact, unavailable in the present, which allow the bear to be apprehended as fearsome . . . Another child, another bear, and we might have another story.[70]

In short, affects and affection stem first from an idea or image: that is, upon a cognition or perception. We must perceive the bear or conceive a (sad? happy?) thought to experience affection and the passage of affect. Thus perception, cognition and affection should be conceived as forming a circuit; perception feeds into affection and cognition, which in turn shape future perceptions, cognitions and affections.

I am not the first to offer this warning about taking the idea of affect as pre-subjective too far. Grossberg also worries that such scholarship tends to conceive 'a kind of immediate effectivity of affect on the body . . . You know, you flash these lights at people and there is some kind of bodily response. Well there isn't! Affect then becomes a magical way of bringing in the body.'[71] Rather than conceiving affect as automatic or even beyond description, the scholarly task becomes twofold: outlining the various affections of consumer media experience and also detailing the modes necessary to trigger such affections. Thus *Special Affects* follows Grossberg's call to 'do the harder work of specifying modalities and apparatuses of affect . . . Organisations of affect might include will and attention, or moods, or orientation, what I have called "mattering maps", and the various culturally and phenomenologically constituted emotional economies.'[72]

This is not to deny the difference between affect and perception or cognition, since affection designates a non-representational mode experienced directly, corporeally, whereas perception–cognition represents the world to us in images (broadly conceived). Yet affect and affection result from these primary, representational modes of perception and cognition. Affective experience is irreducibly bodily, yet affections emanate from a prior mode, an orientation experienced by the person often as a subconscious awareness of their virtual relationality. Likewise, describing affect as pre-subjective or pre-cognitive does not mean that affections are pre-cultural, since they are developed, conditioned, habituated and produced by cultural experiences. People from different cultures will react with disgust or delight to certain types of food, depending upon their cultural orientations and upbringings. Culture relays into affect just as affect relays into culture, in an ongoing feedback loop. Indeed, modes are fundamentally cultural and historical; they are orientations that constitute a shared world. In other words, modes are not universal or transcendent; as consonant with an immanent ontology, modes remain historical and contextual. Animistic mimesis and the daydreaming consumer emerge at a particular time and place. Modes are not stable and eternal substances like Platonic forms but are historically constituted virtual bodies.

When habitually engaged, modes shape culture. Through the various translations, people learn the 'message' of the medium, in McLuhan's sense.[73] We learn about the potential of the mode; the mode goes virtual. The 'message', if it had to be reduced to linguistic paraphrase, would simply be, 'This mode is possible' or 'Certain subjects and practices are now perceivable due to the emergence of this mode.' Some may miss the 'message' or interpret it in contradictory ways, but the translations provide 'lessons' in the potentials and possibilities of the mode none the less. Modes are virtual structures actualised in various moments by specific dividuals. Their actualisation may be resisted or blocked, but the mode exists and persists nevertheless, making bodies visible and ideologies articulable.

Modes are therefore not about presence, a substance of place, identity or ideology that guarantees their outcome. Disney's mode of animistic mimesis, as we shall see, enables a newly visible daydreaming consumer and a newly articulable Disney version of the American Dream, with impacts on the shape of consumer culture distinct from those of classical cinema. The daydreaming consumer is not simply a person who watches Disney movies, or a bourgeois child, or a duped consumer. The daydreaming consumer is the subject made visible through their modal engagements; they become perceivable due to bodies plugging into the mode. A mode makes certain perceptions possible, thereby making certain modal bodies visible as well. In short, neither subject positions nor ideologies create a mode. A mode's economy originates perception, opening the possibilities of appearance, subjectivity and signification. As Disney's animistic mimesis spreads, the daydreaming consumer becomes visible and a Disney version of the American Dream becomes sayable. As the sparks ignite into full-blown fires, culturally shared and recognised, the mode and its affections become available for capture by regimes of value and ideology, as we will discover with respect to American consumer culture.

On History

How, then, does our retelling proceed through the concepts of modes and affects outlined above? Basically, this history does not attempt to portray history 'as it really was' but instead looks back at Disney from the perspective of today, putting the past and the present into a constellation, as attempted by Benjamin in his unfinished *The Arcades Project*.[74] I scoured the historical record for evidence of the affections felt from watching early cinema, early animation, classical cinema, and full-length Disney features of the 1930s and 1940s. From there, those descriptions of affection are connected to a critical analysis of the form of various movies, as detailed primarily in an image typology including the movement-image (classical cinema), the motion-image (early animation) and the mutual affection-image (Disney animation). Constellating these image-forms with the historical affections allows us to outline the basics of the different modes studied here, detailing their virtual relations, metaphoric expression and economic structures. Chapter 2 performs this procedure for the classic cinematic mode. Then Chapters 4 and 5 do so for graphic narrative animation and Disney's animistic mimesis. We begin with classical Hollywood because tracing the emergence of animistic mimesis requires comparison, given the significant cultural, institutional and technical links between cinema and animation, and because many commentators see Disney as an attempt to imitate classical cinema.

After detailing the modes, the following chapters (Chapters 3 and 6) illustrate how these modes – these virtual bodies – become translated into the practices of the culture industry. Classical cinema and animistic mimesis are differently translated into modes of consumer practice, enabling newly visible consumers and commodities that help fuel the consumer boom of the period. These newly visible consumers and commodities demonstrate a significant conclusion of *Special Affects* – that there is a fundamental connection between media and consumerism.

What follows, then, is a layered history – a history of affect, an image history, a modal history, a consumer history and a rhetorical history. The first few chapters begin with a history of affect and mode, demonstrating that one result of the emergence of media is a widespread *spark*, a sense of amazement, wonder, the fantastic or astonishment. Sparks fly as media punctuate perceptual experience, creating distinct affects that motivate the development of modes. Such modes result in particular types of images.

Just as Deleuze details the movement-images of classical cinema, we will outline the motion-images of early animation and the mutual affection-images of animistic mimesis. Chapters 2, 4 and 5 follow this basic pattern, first detailing the affective sparks, then depicting the medium's virtual -abilities, how various modes relate the medium's capacities to the viewer in an economy, and finally what images result. In short, each of these chapters follows the translation of a medium and its affects into a mode of perception and its images.

From there, *Special Affects* traces, in Chapter 7, the ideological transla-tions of these new modes and affections, further demonstrating the unique contributions of Disney animation to consumer culture, as distinct from classical cinema. The ideological translations result in a change of the American Dream narratives associated with live-action cinema into the Disney version of the American Dream. Basically, the Dream changes from the explanation that certain behaviours make dreams a reality to a 'magical theory' of social change. In the Disney version, all one needs is a dream; the emphasis on comportment such as hard work is jettisoned. Instead, dreams come true for those who wish upon a star. With such a translation comes a new constellation of metaphors through which the tales are told, such as genius, fantasy, imagination, children, magic, wonder and innocence.

From the perspective of affect advanced here, the emergence of the Disney version and this constellation of metaphors are not due to imposi-tions of the powerful, or the result of the 'realities' of exigence, or through the false imaginings of the oppressed. Ideologies like the American Dream are not representations of the powerful few but, as Benjamin says, expres-sions or *collective* dreams.[75] The base does not determine the superstruc-ture; the economy does not determine culture. Instead, cultural practices are the expression of economic conditions, just as a dream might express the sleeper's physical conditions in fantastical code. As certain consumers, commodities and practices become perceivable due to the emergence of a mode, rhetoric like the Disney version becomes sayable. The Disney version is a translation of the mode of animistic mimesis, the collective 'making sense' of these experiences.[76] In short, consumerist ideology is not reconstituted because it is a meaningful cover for 'real interests' (although it is seized upon to serve such purposes – molarised, in Deleuze's terms) but because it 'makes sense' in light of these modal, affective experiences, explaining why the abundant critiques of consumerism and Disney have fallen short. Such criticisms have difficulty whisking away this ingrained feeling, this 'making sense' of the American Dream due to the experiences of communicating through these modes.

Viewing history as a collective process of 'making sense', the reader should not read it as his-story, an oversimplified, reductionist account attributing change to the actions of powerful men (typically men) while nullifying and erasing the diversity of influences and factors. In short, I am not arguing, myopically, 'Disney did it.' Instead, animistic mimesis should be understood as emergent, as a complex mode resultant from the reciprocal and resonant influences of multiple motivations, materials and agents, including producers and consumers. Likewise, the 'making sense' of animistic mimesis is not an individual, rational, linear process but a collective, messy and extended one, a process in which a logic of sense and sensation unfolds. Since the time of Disney's first full-length features and continuing through to today, numerous people have attempted to 'make sense' of animistic mimesis by translating it into the American Dream template. Animistic mimesis provides a material origin, constituting an 'original' substance for subsequent translations that uniquely shape aspects of consumer culture.

Thus *Special Affects* understands historical emergence as a series of translations. Translation means the movement from one medium (like cinema) to another (like animation), a process that entails both borrowing from and transforming the original mode. Disney's animistic mimesis is a complex translation of classical cinema, prior animation and other cultural practices that emerges through a wide array of interacting flows and forces. I retell Disney history as a series of translations from cinema and earlier animation, demonstrating how animistic mimesis subsequently becomes translated into consumer practice and ideology.

This retelling helps draw conclusions relevant for the past and for the present, altering the received wisdom on this moment in media history and providing insights into the affect economy and control society today. First, as developed in Chapters 3 and 6, *Special Affects* denies the conflation of Disney's and classical Hollywood's impacts on consumer culture, revealing instead that Disney uniquely contributes to consumerism by becoming a major precursor of the affect economy and a predecessor of digital media and control society. Due in part to Disney's translation of the classical cinema, the culture industry learns that *selling modes rather than products will be the primary task in the digital, affect economy. In short, the mode is the message.* Those companies who best develop, own and control different modes will best be able to attract consumers' attention and thereby capitalise on their affections.

Second, since animated characters were so easily reproducible, Disney has long been waging copyright battles similar to those that have flared with ferocity around digital media. Disney thus was one of the first combatants in the battles over copyright and access prevalent today with digital media: battles that are, precisely, battles for control. In addition, Disney began during this period to re-envision their consumers as dividuals – people understood as divisible conglomerations of affects. According to Deleuze, the emergence of an understanding of subjects as dividuals constitutes a primary element of control society. Dividuals are not individuals understood according to demographic boxes and disciplined in the confinement of institutions but are subjects conceived according to their different affects, which are tracked and targeted via digital surveillance technologies. Walt Disney described his consumer as the 'Mickey audience', made up not exclusively of actual children but of anyone who could feel the wonder, marking Disney as a primary predecessor of control society.

Today, this affect economy and control society constitute a sociocultural environment marked by rapid, repeated mode-switching in the hunt for new affections, as the final chapter illustrates through an analysis of the contemporary Disney movie *Wall-E*, a movie that heavily critiques consumer lifestyles. Despite the critique, Disney makes millions because they sell the mode, not the message, revealing a connection between media and consumerism beyond the purchase of media products, one with significant implications today. Yet *Wall-E*'s critique points to the proliferation of virtual bodies due to a computer-mediated consumer culture, one marked by frequent and rapid mode-switching and resulting in intense pressures on attention that hold significant and potentially dire consequences for the planet. The warning, I think, is apt and should demand more attention to the mediated, cyborg bodies that continue to emerge. Disney alone is not responsible but, in what follows, I stress their unique contribution to an alliance between media and consumerism that has left us in the contemporary predicament so many have begun to feel and name.

CHAPTER 2

Astonishment and the Fantastic in Live-Action Cinema

By the time of Disney's 1930s and 1940s full-length features, live-action film had become the feature attraction. Mickey, Felix the Cat and other animated stars received face time on the silver screen only as seven-minute shorts tacked on to the features. They ran alongside newsreels, previews and other acts on the 'film bill'.[1] The film bill harkened back to an earlier time in cinema history beginning just twenty-five years prior, an era Tom Gunning bills as the 'cinema of attractions'.[2] The cinema of attractions describes a pre-classical film practice located in the vaudeville stage and travelling shows, not the nickelodeons (5-cent theatres) and Hollywood studios of classical cinema. At these shows, audiences witnessed a performance featuring a series of attractions, each seeking to produce 'peak' or 'aggressive moments' generating the 'shock' or 'astonishment' central to the attraction's attraction.[3] Attractions were not limited to reproducible media; music, comedy, live performances, animated images, live-action films and many other attractions shared the same stage and competed for attention.

By the time of Disney's full-length features, however, the classical cinema dominated. Movie theatres dotted the globe, with fifty million watching motion pictures weekly in the United States, equivalent to one-half of the population.[4] Studios had established institutional roots, big budgets and industrial production methods. Film had produced its first recognisable auteurs and stars, and birthed its first mature mode, the classical mode. As a result, almost every other cultural form felt an irresistible pull to become more cinematic, including painting, novels, theatre and animation.[5] Hollywood had developed a mode that would significantly shape American culture as well as transforming the consumer and commodity. From the perspective of 1929, it indeed seemed that cinema embodied the essence of modern consumer culture and that animation would remain a silly sideshow, a mere footnote easily ignored or readily incorporated into analyses stressing Hollywood's dominance.

Hollywood's influence explains why we will spend this chapter, in a book about animation, detailing the translation of the cinema of attractions into classical cinema.[6] Disney's animistic mimesis translates the classical mode, emerging in a context where live-action drove studio imperatives and had repeatedly attracted audiences. A quick word on the concept of translation is necessary. Translation here does not mean a simple transfer from one language to another, instead following Benjamin's 'Task of the Translator'. Benjamin portrays translation as a creative, even constitutive practice.[7] A literal translation strips the original of its truth and beauty, empties it of its essence by reducing it to mere information. A good translation, 'instead of resembling the meaning of the original, must lovingly and in detail incorporate the original's mode of signification, thus making both the original and the translation recognizable as fragments of a greater language'.[8]

As a mode, translation operates according to an economy between fidelity and freedom, or the translatable and non-translatable. The original issues a demand for survival, a demand to spread, to which the translator responds. This demand induces a trajectory towards fidelity; the translation seeks out the translatable in the original. At the same time, however, the original remains unique because something remains that is not translatable. The original is a singular fusion of content and form, a way of signifying and not simply something signified. This 'nucleus', although the primary concern of the translator, is forever elusive, non-translatable.[9] Such non-translatability thus exerts a pressure on the translator towards freedom. The translation must necessarily break apart the fusion of content and form; the movement from one medium to another requires transformation. As such, translators must take some artistic licence in order to translate the nucleus most closely, its mode of signifying.

Operating through this economy, translation does not simply represent the original but constitutes a larger ensemble of modes, shared by the original and translation. In other words, translation reveals what is shared (the translatable) and what is transformed (the non-translatable) in the movement from original to a new mode. In this way, translation illustrates and embodies the kinship between media, the properties shared *and* altered in the movement from one medium to another. In short, the theory of translation is the theory of the change of modes; through translation, the life of a mode unfolds – emerging, growing, maturing and then transforming as it is translated anew. Thus translation is the constitutive cultural process. The translation of forms constitutes new modes, as in the translation of the graphic narrative mode into animistic mimesis. Tracing these translations allows us to see the similarities and differences in modes, and, as such, will help uncover, in the final chapter, what is new about digital media, in distinction from the animation of this time period.

In this chapter, I trace the translation from the early 'cinema of attraction' to the classical mode. Since we are retelling a moment in media history, much of this chapter relies on previous scholarship, especially the work of three scholars – Benjamin, McLuhan and Deleuze. Writing at different times, each theorist frequently employs the concept of modes, and each draws on the concept to offer a different take on media history. Benjamin tells this history as the decline of an auratic mode due to the rise of reproducible media such as cinema, which result in a mode characterised by 'reception in distraction'.[10] McLuhan tells this history as the transition from a literate, print-based, 'hot' culture dominated by visual space to a 'cool' electronic culture marked by aural space. Finally, Deleuze depicts the transition from the classical cinema's regime of movement-images to the time-images of much postwar cinema.

Given these theorists' affinities to the approach developed in *Special Affects*, I employ their insights to triangulate my retelling of cinema history with these previous versions. Of course, these theorists at times conflict or contradict, so this should not be seen as an argument that their different histories are wholly consonant. Instead, I piece together the insights of these theorists to help create a refined retelling of media history. Not exclusively the decline of auratic modes, or the movement from acoustic to visual space, or the transition from movement-images to time-images, this retelling sees history as a series of translations enabled by the virtual potentials of media and audiences. These modal translations are actualised in different types of images and manifest in distinct consumer practices and ideology. Through this retelling, I illustrate the fundamental connection between media and consumerism, with Disney representing a precursor of the affect economy and a predecessor of digital media and control society.

Unfortunately, conflation remains a tendency in Benjamin, McLuhan and Deleuze alike. As we will see, Benjamin and Deleuze conflate animation and cinema, with animation being part of cinema for Benjamin and part of the movement-image for Deleuze. Instead, I contend that Disney's animistic mimesis does not innervate the same affective experience as classical cinema because it presents a hybrid movement- and time-image. McLuhan does not reduce animation to cinema, depicting animation as an iconic form based in acoustic space opposed to the visual space of cinema. However, McLuhan tends to conflate media technologies into singular categories like 'cinema' and 'animation', treating each medium as distinct rather than recognising the diversity of modes in animation and cinema alike. Indeed, an essential part of Disney's animistic mimesis is the imitation of classical cinema, creating a visual space based in Renaissance perspective that McLuhan opposes to the iconic perspective of much animation.

This chapter helps situates Disney's translation in the context of classical cinema, allowing us to ascertain later what Disney borrows and transforms from the classical mode. Before the classical mode, however, cinema also underwent a series of translations, transforming the cinema of attractions but also borrowing heavily from theatre and literature. The classical mode draws on two sparks – the fantastic and astonishment – that together compose an economy between realism and fantasy. The classical mode entails *perception of discontinuous shots as a continuous whole*. As a result, the classical mode produces movement-images as an interface, piecing together action-images, perception-images and affection-images through organic montage into an indirect image of narrative time. Throughout its heyday, classical Hollywood leaned heavily on action-images and relied upon American Dream narratives, according to a template in which heroes adjust their behaviour to the milieu to save the day. How, then, did the classical mode emerge? How did cinema relate to the viewer in such a manner as to produce the sparks of astonishment and the fantastic?

Astonishment and the Cinema of Attractions

What affection was sparked via the modes of the cinema of attraction? The answer, in brief, is a spark of life. Cinema was often described as astonishing, amazing or marvellous due to its lifelike or realistic portrayal of movement. Although these adjectives are considered synonyms, I will label cinema's initial spark astonishment, especially since Gunning employs this term.[11] For our purposes, astonishment designates the spark from perceiving lifelike movement occurring in the here-and-now that took place in another time and space.

During early cinema, astonishment was a common reaction, especially to the lifelike movement featured in the earliest offerings by Edison's Vitascope and the Lumière brothers' Cinematographe. In 1896, the *Optical Magic Lantern Journal* exclaimed, 'The greatest boom the lantern world has ever seen is that which is still reverberating throughout the land – the boom of the living photograph,' and by 1899, Henry V. Hopwood wrote a book describing the new images as *Living Pictures*.[12] On the 22 April 1895 premiere of the Vitascope, the *New York Daily News* remarked, 'The representation was realistic to a degree. The most trifling movements could be followed as accurately as if the dancers had been stepping before the audience in proper person.'[13] From sea to shining sea a year later, the *Los Angeles Times* also lauded the realism, 'The life-like reality of the pictures is said to be startling . . . The changing expression of their faces, their graceful movements, the play of hand and lip and eye, are said to be faultlessly reproduced.'[14] At the 1896 showing of *Rough Sea at Dover*, Robert Paul recounts that this 'actuality' film of a large wave created quite a stir: 'The thing was altogether so realistic and the reproduction so absolutely accurate, that it fairly astounded the beholder. It was the closest copy of nature any work of man has ever yet achieved.'[15] Musser reports that the realism was so vivid that patrons in the front rows became disconcerted and inclined to abandon their seats.[16]

Similar reactions were common enough to become film lore, labelled the 'train effect' since it was often films of approaching trains that caused audience members to flinch, stir and perhaps run away in terror.[17] Although Stephen Bottomore contends that the extent of the panic was likely overblown for publicity purposes, the reports are consistent and widespread enough to conclude there was 'some truth in them', especially the accounts that audiences experienced a physical response, at times flinching at the oncoming waves or trains.[18] The lifelike realism of such images provoked the flinching, and the flinching attests to the spark of astonishment, the intensive sensation felt from witnessing time and motion that seem so real yet are divorced from the here-and-now. Bottomore draws a similar conclusion: 'One might argue that the myth of the train effect is part of the "universal human response" to the early cinema: a way of resolving a certain discomfort about a new and uncomfortably realistic new medium.'[19]

Audiences were accustomed to seeing lifelike images in photos, but the realism of lifelike movement astounded, producing cinema's first spark. In fact, the Lumière brothers played upon the transition from photograph to film, beginning their projections with a still image that starts to move after a few seconds. The movement transformed the photograph from the mundanity it was by the end of the nineteenth century to a novelty, shocking even those such as George Méliès, who would later become film practitioners. Upon seeing his first movie, Méliès scoffed when the film begins with a static image, remarking, 'They got us all stirred up for projections like this? I've been doing them for years.'[20] Suddenly, as the wagon begins to move towards the spectators, Méliès felt cinema's astonishing spark: 'Before this spectacle we sat with gaping mouths, struck with amazement, astonished beyond all expression.'[21] Méliès experienced one of cinema's primary affects, becoming astonished before his conscious mind could compute what he had seen.

The structure of many early films, called 'actualities', reflects the astonishment over lifelike movement. Most commonly associated with the Lumière brothers, actualities display everyday occurrences such as trains or people leaving a factory. Actualities quickly faded in film practice as the novelty wore off, yet they constituted one of the first filmic forms. As Levio Belloi details, actualities did not simply capture 'actual' everyday moments but depended upon a particular staging that evokes a perceptual frame and limits the reactions of those unsuspectingly caught by the camera.[22] This form allowed the cameraperson to control the events photographed, presenting an illusion that actuality was simply reproduced, not staged.

How, then, did the form of actualities spark astonishment? How can we describe the mode of relation between medium and viewer in early cinema? This early mode, evident in many actualities, relates the space–time reproducibility of cinema to the viewer's perception of living movement and their sense of here-and-now presence. The term reproducibility comes from Benjamin in his famous 'Work of Art' essay, which he ties to photography and cinema.[23] Photography enables a reproducibility of the static space in front of the lens, while the movie camera enables a reproducibility of movement. Although stemming from photography, it was not until the 1860s invention of celluloid and Eadweard Muybridge's 1870s motion-study photography that motion pictures became possible. In response to a bet over whether all four hooves of a galloping horse leave the ground at the same time, Muybridge developed a system for taking rapid snapshots at equidistant intervals. Muybridge thereby demonstrated photography's ability to turn instants into images. In the context of cinema, Deleuze calls these instants 'any-instant-whatever', indicating how no image has privilege over any other, each instantly dissipating as the next passes before the projector.

The passing of any-instants-whatever creates the potential for cinema's reproducibility of movement. Such reproducibility is crucial for cinematic perception and production since, as Benjamin states, reproducibility makes the moving images detachable and hence transportable.[24] Where are these image transported? Reproducibility allows movement to be transported to various and widely scattered locations. Without reproducibility, there would be no editing and no mass audience. First, without reproducibility the editors would not be able to piece together different moments to create the montage and cutting (what I will later call transposability) necessary for classical cinema. Second, reproducibility allows audiences across expanses of space to view the same movie. Reproducibility means that the here-and-now of the photographic objects can be stripped away, permitting the movement of the image to a space closer to audiences and editors alike.

Benjamin describes the perception of a here-and-now as the *aura*, which is perhaps better conceptualised as an auratic mode. The aura is

> a strange tissue of space and time: the unique apparition of a distance, however near it may be. To follow with the eye . . . a mountain range on the horizon or a branch that casts its shadow on the beholder is to breathe the aura of those mountains, of that branch.[25]

We can interpret Benjamin's quotation as a distance in *time*, no matter how close in *space*; the auratic mode entails *perceiving a present object as evidence of an invisible duration.* We can hike a mountain range or rub noses with the Mona Lisa, but an aura remains, a sense of the great duration of its existence and our absence. For a work of art, this sense of distance comes from cultural practice; the work's embeddedness in tradition gives it a sense of singularity, of a distant, invisible life.

For Benjamin, then, photography betokens the decay of the aura. Since photography rips the object from its singular existence and potentially spreads multiple copies over space, it becomes difficult to perceive the photograph as having an aura. The object pictured might be singular, might attest to a great expanse of time, but the photograph itself is industrial refuse, the scattered remains of a secular, consumer world and not a sacred, transcendent one. Reproducibility drains the aura, enabling the work to be moved closer to the audience and thereby overcoming that 'unique apparition of a distance' present in the perception of a singular here-and-now. Benjamin concludes that film takes this process even further, making it the most powerful agent of the aura's destruction.[26]

The astonishment of early cinema, then, can be seen as a rupture in the auratic mode, enabled by the reproducibility of cinema. This rupture occurs by splitting two folds that, until that time, had always been unified in human perception – the sense of presence and the perception of living movement. Before reproducibility, perception of living movement was accompanied by a sense of presence; that is, any perceived movement also had presence in the here-and-now. After film's reproducibility, viewers could infold perceptions of living movement without sensing presence. Viewers could perceive movement that – due to the flatness of the screen, lack of colour, knowledge of the artifice, and other orientations – they did not sense a presence from and knew occurred elsewhere, in a there-and-then and not here-and-now. In short, the reproducibility of film enables a split between the viewer's space–time and the screen's space–time. This splitting disables the auratic mode, precluding the viewer from seeing the image's here-and-now as their same here-and-now. In its place, we have the first cinematic mode, in which the reproducibility of film is related to the viewer's capacity to sense presence and recognise living movement in ways that innervate astonishment.

The spark of astonishment, then, flows forth from the splitting of the viewer's folds, enabled by the reproducibility of cinema. Cinema's reproducibility allows the presentation of the image's time in a completely different space, divorcing the here from the now. The space–time of viewers, their sense of presence, becomes split from their perception of living movement on screen, which features another space–time. The viewer perceives lifelike movement that does not take place in the present, split between their here-and-now perception of movement and their sense or knowledge that this movement re-presents there-and-then. Viewers perceive movement without presence, or presence without aura, potentially innervating the spark of astonishment.

Such affections become a major resource for producers. Even when audiences no longer feel a sharp affection, cinema still draws on this affection, garnering some of its attraction from its reproducibility of lifelike movement. Even when the novelty of actualities wears off, the fold in space–time remained astonishing, as evidenced by the popularity of films featuring the audience's local community. People flocked to the theatres, hoping to catch a glimpse of themselves or people they know.[27] Exhibitors informed townspeople of the attraction of such local views: 'You can see pictures of your very own town, your very own fire department, and what is more, you can see yourself.'[28] If viewers saw themselves or other audience members, the folded self became visually apparent, a self split between their present body and past body displayed on screen. Musser mentions the potential desirability of such folding in the Vitascope scene, *Herald Square*:

> When the film was shown at Koster & Bial's Music Hall, spectators may have had the pleasure of seeing the exterior of the building inside of which they were sitting . . . In this play with space, outside became inside – a somewhat disconcerting experience, greatly heightened by the lifelike quality of the image.[29]

In sum, astonishment represents the first special affection of cinema, one that became a major economic resource in the early twentieth century.

From Astonishment to the Fantastic

Astonishment, however, constitutes only one affection from early cinema, and the cinema of attractions developed many modes, not only the one evident in actualities. Indeed, by the turn of the twentieth century, this spark of live-action film had already begun to wane. Seeing 'actualities', the lifelike movement that so astounded viewers, became mundane as numerous exhibitors displayed films across the country. Musser reports that vaudeville shows started using films as chasers, the final act that ran as audiences left the theatre, and viewers started leaving the show early when the motion picture chasers appeared. This 'general indifference' to film programmes led to a widespread economic crisis from 1900 to 1903.[30] As the astonishment over lifelike realism wore thin, actualities no longer offered a viable commodity, unable to compete with the many other attractions composing the vaudeville stage, fairs and travelling shows. Cinema would bounce back from this decline by discovering another spark and taking the first steps towards the classical mode. Cinematographer Charles Pathé outlined the coming translations as early as 1902:

> When the kinematograph appeared, its only goal was to demonstrate the progress of science and human wisdom, which is to say to bring photography to life. The least everyday event sufficed. The same is no longer true today, when exhibitors have raised it to the level of theatre.[31]

These translations emerge in an entertainment culture located primarily in fairgrounds, vaudeville stages, carnivals, circuses and other public venues. Such locations featured different 'attractions' enticing the modern consumer, 'attractions' being the word that, by the time Eisenstein incorporated it into his theory for the montage of attractions, 'had been on everyone's lips, or almost, for *nigh on thirty years already*'.[32] Early filmmakers had to adapt to these viewing environments since movies lacked the institutional home that the later nickelodeon boom would provide. Before this time, filmmakers had to address a cultural environment accustomed to the attraction format.[33] Such an entertainment environment should remind us that consumer capitalism has been mining affect for some time, well before scholars pronounced the rise of an affect economy. Attractions were designed to shock, amaze, astound or otherwise tickle spectators.

Since filmmakers had to address the economic force of attractions, and since lifelike movement alone no longer astonished, filmmakers began developing other means. Many cinematic modes emerge, collectively constituting the 'cinema of attractions'. Gunning even goes so far as to claim that attractions represent the aesthetic form of modernity.[34] Just as attractions offer a series of affective shocks and pleasurable distractions, the fast pace and tumultuous change of early modernism seemed to make experiences of shock and distraction an everyday fact of life. Thus Gunning concludes that the cinema of attractions continued the modern trend

towards 'a new culture of consumption which arouses desire through an
aggressive visuality'.[35] Cinema shared in this trend with fairs, circuses,
vaudeville acts, department stores and amusement parks, each part of a
'modern channeling of visuality towards the production of desire essential
for the creation of consumer culture'.[36]

From this epochal angle, Gunning's thesis appears correct. The cinema
of attractions contributed to a consumerist environment stressing visual
spectacle and aiming for affective response. Indeed, many scholars,
worried about the limitations of technological determinism, have instead
placed film in this context, positing a 'modernity thesis'.[37] Under a modernity thesis, film becomes explored as a contributor to a broader formation
called modernity. In animation studies, for instance, Esther Leslie ties
early Disney to a modernist aesthetic, one that she argues Disney abandons as they move to replicate cinematic realism.[38]

While the warnings against a teleological determinism remain well
founded, the modernity thesis conflates the impact of various media,
modes and affects under the wide-ranging and ill-defined banner of
modernity.[39] In short, modernity theses end up repeating the gesture
critiqued in the introduction – erasing differences in mediated experience
and conflating the impact of various media. According to the modernity
thesis, Disney animation and Hollywood cinema contribute similarly to
consumer culture and the formation called 'modernity'. Again, such a
thesis is undeniable from a certain level of analysis, one that attends to
social formations more globally and over long historical epochs. Affect
theory, in contrast, directs our attention to differences in mediated experience and cultural consequence, differences often erased by an epochal
point of view. What is needed, then, instead of modernity theses or
technological determinism is attention to the differences in modes and
affections emergent in different historical moments. Indeed, in this early
period, many filmic modes existed, including seeing films as actuality, as
visual newspapers, as magic tricks, as travelogues, as the recording of a
play, as erotic spectacle, or as narrative with spatio-temporal structures
very different from the later classical mode.[40] Musser shows that, rather
than quick distraction and pleasurable spectacle, some early films were
presented as objects for aesthetic judgment or as reproductions of fine art
designed for the sustained reverie of a contemplative mode. Since the films
were incorporated into live shows, the performers employed the films for
many purposes, constituting numerous modes along the way. Conflating
all of these modes under a single 'mode of attraction' erases this diversity.

Therefore, we should understand the cinema of attractions not as a
single mode, but as outlining a factor contributing to film's modal econo-

mies. Attraction was not so much a mode as a force; audiences of the time expected attractions, and this expectation constituted a flow of energy enticing consumers and producers alike. Early film developed many modes to tap into this energy, discovering in cinema not only the potential for astonishment over lifelike realism but also the potential for amazement over the display of fantasy. We will call this other spark the fantastical, indicating the physical appearance of something that seems to exist only in the imagination. The fantastical is the affective experience of seeing what cannot be seen, which can also be described as the affection resulting from the split between human eye and camera eye. Many commentators attest to this fantastical spark of the cinema, extolling the realistic fantasies of cinema, describing it as a camera-eye that explores fictional and non-fictional worlds from the ancient past to the distant future, the deep undersea to outer space. Amazed viewers connect cinema to the supernatural worlds of dreams, fairy-tales, legends, myths and science fiction. For instance, in 1912 Heinz Ewers praised Edison as the inventor of the movies because 'he returned fantasy to the matter-of-fact world'.[41] In 1911, Adolph Slaby exclaimed that in the movies, 'Every dream becomes real.'[42] By 1914, scholar Hugo Münsterberg concluded, *'The massive outer world has lost its weight, it has been freed from space, time, and causality, and it has been clothed in the forms of our own consciousness . . . It is a superb enjoyment which no other art can furnish us.'*[43]

Many early theorists also testify to this fantastical spark, describing the cinema as a machinic eye or vision machine with powers to reveal dreams and fantasies. Essentially, they describe the amazement of folding between human and machine eye, of seeing with human eyes what only cameras can reveal. Surveying these early film theorists, Viva Paci describes their shared affection as the result of cinema's 'ability to touch viewers, to shock them, through suddenness, attacks, and assaults' by not re-presenting the real world but by offering 'hitherto unseen ways of shaping time'.[44] Benjamin labels these unseen ways the optical unconscious. The camera opens up a whole new world by greatly magnifying things, or swooping across their surfaces, or approaching them from a difficult angle, or slowing down or speeding up movement, revealing previously unseen and unknown aspects of reality. Benjamin concludes with a tone of amazement evincing this fantastic spark:

> Clearly, it is another nature which speaks to the camera as compared to the eye. 'Other' above all in the sense that a space informed by human consciousness gives way to a space informed by the unconscious . . . Many of the deformations and stereotypes, transformations and catastrophes which can assail the world in films afflict the actual world in psychoses, hallucinations, and dreams. Thanks to the camera,

therefore, the individual perception of the psychotic or the dreamer can be appropriated by collective perception. The ancient truth expressed by Heraclitus, that those who are awake have a world in common while each sleeper has a world of his own has been invalidated by film . . . by creating figures of collective dream, such as the globe-encircling Mickey Mouse.[45]

Here, Benjamin conflates animation and cinema, perhaps because both mediums may access the fantastic spark. Yet cinema's fantastic is different because it entails seeing lifelike movement that could not be seen before. In short, cinema innervated two different sparks in its early history, a spark of astonishment over lifelike movement and a spark of amazement over the fantastical, of the optical unconscious, of seeing what could not previously be seen. The fantastical spark flows forth from a mode that relates the camera's manipulability to the viewer's folds of visual perception and imagination. Manipulability designates the camera's capacity to manipulate space and time, such as slowing movement down, stopping it or speeding it up, as well as moving closer to or through space in ways not possible with the human eye. Prior to this manipulability, people could only see things with their eyes and had to imagine other transformations in space, time or form. As Benjamin notes, the manipulability of cinema allowed viewers to see things previously only imaginable. Fantasy images became materialised. Such manipulability constituted images that looked like those most frequently experienced in the imagination, fusing the foldings of visual perception with those of the imagination. In short, the fantastic labels the spark of affection felt from the fusion of vision and imagination, from seeing images with eyes previously only perceivable in minds.

In the sparks of astonishment and fantastic we can discern the beginnings of a cinematic economy between the realistic or lifelike and the fantastical upon which the classical cinema will draw. The attraction of lifelike movements constitutes one force affecting viewers, whereas the other pole comes from cinema's fantasy worlds. Benjamin finds both forces in film, noting how film first moved viewers by exploring 'the necessities governing our lives' and its 'commonplace milieu', and then by opening up the 'vast and unsuspected field of action'.[46] Both forces also exist from nearly the outset of film. Early filmmakers shot travel destinations or other actualities, while others constructed fictional plots and magical illusions. To film theorist Siegfried Kracauer, 'Their prototypes were Lumière, a strict realist, and Méliès, who gave free reign to his artistic imagination. The films they made embody, so to speak, thesis and antithesis in a Hegelian sense.'[47] Whereas Lumière films showed actual trains moving, Méliès pictured model trains floating into outer space in *The Impossible Voyage*.

Over cinema's history, practitioners and theorists repeatedly evoke and extend the poles of this economy. Many filmmakers created movies featuring fantasy worlds, dreams, hallucinations, or fictional settings from the distant past or deep future, from the recesses of sleeping dreams or waking fantasies. Art historian Rudolph Arnheim even decried the tendency towards naturalistic realism, seeing it as the result of economic impetuses rather than artistic ones: 'Every step that brings film closer to real life creates a sensation. Each new sensation means full houses.'[48] To Arnheim, these influences were unfortunate. The financial pressures led cinema further away from its true calling, an artistic portrayal of the fantastical.[49] Others chose to praise realistic imagery and style. Director André Bazin, for instance, esteems the work of the Italian neorealists, who rely on a documentary style, non-professional actors, and actual settings and situations while discouraging editing and camera tricks. Bazin praises the replication of reality as cinema's guiding myth, 'a recreation of the world in its own terms, an image unburdened by the freedom of inter-pretation of the artist or the irreversibility of time'.[50] Likewise, Kracaeur insists that films are more satisfying if they build from realism.[51] Films should stick closely to physical reality in order to claim 'aesthetic validity' because

> whenever a filmmaker . . . ventures into the realm of fantasy, he runs the risk of defying the basic properties of his medium . . . (H)e seems no longer concerned with physical reality but bent on incorporating worlds which . . . lie outside the orbit of actuality.[52]

Although these debates were often heated, neither side can be described as 'correct' because cinema does not constitute an opposition between realism and fantasy but an economy, with both forces in play and different modes modulating those forces. Cinema's reliance on the photograph, the photograph's assumed fidelity, the fascination with reproduced move-ment, and the economic incentives of advances in naturalism all work to create realism as one pole, drawing on the energy of astonishment. Cinema's use of editing and montage, the wonder over trick shots and moving cameras, the economic incentives of the attraction, and the influ-ence of other art forms all work to create the imaginary as the other pole, drawing on the energy of the fantastical. Focusing on either misses the terms of their mutual relation. Cinematic modes include real movements and fantastical ones, real spaces related to imaginary spaces, real time related to imaginary time. The cinema brings the two into relation, con-necting the real and fantasy, tapping into the forces of cinema's lifelike and fantastic images. The classical mode will do so by translating -abilities from the cinema of attractions, theatre and literature into a perception in which *discontinuous shots are perceived as a continuous whole.*

The Classical Cinematic Mode

Although the classical cinema draws on this economy between fantasy and realism, classical Hollywood constitutes a different mode for inner-vating the sparks of astonishment and fantastic. The classical mode translates the cinema of attraction, both sharing some aspects with it and also transforming it. The classical mode shares the force of attraction of the single shot, what we might awkwardly call cinema's 'attractability'. The attractable shot becomes one element of the classical economy. Films before the classical mode were mostly one long shot, with a sin-gular framing, shown frontally, without camera movement or montage. The shot itself was whole, the autonomous unit containing the content. Whereas the classical mode makes the continuous whole internal to the film, early cinema's whole was the exhibition, external to any one film. The whole show was a discontinuous string of attractions, linked by performers, while the films are typically one continuous shot contribut-ing to this whole. The films contain movement within the shots but do not internally constitute a continuous narrative.[53] Early cinema presumed that the viewer and camera-spectator were identical, both watching an attraction unfolding before the lens. Movies did not put the viewer and camera into a dynamic relation, requiring audiences to interpret the relation between shots and to record the whole. Whereas early viewers engaged in mostly a bipartite relation between the public audience and filmic attraction, classical viewers must negotiate a tripartite relation including the camera and narrative world. Early cinema relates the single shot to the whole event; the shot is a discontinuous segment of a con-tinuous exhibition of attractions. There is no whole movie, and hence no perception of narrative in the classical manner.

The classical mode taps into the force of attraction yet modulates it differently. The whole becomes internal to the film, and the attraction becomes a single element. In other words, classical cinema uses the camera and editing to construct an independent spectatorial space–time, transforming the spectator 'from a participant in a concrete and variable situation of reception to a term that informs the structure of the film as product'.[54] The spectator is no longer assumed to be part of a public audience but is presumed to be an individual viewer deciphering a nar-rative whole. The shots that constituted the whole attraction in early film remain; viewers are still attracted to, or astonished or amazed by single, spectacular shots. As Gaudreault remarks, attractions are everywhere in classical cinema as well, such as in chase scenes, special effects and gags, even to the point where they may be called 'the kernel' of most views.[55] Yet classical cinema differently modulates these attractions, counterposing them not to a whole show of different attractions but to the whole narrative. To put it otherwise, the attractions remained (in the discontinuous shots) but the classical mode adds the attraction of the whole.

In short, the classical mode puts two capacities of the cinematic apparatus into relation – the capacities for discontinuity and for continuity. These capacities stem from cinema's two technological pre-conditions – the discontinuous snapshot and the continuous projector. The snapshots create discontinuity through the reproducible capture of space, whereas the projector and reel create continuity in duration. Photographs create discontinuous images plucked from the flow of time. Then, the movement mechanism projects the images in succession, creating continuity. Likewise, classical filmmakers work with this economy between the continuous and discontinuous. Their task is to construct a continuous whole from the linkage of discontinuous shots. For the filmmaker, accomplishing this task entails an art of the whole (montage, editing) and an art of images (framing, shooting). The filmmaker shoots scenes and then edits, arranging the shots for their continuous projection. By shooting and editing the filmmaker creates the two basic elements of classical film, the shot and whole, with the whole in the classical mode being a narrative. The discontinuous snapshots make up a continuous shot and the discontinuous shots make up a continuous whole. These two arts thus represent the two poles of a classical cinematic economy, of discontinuity and continuity, frame and whole. As Deleuze discerns:

> Hence the situation of the shot, which can be defined abstractly as the intermediary between the framing of the set and the montage of the whole, sometimes tending towards the pole of framing, sometimes tending toward the pole of montage. The shot is movement considered from this dual point of view: the translation of the parts of a set which spreads out in space, the change of a whole which is transformed in duration.[56]

The classical cinema enables the perception of discontinuous shots as a whole narrative by translating from theatre and literature alike, drawing on the capacities of cinema that we will call translocatability and transposability. In these translations, classical cinema borrows techniques, stories and practices from literature and theatre but also transforms them by differently relating to the audience, splitting the space–time of the viewer from those of the spectator-camera and diegesis. Like the cinema

of attractions, literature and theatre operate through a bipartite relationship between audience and diegesis. Cinema adds a third interface, the
camera-spectator position, requiring that viewers relate not only to the
image content but also to camera movements, placements and duration in
order to decipher the whole.

This camera-spectator constitutes cinema's virtual potential for transposability and translocatability. Transposability designates the potential to
change the spectator's point of view, moving their position throughout the
diegetic world. Translocatability designates the potential to direct spectator attention through such techniques as framing, lighting and camera
movements. Translocatability is different from transposability because
the latter designates the movement from shot to shot while the former
designates techniques within shots. Both transposability and translocatability contribute to the classical mode's economy between discontinuity
and continuity, shot and whole, and thus each taps into the forces of
realism and fantasy, astonishment and fantastic. Transposability helps
constitute the whole by allowing multiple shots to be pieced together, but
it also creates discontinuities by cutting into or away from the current
scene. Translocatability helps create a continuity of space by suggesting
that off-screen space exists and is connected to on-screen space. As the
camera pans to show something to the side, attention is redirected and
the screen's frame is revealed not to be a boundary. Yet translocatability
also introduces discontinuities into the scene by redirecting attention,
discontinuities that often punctuate the rhythms of progression. Likewise,
translocatability can be used to show a realistic scene or to create the
optical unconscious, just as transposability can construct either the most
realistic or the most fantastic narrative.

Although translated from literature and theatre, cinema's transposability and translocatability remain unique. While the theatre includes
motion, it lacks transposability. The viewer's point of view is typically
singular; they rarely move around the room to find better angles and certainly do not repeatedly alter position. In contrast, the cinema spectator's
point of view may be transposed. The viewer is shown close-ups closer
than any actual perspective and then the landscape from a distance. The
viewer sees from the protagonist's point of view, then antagonist's, then
sees both from the side. The spectator jumps across time or space, moving
from one building, city or even planet to the next. The theatre can change
times and places but usually requires a change of staging to do so. The
instantaneous shifting, especially the rapid transposing common in many
movies, is difficult if not impossible in theatre.

Transposing entails relating the spectator's position to the diegetic world, through multiple shifts in point of view. Theatre faces numerous difficulties in similarly relating spectator and diegetic space. Theatre actors may adapt to the audience, but theatre nevertheless demarcates viewer space from narrative space. Conventionally, a 'fourth wall' separates viewer space from performance space. The performance occurs on a stage, a word that indicates its difference from real, everyday space. Very literally, everything on stage is staged. Of course, some *avant-garde* productions attempt to violate the fourth wall. Yet important differences remain. Even when the fourth wall is violated, this occurs in order to bring viewers into the diegetic space; the viewer becomes part of the performance. The viewer's real space is not related to the diegetic space; it is included within the theatrical world. Even if we go to see the most *avant-garde* performance challenging the fourth wall, we still go to the theatre, a location clearly bounded and designated for diegetic worlds. Such performances, in fact, recognise the marking off of diegetic space as a fundamental condition of theatre and seek ways to play with or problematise this condition.

Further, theatre's demarcation of viewer and diegetic space means that the distinction between on-stage and off-stage does not make sense when applied to the screen. The camera-spectator can go anywhere in the movie world; the whole world's a stage. The theatre can portray all types of fantastical worlds, but it can only do so on the stage. Thus theatre is more limited to the logical use of space than the transposing cinema. The movie screen has an edge but this edge does not work like a frame in the same way. The classical cinema's frame remains open to a whole, continuous world, not enclosed within the stage space, and thus cinema comes equipped with the potential to transpose throughout this world.

Unlike theatre, literature holds the potential for such transpositions. Literature also arranges and links scenes to tell a story. In both cinema and literature, audiences read a narrative through linked scenes told from particular points of view. For McLuhan, these shared properties with literature were crucial to cinema's popularity, and the influence of literature on film is well established, with many movies based on books and with directors employing conventions drawn from prose.[57] Cinema, especially in the classical mode, works through a narrative legibility and transposability similar to literature.

Cinema's transposability and translocatability remain distinct from literature, however, because the primary substance and content are different. Words constitute the primary substance of literature, which depends on description to create image content. Literature moves from words on the page to a reader's interpretation. The second step is a creative transformation, one that will vary from reader to reader, who form mental pictures. In contrast, cinema's legible images are shared as collective reality; each viewer sees the same images from the same points of view, even if they interpret them differently. Literature can describe points of view, but these cannot position (transpose) the viewer or redirect their visual attention (translocate). Both narrative space and reader space stay confined in their own worlds. The reader's actual perspective never changes; they remained gazing downward, a couple of feet from the pages. In cinema, the viewer's perspective is altered in relation to the diegetic world, via spectator space. The spectator space is displayed rather than described. In other words, the difference in substance results in a difference in content between the interiorised legibility of literature and the exteriorised legibility of cinema.

To elucidate, a distinction between viewer, spectator and narrative space–time will be helpful. Viewer space–time indicates the present space–time of the person watching the movie or reading the book. The narrative space–time means the world portrayed on the paper or the screen. Spectator space–time describes the 'textual' positioning and locating of the camera in relation to the narrative world. This is the 'spectator in the text' that has been a focus of much film theory.[58] In literature, narrative and viewer space–time remain distinct. With a book, everyone assumes the divide between narrative and reader space. It does not matter where the reader reads, and authors have no way of knowing where the reading occurs in order to adapt narrative space. In addition, cinema differently splits the temporal experience. Scholars of literature distinguish between story time, narrator time and reader time, the time it takes to read. Reader time varies for each reader and even each reading; the audience determines the time spent. In fact, it does not make sense to say a sentence has duration. The sentence, when read, has duration, yet this varies for each reader and may even be skipped (aghast!). The reader can stop, ponder, doze, reread, skim, skip ahead; the reader determines the pace. Literature can shape narrative time but can only suggest audience time; the times cannot be put into relation.

Cinema, in contrast, can relate the viewer, spectator and narrative time. Each frame lasts exactly 1/24th of a second since the apparatus projects at twenty-four snapshots per second to ensure smooth movement. Each picture is thus a duration, exactly and always 1/24th of a second. The substance is a moment in time, what Deleuze calls a mobile section of movement. Time/motion goes into the camera, is split up into instants and then projected back into time/motion. As a result, spectator time never varies. Even if I leave for the toilets, the movie continues to run.

Obviously, DVD players add some control, but the film's length is still not changed by viewers. Only cinema captures and directs viewer time by splitting it from spectator time. In order to see a film, we must invest a precise amount of time because the film is filled with that much time. Directors can present objects for as long as they wish, and duration becomes a crucial part of the experience.

By the term translocatability I intend this ability to control duration and relocate spectator attention. With translocatability, filmmakers can direct spectator time. Translocation includes zooming in on a bloody fingerprint, panning to follow a character exiting a room, dollying along the side of a building, or any other camera motion, including slow motion and the like. With these motions, eyes are translocated, moved from one point of attention to another. These movements also include various fades, irises and dissolves redirecting and colouring attention. Translocatability is an essential element of filmmaking and reception. The narrative unfolds by using viewer time, directing five seconds of attention here or a minute there. With literature and graphic arts, the works cannot use viewer time or relate it to the narrative time. Books and paintings can beckon or suggest audience time but not control it. The painter cannot determine if viewers glance or gaze and thus cannot use the difference to suggest meaning. In contrast, cinematic modes often require interpretation of how long we look.

Take a montage sequence. Sometimes, a montage sequence condenses an expanse of time through a few representative scenes, such as Rocky's year-long boxing training portrayed through a few alternating shots. Such montage sequences control viewer attention in order to express something; viewer time becomes material for narrative effects. Another example is the close-up, often used to convey affect. The camera moves in on a face to show its intensive reaction. Close-ups manipulate space–time, frequently showing the expression for longer than the actual response could have lasted. Furthermore, the close-up rips the face from the narrative sequence to hold it up for expressive display, detaching the face from its surroundings to put it in relief. In Deleuze's terms, the close-up 'abstracts [the face] from all spatio-temporal co-ordinates, that is to say it raises it to the state of Entity'.[59] Benjamin's optical unconscious also describes ways that the camera can direct attention and control viewing time, such as slow motion. Slow motion extends movement, often creating heightened suspense by mimicking a suspenseful experience, which seems to hang in the balance for longer than clock–time attests. The camera's potential for moving, stretching, isolating, slowing down or speeding up, enlarging or reducing allows a measure of control over viewer time and colours attention.

This transposability and translocatability of cinema is related, in the classical mode, to the viewer's potential for infolding: namely, their capacity for taking up a perspective, for sensing position (proprioception) and for remembering. Drawing an analogy between the viewer's perception and the camera, Christian Metz notes that two of these capacities are crucial for cinematic perception: 'Releasing [the film] I am the projector, receiving it, I am the screen; in both these figures together, I am the camera, which points and yet which records.'[60] Watching a movie, viewers must project, taking up a point of view, and also record the sequence of images. In other words, the viewer acts similarly to a movie camera, both projecting their eyes and recording with their memories.[61] Such projection is not an automatic process, as McLuhan's anecdote about an African tribe's struggles with interpreting motion pictures illustrates. The audience did not understand that they were supposed to take up the camera's perspective. Instead, seeing the screen as a logical and bounded space separate from themselves, they wondered what happened to the chicken that wandered off the screen.[62] Following the translocations and transpositions requires the viewer to know how to actualise their capacity to take up the camera's perspective, peering into the cinematic world from that point. The viewer receives what the camera sees by taking the camera's position, establishing a point of view.

The viewer's recording entails remembering the plot or following dialogue but is also more significant than these basic procedures. The viewer must also record the transpositions and translocations, the points of view and camera movements offered. This is why most theorists accord so much import to montage. Directors often convey meaning through the relationship of images, linking images to create symbolic meaning (a person being killed contrasted with a lamb to suggest innocence) or to create a temporal relationship (Rocky's training). Audiences follow the meaning and plot by recording the sequence. In addition, recording when the camera pans to blood on the villainess's glove is crucial to comprehension. Viewers instinctively know that the camera moves in relation to them, and thus quietly ask, 'Why did the camera show me that?' As Deleuze notes, '(T)he frame teaches us that the image is not just given to be seen. It is legible as well as visible.'[63]

What transposability and translocatability enable, then, is a split between the viewer's foldings of perspective, recording and positionality, or, more simply, between spectator space–time and viewer space–time. Prior to transposability and translocatability, any time a person took up a perspective, that perspective was tied to their spatial position. One could peer into the world, but only from their individual position. Thus proprioception and visual perspective were always fused. Even when we look into a painting done with Renaissance perspective, the perspective is not transposed or translocated; the perspective is singular, fixed, and directly articulated to an assumed position of the viewer's body. In experiencing cinematic transpositions and translocations, this fusion becomes severed. The camera perspective changes, whereas the viewer's body remains positioned in the same space. There is a splitting of proprioception and visual perspective that remains crucial to some of the special affections of classical cinema – including those of shot and whole, whether realistic or fantastic. Likewise, anything a person remembered was tied to our position in space; we simply had to be there to form a recallable memory. With the transpositions and translocations of cinema, viewers could now witness unfolding events without their bodies being present in that world.

Enabling the manipulation of relations between diegetic space and viewer space via spectator space, transposability and translocatability alter the viewer's proprioception by splitting it from typical modes of remembering and visual perspective, which were previously fused to bodily position. It is not, as many have claimed, that the viewer 'enters the screen'. The viewer's space does not change; the viewer does not physically change position. The reverse is more apt. The diegetic space comes out into viewer space: that is, it changes shape in relation to viewers. Noting this reversal, Benjamin sees film as extending the masses' desire for closeness.[64] The moving pictures come closer – in more intimate relation – to the viewer, moving in relation to their space. The screen's world can come nearer or go further away; the spectator can be positioned above the dialogue or below the table. The spectator can take the perspective of a god or an ant.

This bringing closer attests to the viewer's folding between their space–time and that of the spectator, a folding that also happens to actors (and again reminds us of the shared nature of modes that influence producers and consumers alike). Unlike theatre, actors perform in a space–time distant from the viewing. Thus distanced from actors, the audience is brought closer to the role. As the camera moves in for a close-up, or away for a long shot, or takes the protagonist's perspective, the viewer is brought closer to the role. The diegetic world changes shape in relation to the spectator. Indeed, film separates the actor and role in a way denied in theatre, with two consequences.[65] First, the splitting of role and actor precludes the actor from adapting to the present audience. The film actor's performance is folded between actor and role, occurring in various locations over an elongated and often disjointed period of shooting. Thus the actor's performance becomes fragmented, subject 'to a series of optical tests'.[66] The actor performs for the apparatus, rather than a live audience, subjecting their image to the test of how it will appear when transferred to the screen. The actor still seeks to impress the audience, but does so via an intermediary. They presume the spectator's transposability, and act with one eye to this camera–spectator, hoping their images project a captivating and distinct imprint.

Second, audiences gain critical separation from the actor's aura while moving closer to the role, through the camera–spectator position. As Benjamin remarks, '*Consequently, the audience takes the position of the camera; its approach is that of testing.*'[67] The role is existent only on the screen, taking place through the camera, which 'continually changes its position with respect to the performance'.[68] The viewer relates to the spectator-camera position located in the world of the role, a world in which the actor is absent. With the actor dismissed, so too is their aura dispelled. The unique phenomenon of a distance relies on the presence of live actors, whose embodied selves attest to their singular expanse of time. A theatre actor's performance has aura because it is experienced as an integral whole of actor and role. With the actor gone in film, the aura dissipates and the role is brought closer to the audience. Viewers never see the actor and thus rarely experience the temporal distance of an auratic mode. Instead, films present merely 'shadows' of actors, shadows composing their role.[69] Separated from actors, spectators are transposed and translocated in relation to the role.

Such splitting remains essential to invoking the special affections of classical cinema, allowing films to tap into the astonishment of realism without being too real (close but not too close) and the fantastic feelings of imagination without being too unreal (far out but not too far). First, the transpositions and translocations create an enhanced realism, an affection by lifelike movement, whether viewers become fully astonished or not. The frequency of classical cinema's translocations and transpositions means viewers must repeatedly comport to other, unfolding and shifting spectator and narrative space–times, rapidly adjusting from one shot's attraction to the next. Benjamin calls this viewing experience a 'reception in distraction', claiming that such reception works more through habit – through bodily comportment and adjustment – than through conscious processing.[70] People learn to watch movies similarly to how they learn to negotiate architecture – not by reflection but by practice, by adjusting to space. Many Deleuzian film scholars concur that understanding cinematic desires requires attention to the body, the kinetic, the tactile, habit, affect.[71] The dizziness produced by Hitchock's camera in *Vertigo* (1958) or the shock felt from the booming speakers during a giant explosion are essential to the experience. This recognition of cinema as a bodily, sensual experience suggests the significant import of translocatability. The term translocate has many denotations that connote this affective experience, such as unsettling, upsetting, budging, churning, boosting and stirring. Through camera translocations, cinema creates sensations of movement, received affectively. The body's ability to sense motion is activated, creating a temporal experience unique from literature and theatre.

Indeed, such reception in distraction contrasts with the preferred mode for literature and the fine arts. Admirers of these arts trumpet an ideal of contemplative reception. Viewers or readers should look and relook, read and reread, pause to think. Although the ideal is rarely achieved, the idea expresses something important about the temporality of reception. With the contemplation of art, the audience enters into the work: that is, they construct the work by investing their viewing time. The viewer becomes part of the work; their investment of time gives the work an unfolding. Since beholders of literature or fine art control the reception time, substantial contemplation is held as the ideal and contrasted with distraction, those viewers who do not invest the 'appropriate' time. Normative arguments seek to discipline audiences into a contemplative mode. *Film takes this instruction out of the realm of didactics and into the realm of mechanics.* Cinema's translocatability enables control over reception time. Instead of requiring conscious investment, filmmakers can directly address the body, shaping and relocating attention. In the classical mode, viewers surrender their time to film control. They invest a certain amount of time, and the film directs where and how their attention moves. The viewers, in Benjamin's words, 'absorb the work of art into themselves'.[72]

More precisely than Benjamin, what happens is not the viewer entering the film but the relating of viewer space–time to narrative space–time through the interface of spectator space–time. The transposability and translocatability of the spectator relates viewer and narrative space–time. This delineation should be made because the conflation of viewer, spectator and screen space–time has been the source of much confusion. For one, many film theorists suggest that the viewer enters the screen. Theorists conclude that this positioning elicits viewer identification, with viewers at times becoming so absorbed as to react affectively. Certainly identification occurs, but the claim that viewers enter the screen remains imprecise because it conflates viewer and spectator space. At times, viewers look *through* the spectator into the world; at others, however, they look *at* the movie, taking note of the special effects, framing, quality or realism of the scene. The viewer interprets not just the things shown but also the spectator's position in relation to that world. Why am I shown these things? Why did the camera flash to the doorknob? In the classical mode, viewers must oscillate between witnessing the diegetic world through the spectator position and interpreting the movie from their own.

Rather than entering the screen, viewer space remains separate from the screen, whereas the spectator space enters, or more precisely frames, the screen. Spectator space is mostly made 'invisible' in classical cinema but exists between viewer and filmic world. Viewers are split between the spectator and their own position. This split is fundamental to the other pleasures of classical cinema: namely, the pleasures of the fantastic. The separation of viewer and spectator space leads to a cognitive recognition of the separation of real and fictional worlds: that is, viewers know that they are watching a movie. As Carroll points out, viewers would be unlikely to respond in the same way if they are fooled into believing these were real events: that is, if they actually enter the screen. 'Who wants to be bombarded by the Empire's laser cannons?'[73] Yet in *Star Wars* (Lucas, 1977), viewers can experience a thrill from bombarding lasers precisely because of the split between viewer and spectator space. They can watch through the spectator without facing the danger. Thus, while being thrilled by the (astonishing, lifelike) suspense of the Empire's attack, viewers can respond differently, more able to enjoy the action without the doom that would come from being in the scene. By transposing the spectator, viewers can relate to the screen from a safe distance, generating different cognitive and affective responses.

The contention that the viewer enters the screen has a flip-side that equally conflates spectator and viewer space. Other film theorists, like Metz, presume that viewer and screen space are radically separate. Metz acknowledges that viewers know they watch a movie; the viewer realises that the screen referents are radically absent.[74] This means that viewers remain strictly segregated from the screen, rather than entering, like the segregation of people and their mirror image. Film is thus 'like a mirror', with one other crucial difference – 'there is one thing and only one thing that is never reflected in it: the spectator's own body.'[75] So, for Metz, the absent viewer and the segregation of the screen demarcate two different relations of presence and absence. The referents are absent from the viewer, and conversely viewers are absent from the screen. This condition makes the theatre and cinema fundamentally different, since 'the filmic spectacle, the object seen, is more radically ignorant of its spectator . . . than the theatrical spectacle can ever be.'[76] Movie voyeurs watch as if through a keyhole, absent from the unaware actors.

Metz's conflation of viewer and spectator space makes this a tenuous distinction between theatre and cinema. With theatre, the fictional referents are equally absent, even if the actors are present. As Carroll quips,

I can't reach out and touch one of the yellow bricks on the road to Oz; but then I can't wear Lear's crown either . . . In both fictional film and theatrical fiction, the characters are absent from the continuum of our world in the same way.[77]

Audience presence in the theatre does allow performers to adapt to their responses, yet actors usually perform *as if* the audience is not present and the audience usually watches without making their presence affect the events. More importantly, one cannot say that the filmic spectacle remains radically ignorant of viewers. Filmmakers might, like a novelist, remain radically ignorant of particular viewers but both are constructed with a generic audience in mind. In the classical mode, actors act 'naturally', as if the camera-spectator is not present. Yet the actors still act for the spectator-camera. In fact, the entire filmic performance is staged for the camera, creating spectator space–time to mediate between viewer and narrative.

Rather than a radical absence of viewer from diegetic world and world from viewer, cinema's transposability and translocatability contribute to a more complex relationship mediated through spectator space. Viewers gain presence in the filmic world through the spectator, garnering pleasures of presence while still maintaining safe distance. By relating viewer position to the spectator, viewers achieve a hybrid form of absent-presence. The conflation of viewer and spectator space, then, allows two imprecise evaluations: that the viewer enters the screen or that they are radically absent from it. Instead, the conceptualisation of transposability and translocatability allows us to delineate between spectator space–time and viewer space–time, revealing the dynamic relations of the classical viewer's foldings. Spectator space–time mediates between filmic world and viewer, in many complex ways belied by the conflation of viewer and spectator space.

In Chapter 3, these splits between viewer and spectator will be crucial for understanding the classical mode's contribution to a lifestyle mode of consumerism, splitting self and style, but for now a summary is in order. Transposability and translocatability describe the two -abilities of the cinematic medium actualised in the classical mode. The cinematic medium allows the spectator to be transposed and translocated in space–time, creating the possibility for the perception of discontinuous shots as a whole narrative. Of course, the viewer might not accept the spectator position; they might, instead, engage in a kind of reverie or focus on aspects not placed in central focus. In fact, many viewers reportedly do.[78] They do not relate themselves to spectator space. Yet cinema creates the potential for relating viewer space to spectator space; these are virtual -abilities, not determinations. Likewise, the modes are pre-personal and pre-subjective.

The viewer *can* see as the spectator. The cinema *can* transpose the spectator. As bodies actualise these -abilities, the classical mode will entail *perceiving discontinuous shots as a continuous, whole narrative* and thereby compose interfaces that Deleuze calls movement-images.

Managing the Split: Movement-Images as Interface

The split between viewer position and their perceptions (recording and projecting) requires careful management, lest the viewer's split sense of proprioception makes them feel lost in all the transposing and translocating. How, then, were transposability and translocatability actualised in classical film? How did the classical mode create an interface for managing this split? Perhaps one reason why commentators label it 'classical' is because filmmakers typically restricted the uses of translocatability, instead borrowing techniques from theatre. Mostly, classical theatre directs attention to the human actors through framing, staging and lighting. Spotlights or backdrop lighting reveal the focal part, or the main action takes place front and centre. Actors turn slightly to face audiences, orienting actions toward viewers, and those wearing the most distinct costumes are typically the main characters. Likewise, classical cinema frames human characters, directing attention to their words, movements and positions. Through translocation, David Bordwell remarks, 'the classical cinema declares its anthropocentric commitment: Space will signify chiefly in relation to psychological causality.'[79] The classical mode translocates spectator attention towards actions and their psychological causes; human action is the centre of interest.

Of course, cinema offers the potential for translocatability in ways denied to theatre, mainly through camera movements. For instance, if an action begins on the sides of the frame, the camera will pan to centre and draw attention. Attention can be translocated when a character's reaction to something off screen anticipates the cut to what they are seeing. At other times, the camera will track or dolly to follow a character in motion, maintaining their central framing. With each camera movement, the spectator's attention is translocated in ways denied to theatre, which does not control the spectator's projections. Over time, classical cinema begins to develop more camera movements for translocating attention, but, as we will see further with *20,000 Leagues* in the following chapter, the classical cinema remains primarily beholden to the techniques of theatre.

Classical cinema's translocations primarily adapt devices from theatre, including framing, lighting, staging in depth, deep focus, centring, balancing, frontality and the 180-degree rule, adding only a few camera movements. First, the frame is centred on a human character and typically filled from left to right to create balance. A common example is when two characters take positions across from one another, signalling that they will be the participants in conversation. Most often, the scene begins with a centred frame, but at times an actor might translocate attention by moving across the camera to fill an empty spot. The classical mode also furthers the human focus by mostly employing medium or three-quarter shots, from the knees up. In comparison to much early cinema, the actors are brought closer to the camera so that the viewer can discern facial and other bodily movements. This closer framing, known as the 'American foreground', also encouraged the shift to location shooting and three-dimensional sets, with walls, furniture and other props extending into the background, giving a greater depth of scene. The general lighting also contributes depth, and selective lighting helps centre attention on significant characters. Props and costumes serve a similar centring function, ornamenting main characters and drawing attention to their individuality. The combination of centring, lighting, staging in depth and deep focus shots places the spectator on the screen's edge, gazing into the depths of a narrative world.

With the spectator so located, directors follow a 180-degree rule, whereby action takes place in a half-circular region across from the spectator. Directly across from the spectator-camera is an invisible line; all action takes place in the 180-degree area across that line. Often, this results in circular shots where the characters form a half circle around the camera-spectator at the centre of the circle. Instead of closing ranks and completing the circle as most people in conversation typically do, each character is positioned so as not to block the spectator's view. As is common in theatre, characters face the audience, spreading out in space along the arc of the 180-degree half-circle, a characteristic known as frontality. At times, the shot will show a whole circle as well, with characters in the foreground, backs turned to the spectator, connecting the two ends of the centre line, but these characters do not cross the centre line and simply form a circle within the 180-degree area. Like classical theatre, classical cinema carefully manages the translocations of attention to 'create expectations about the most important elements in a scene . . . The classical composition took care to guide the spectator's eye to the pertinent actions without effort.'[80]

Deleuze describes this careful managing of the split between spectator and viewer as the unification of sensory-motor space. The classical cinema translocates and transposes in ways that fuse the viewer's sensory-motor space to the spectator's in order to facilitate an ease of perception. By linking these sensory-motor spaces, classical cinema creates an interface called movement-images. Transposing the spectator and translocating their attention allow classical filmmakers to present images of movement, of both the mobile section and the whole. It is not just because viewers perceive movement that classical cinema creates movement-images; instead, audiences perceive movement because the image is an image of movement – rather than an illusion of movement, as commonly understood – that carefully links the sensory-motor space of spectators to viewers.[81]

What, then, is movement? According to Deleuze, through an interpretation of Bergson, movement is 'a mobile section of duration, of the Whole'.[82] Think of walking across a room. The movement is the whole course, the duration crossing the expanse of space. You could, as Muybridge did with photography, cut that duration up into instants, but then you do not have movement. Muybridge's photos remain eerily still despite people being caught in action. So movement can only be conceived in relation to the whole, or the duration. There are, of course, a series of actions, such as raising your right leg then placing it down. These series are what Deleuze means by a 'mobile section'. So, movement is both the mobile sections and the duration, the whole. This whole is necessarily open, not a closed set. It is a duration, and thus cannot be given to anyone, stopped, objectified, contained, set. The whole movement exists only across time but is experienced only as a mobile section in time. We see, again, an economy between discontinuous sections and continuous whole. Movement operates by piecing discontinuous mobile sections into a continuous whole.

In fact, from the perspective of viewers and moviemakers alike, classical cinema produces movement-images, both mobile sections and the whole. The viewer perceives a whole movie, an open duration whose parts are only understood through the relation of its mobile sections. For the classical mode, this whole narrative is linked together by a kind of question-and-answer process.[83] Viewers engage in interrogation or hypothesis formation; each mobile section raises or answers a question, and the series of questions and answers provide a whole story. The discontinuous series of questions and answers results in a whole account. Deleuze describes this whole as open because the whole openly receives each question and answer. The whole is open to every shot, and every shot forms a link in the chain composing the whole. In the classical mode, this chain is cause and effect, action and reaction. The various shots are linked via a forwardly propelled cause–effect chain. One scene shows an action. The viewer wonders what will happen next. The next shows reaction, answering the original question but probably opening another, until all questions are answered. The classical mode creates a 'game of controlled expectation and likely confirmation', but in the end, the spectator-camera sees everything necessary to decipher the whole.[84]

The classical cinema composes movement-images through particular actualisations of cinema's transposability and translocatability. The translocations frame the images, creating different varieties of the mobile sections, whereas the transpositions link the images together to compose the whole. Within the shot, mobile sections are composed of three primary types: the perception-image, affection-image and action-image. The classical mode relies heavily on action-images, which are easy enough to understand. Action-images present an action or behaviour. For instance, in *20,000 Leagues* we see action-images when Ned battles the giant squid. These action-images display a relation between a milieu and embodied behaviour: 'The milieu and its forces incurve on themselves, they act on the character, throw him a challenge, and constitute a situation in which he is caught. The character reacts in his turn . . . He must acquire a new mode of being (*habitus*) or raise his mode of being to the demands of the milieu and of the situation.'[85]

Action-images dominate the classical mode, but perception-images and affection-images also play a role. The perception-image is basically an image that shows us something or shows someone perceiving something. In *20,000 Leagues*, the camera pans to a large shark circling Ned and Conseil as they hunt for treasure. Affection-images will be discussed further in the following chapters, but for now they can be summarised as images of people being affected, such as a look of shock, horror or elation. After seeing the shark, the camera pans back to show us Ned and Conseil react with fright. Affection-images present expression, and we read the quality or power of that expression. The close-up is the most common technique, and anyone who has seen Dreyer's *The Passion of Joan of Arc* (1928), a silent movie that tells the story of Joan's trial and execution almost exclusively through expressions on her and her accusers' faces, has witnessed the affection-image *par excellence*.

Classical translocations make the spectator, in David Bordwell's words, an 'ideally placed onlooker'.[86] The spectator sees the world through a window or knot-hole in the diegetic space, a space that typically is frontally presented, centred and framed in order for the viewer to locate the appropriate focus of attention easily.[87] The spectator's location is ideal, not for seeing everything in the diegetic world, since at times the framing obscures the scene or something takes place off screen. Their location is ideal, however, for seeing the affections, perceptions and actions composing the whole. The spectator is translocated so that they see everything necessary to complete the narrative. Bordwell describes this as an omni-presence of the spectator; translocation ensures that the spectator is located to see the mobile shots composing the whole story. In other words, the spectator's position is ideal for viewers to see the perceptions, actions and affections necessary to record the series of questions and answers, actions and reactions, structuring the narrative.

How, then, does the classical mode employ transposability to link these images and constitute the whole? Montage creates the continuous whole by linking together discontinuous shots. Through montage, the movie presents an *indirect image of time*: that is, a whole that is deduced from the relationships of the various shots. This is an indirect image because the viewer pieces together an approximation of the time of the narrative; we are not given this whole all at once but perceive it indirectly. Montage thus creates narrative time, the continuous whole. There are many different types of continuity that a montage might express, such as D. W. Griffith's continuity in the conflict between good and evil that is largely replicated in *20,000 Leagues*. Deleuze describes classical montage as organico–active. The classical mode conceives of the whole as an organism, an organic unity. From a set of differentiated parts (men and women, good and bad), a unity is formed. The parts 'act and react on each other in order to show how they simultaneously enter into conflict and threaten the unity of the organic set, and how they overcome the conflict or restore the unity'.[88] Ultimately, the indirect image of time presented by organico–active montage is Time as a circle, a unity achieved as we move from situation to resolution, ending with the common 'happy ending', such as in *20,000 Leagues* where Ned ousts Nemo.

Deleuze describes the classical mode's montage as organic because it creates an organic sense of space, a continuous world, that Deleuze calls the milieu or situation. 'This is realism.'[89] The organic montage creates a 'realistic' milieu that motivates, shapes and contains character actions. In other words, the transpositions convey a sense of continuous space by carefully orienting viewer space to spectator space. From one transposi-tion to the next, sometimes the space is contiguous and sometimes non-contiguous, but across them all the transpositions reinforce the viewer's spatial orientation by showing space from multiple, consistent angles. Deleuze describes this as establishing a sensory-motor linkage since trans-positions are minimised that do not synch with the normal sensory-motor perception of viewers. Scenes generally begin with establishing shots, often long shots of the scene, and then cut in closer to provide viewers with spatial orientation. If a character exits left, after the cut they enter right. Eyeline matches (someone is shown looking off screen then the cut shows what they are looking at from the character's eyeline), shot–reverse shots (SRS – where we see a conversation from over a person's shoulder and then alternate to behind the interlocutor) and point-of-view shots (where the camera takes a character's position) all transpose the spectator to create the viewer's sense of continuous space. When the spaces are non-contiguous, crosscutting and parallel editing occurs whereby the spectator is transposed between two spatially separate events, both occurring within the same continuous world. Such transpositions orient the viewer to adjacent spaces.

Classical Hollywood montage is organico-*active* because the whole constitutes a cause–effect chain of affection, perception and action dominated by action-images. Action motivates cycles of reaction until the whole is complete. As action-images, the classical mode almost invariably subscribes the causality to psychology. Mere motion is mechanical, without thought, but action requires intentionality and psychological motivation. Thus Deleuze describes the first pole of the action-image as the 'milieu' and the second as 'behaviour'. The milieu presents certain motivating qualities or powers and the behaviour responds. It constitutes a behaviourist model because psychology drives action; it reduces causality to psychological reaction in response to situations. Such behaviourism dictates two primary kinds of characters – types and stars – because each contains psychological motivations that are readily perceived. Types get their easily recognisable motivation from their generic status; the stars are more individualised, given unambiguous traits so that the viewer can easily decipher their motivation.

Given this behaviourist model, the most common narrative line runs from situation to action to transformed situation (SAS'). For instance, *20,000 Leagues* contains mostly action-images and moves through the SAS' cycle, from situation (capture in the *Nautilus*) to action (attempts to escape) to transformed situation (death of Nemo). The narrative is fundamentally psychological; it sets up a basic duel between Nemo's dark disposition (motivated by his experience of war) and the Professor's sanguinity (motivated by a belief in science). This SAS' cycle constitutes the basic template for the Hollywood version of the American Dream, in which those engaging in correct behaviour rise above the situation. As an image, the Hollywood American Dream is mostly an action-image, with two poles:

> on the one hand the idea of a unanimist community or of a nation-milieu, melting pot and fusion of all minorities . . . on the other hand the idea of a leader, that is, a man of this nation who knows how to respond to the challenges of the milieu.[90]

In *20,000 Leagues*, Ned represents the man of the nation who responds to the situation. He saves the Professor and the ship from the squid. The other pole, the unanimist milieu, is represented by the Professor and challenged by Nemo. The Professor believes technology can bring the abundance necessary for a true melting pot while Nemo sees only hatred and division. Ned saves the day, and we are led to believe that some day these marvellous inventions (the American Dream) will become reality.

Deleuze contends that the classical mode's organico-active montage and American Dream template 'produced the universal triumph of the American cinema'.[91] In fact, the mode was so consistent that he argues the American cinema 'constantly shoots and reshoots a single fundamental film'.[92] By the time Disney began shooting live-action movies like *20,000 Leagues*, such movement-images were in crisis due to this dulling repetition. The American Dream template had become a cliché; profits were declining. Yet Disney's live-action movies, not beginning until the end of the classical period, follow this template to a T; their late arrival to the classical mode marks them as clichés of the American Dream, blunt portrayals of lifestyle consumption. Such an analysis of *20,000 Leagues*, performed in the following chapter, will help us re-explain the widely established connection between the classical cinematic mode and consumerism. The connection, as we will see, depends fundamentally on the perceivability of new consumer bodies engaging in the classical mode, bodies with distinct affections from those of the modes of animation.

CHAPTER 3

Say Cheese! The Cinematic Lifestyle Consumer

The movie . . . offers as product the most magical of consumer commodities, namely dreams. It is therefore not accidental that the movie has excelled as a medium that offers poor people roles of riches and power . . . The life of display that the photo had taken from the rich, the movie gave to the poor with lavish hand . . . It meant that in the 1920s the American way of life was exported to the entire world in cans. The world eagerly lined up to buy canned dreams. The film not only accompanied the first great consumer age, but was also incentive, advertisement and, in itself, a major commodity.

McLuhan[1]

Here McLuhan outlines a connection between classical cinema and modern consumerism that many others have since repeated. Indeed, cinema's influence on consumer culture is practically a tenet of studies of contemporary capitalism. The front cover of Guy Debord's *Society of the Spectacle* features cinemagoers in 3D glasses, Max Horkheimer and Theodor Adorno often equate the culture industry and Hollywood, and Jonathan Beller describes contemporary capitalism as operating through a cinematic mode of production.[2] For these scholars, cinema represents the penultimate example of consumer culture, since it trades in images that garner attention, entice commodity fetishism and generate affection. As McLuhan says, cinema is an incentive, advertisement and itself a major commodity.

Although undeniable from the epochal angle of the modernity (or post-modernity) thesis, such accounts perform two conflations – conflating all forms of consumerism with cinema's lifestyle consumer and conflating the impact of animation and cinema on consumerism. In this chapter, I argue against these conflations, illustrating that the classical cinematic mode contributes to consumer culture in ways distinct from other forms of consumption. The classical mode makes perceivable a virtual body that will become envisioned as a lifestyle consumer, one that the culture industries will seek to sell particular commodities. While cinema retains a definite connection to consumerism, these connections, as well as the predominant theories of the emergence of modern consumer culture, become refined when understood through the perspective of affect and modes. Such analysis will be supported through an examination of Disney's first movie in the classical mode, *20,000 Leagues*. The movie constitutes a cliché of the American Dream and the movement-image regime, which today is likely to evoke affections I can only describe as cheesy, since it offers an aged, blunt representation of a dated mode and especially the virtual bodies perceivable through the mode – lifestyle consumers. Thus *20,000 Leagues* helps us specify cinema's unique contribution to consumer culture – how it makes visible lifestyle consumers and articulable commodities for lifestyle display.

Theories of Consumerism: From Innate Desires to Modal Productions

McLuhan depicts the 1920s as the 'first great consumer age', and certainly by this time the general aspects of consumer culture are well established and consumption has taken on an ideological status, appearing to be a natural, permanent feature of the landscape. Consumerism's triumph, however, began well before this; in fact, many historians now acknowledge that accompanying industrialism was a consumer boom providing the requisite fuel for continued growth.[3] Many different dates and causes of this boom have been proffered. Chandra Mukerji dates the rise to sixteenth-century Europe and the practices of the Elizabethan court.[4] McKendrick, Plumb and Brewer find the origin in the eighteenth century and the commercialisation of fashion.[5] Rosalind Williams traces the consumer boom to the nineteenth century with the coming of expositions and department stores.[6] None of these time periods or developments can be denied a supporting role. Consumer culture emerged as a translation of a variety of practices, a more complex and messier emergence than a single causal origin or time period can account for.

In fact, numerous causes and multiple periods contribute to twentieth-century consumer culture because modern consumerism demanded uprooting, displacing and transfiguring many cultural practices, particularly prior restraints on consumption. Although consumption occurs throughout history, such insatiable, ongoing and brisk consumption rarely existed until recently. The consumer revolution entailed a rapidity and voraciousness almost unheard of in prior eras, keeping pace with mass production and emptying the shelves of swelling inventory. To fuel such changes, the understanding of consumption's proper social role had to be dramatically altered. As Mary Anne Doane, one of the scholars to notice the connection between film and consumerism, remarks, 'Consumerism requires a transformation in modes of perception.'[7] Even if we correctly isolate the time period, this larger question of how consumer modes emerged and spread remains.

This search for a causal origin of modern consumerism has elicited a number of theories. Each theory provides insights into modern consumerism, yet most theories do not approach the question from a modal perspective and cannot account for the specific attractions, affections and manners of the wide variety of consumer practices constituting modern consumerism. Each theory tends to conflate all forms of consumerism, reducing them to a single cause. In fact, they perform a double conflation, reducing consumption to one mode and describing that consumption as driven by one cause. The first conflation overlooks the different ways in which desire is produced, and the second presupposes consumer characteristics, based in a speculative psychologism.

In contrast, modal theory reminds us that desire is produced rather than innate. As Deleuze and Guattari maintain, social constitution results from desiring-production; desiring-production is at work everywhere, driving social production.[8] Desiring-production is the result of 'desiring-machines', which are binary systems, always coupled with another machine, inherently connective or, we might say, *interfacing*. One machine produces a flow and another interrupts or channels this flow.[9] Modes are the code for this interfacing, the precepts for how desiring-machines link with other machines, orienting their capacities with other selves or objects to produce desire. Take the classical mode as example. The movie constitutes a flow of images and the spectator is the plug that diverts the flow into a locus of perception for viewers.

Conceiving desire as machinic production is radically different from theories of consumerism that presuppose innate human desires. Instead, modal theory acknowledges that there exist many modes for producing desire. As such, the fundamental questions about desire shift as well: 'The question posed by desire is not "What does it mean?" but rather "*How does it work?*" How do these machines, these desiring-machines, work – yours and mine? . . . What occurs when their mode of operation confronts the social machines?'[10] Modes answer these practical questions. Modes are how desiring-machines link; a mode is the virtual software of a desiring-machine. Deleuze and Guattari describe these modes as a code built into the machine, responding to 'all sorts of functional questions: What flow to break? Where to interrupt it? How and by what means?'[11] Thus modes assist in the production of desire, helping generate desirable experiences, as we saw with the classical mode's sense of astonishment and the fantastic. By linking or creating flows, diverting or interrupting them, fusing or splitting them, desiring-machines produce bodily affections, which in turn become desirable and potentially habitual. We need not speculate on the motivations or deep psychological reasons for desire – whether, that is, it is about the death drive or pleasure principle, the libido or Numen, some drive or delusion, instinct or repression, projection or fantasy. We can, instead, shift the focus from being to becoming, the emergence and production of desire rather than its representation. We can stay at the surface and understand desire as a channelling of affect.

Such a perspective conceives that there are multiple modes producing multiple desires, rather than one consumer mode responsible for the origin of consumerism. Presupposing a single origin runs into multiple difficulties. For instance, some, such as Thorstein Veblen, claim that consumers galvanise consumerism through their struggle for status.[12] Many theorists such as Pierre Bourdieu, Dick Hebdige, Mike Featherstone, and Mary Douglas and Baron Isherwood follow this 'emulationist' perspective, emphasising how consumers make lifestyle distinctions through commodities.[13] These theorists see consumers as emulating others and distinguishing themselves in a process of meaning-making via commodities. Yet this emulationist theory reduces all consumption to an expression of lifestyle, ignoring, for instance, experiences like watching a Disney move, playing a game or tourism that can be pleasurable without necessarily being attached to lifestyle significance. Second, the emulationist theory does not provide an explanation for why consumers change their wants, especially the characteristic practices of modern consumerism where wants are repeatedly generated and then supplanted. Perhaps consumers seek distinction, but why must they seek it again and again? Third, these theories provide little basis for distinguishing traditional consumption from modern behaviour, particularly the 'insatiability and desire for novelty which is a crucial hallmark of the latter'.[14] Veblen contends that all of human history experiences battles for status,[15] and Douglass and Isherwood remark that it is common anthropological practice to see consumption as principally expressive.[16] In other words, people have been consuming for distinction and meaning since time immemorial, so why the sudden proliferation and increase in celerity?

Furthermore, recognising multiple consumer modes means that not all consumption must be fuelled by prior frustrations and not all must be aimed at novelty, as Colin Campbell, another theorist of consumerism, maintains. Campbell argues that discourses such as Romanticism spark modern consumerism by generating a desire for hedonistic daydreaming.[17] This daydreaming produces pleasure, but when real experiences take place, they never live up to the daydream's perfection. Disappointed, consumers withdraw again into the daydream, shifting focus to new objects.[18] Such modern hedonists continually long for daydreams and repeatedly find frustration. This longing and frustration create a perpetual cycle where the consumer daydreams, galvanising longing, and then consumes, producing more frustration.[19] Yet Campbell's take also conflates many different consumer modes, offering little insight into consumers such as collectors, who do not seek the new but instead the old and established.[20] These consumers prefer the familiar or antique for their already stabilised significance. The same may be said of addicts, who return again and again to the same wells for increasingly inured pleasures.[21] Further, the daydreaming mode might result in frustration, but all consumption does not require frustration to fuel the cycle. In fact, consumers return to certain commodities, such as movies or books, not because they experience frustration but because they experience pleasure. Other renewable desires, such as nightlife and tourism, persist not because of disappointment but because of satisfaction.

A modal perspective eliminates the false exclusivity of these theories and the search for a causal rather than material origin. Rather than asserting that modern consumption is only about novelty or lifestyle distinction, or fuelled by frustration, a modal theory allows for many different types of commodities and consumers, varying according to modes. Many consumer modes contribute to modern consumerism *and it is precisely the proliferation of modes that explains the proliferation of consumption.*

Another dilemma also presents itself from the double conflation of these theories. By reducing consumerism to one cause, these theories rest on assumptions about consumer psychology. For instance, emulationists advance an instinctivist position; people instinctually desire to be social, to fit in or stand out. This premise fails to explain why such desires explode in the early twentieth century. The supposition that people are motivated by distinction results in a 'psychological reductionism about as useful (and convincing) as the older explanation of insatiable consumption as motivated by greed', according to Campbell.[22] Yet Campbell also presupposes a consumer with certain desires without offering much support for how such desires emerge. He assumes that consumers enjoy daydreaming and contends that Romanticism somehow encouraged the behaviour, yet he provides little explanation for how such desires and behaviours were learned and spread, other than to trace similar beliefs to the Romantics.

In brief, most theories of the emergence of modern consumerism assume a particular consumer – the consumer as dupe, as emulator, as daydreamer

– without detailing how such consumers become perceivable and how their desires become articulable to certain commodities. In other words, they each locate the causal origin of consumerism in the consumer's presupposed behaviours rather than exploring modes as material and formal causes. A modal approach contends instead that a wide variety of modes provide the resources necessary for the emergence of modern consumerism, adapting perceptual manners and habits in ways conducive to consumerism. Rather than an exclusionary approach, a modal perspective better accounts for the diversity and complexity of modern consumerism. A modal approach need not deny that emulating or daydreaming consumers exist, but asks the prior question – how do they become perceivable? What makes such consumers and consumption practices visible and articulable? How did daydreaming or distinction emerge as desirable modes? Any account of modern consumerism cannot locate the causal origin in assumed characteristics of a pre-given consumer. Instead, we should trace how desiring-production becomes social production, how modes, as the software of desiring-machines, make perceivable certain consumers and their commodities. Consumers may practise according to these modes, but not because of an inherent instinct, genetics or pure manipulation. Consumers and their practices emerge from a perceivability that is a historical result, made through translations such as the classical cinematic mode and animistic mimesis.

In other words, people do not enter into consumerism as a fixed essence, either as an emulating consumer seeking distinction or a daydreaming consumer going through cycles of emotional release and frustration. The emergence of various consumers and commodities first requires that they become perceivable. By perceivable, I mean two virtual potentials – the visible and the articulable, what can be seen and what can be said.[23] Like all -abilities, the visible and the articulable are not what is seen or what is said but a prior, virtual economy enabling certain things to be seen or be said. Ideas, behaviours and subjects are the result of these -abilities, potentialised by these a priori conditions. A stratum or regime of knowledge is composed from what can be seen and what can be said; knowledge is a practical assemblage built from the visible and sayable.[24] In other words, the objects or subjects we can see and the things we can say depend on a prior visibility and articulability. This includes, for our purposes, producers' knowledge of what consumers potentially exist and what commodities potentially attract them. As people engage in modes like classical cinema, new virtual bodies become perceivable, and culture industries, in turn, seek to articulate commodities to these newly visible consumers. As the classical mode spreads, culture industries begin to perceive a lifestyle consumer and craft commodities for it.

In other words, these other theories of modern consumerism belie the virtual, presupposing the perceivability of lifestyle and daydreaming consumers by beginning with their actualisations. That is, they presuppose the *knowledge how* and *desire to* distinguish or daydream and thus founder on the problematic of social change. Specifically, how did modern consumerism emerge if humans are intrinsically consumers and inherently social? Why did the status competitions or daydreams of previous cultures not devolve into a consumerist arms race?[25] Why does a consumer change their wants and expressed meanings over time? The theories fail to ask the prior questions of a modal perspective such as: How do such consumers become visible? How do various commodities become articulable to this consumer? How do these desiring-machines operate? We have detailed how the mode of classical cinema operates; now, we shall discover how those modes, in translation, make visible lifestyle consumers and articulable lifestyle commodities on which the culture industry will capitalise, beginning with a reading of *20,000 Leagues*.

Disney's Live Action: Clichés of the Classical Mode

In this section, I argue that *20,000* Leagues constitutes a cliché of the classical mode. Why *20,000 Leagues* can be seen as a cliché has little to do with the acting styles or the effects. The squid can still startle; Nemo can still spook. Why, then, can someone today call this movie a cliché? It is a cliché because of how it uses transposability and translocatability. It uses transposability to present a narrative following the template of the Hollywood American Dream, and uses translocatability to direct attention blatantly to the main characters, who stand out from the scene via such classical techniques as lighting, costumes, props, centring, balancing and minimal camera movements. Ultimately, these translocations and transpositions seem to be such a careful management of the characters' images, who oscillate between standing out and fitting into the frame, that the movie reveals itself as a blatant portrayal of lifestyle consumption.

The film represents a fitting choice to demonstrate the classical mode's connection to lifestyle consumption, since a film about a nuclear submarine and its mad commander is not obviously about consumerism.[26] Additional justification comes from the movie's popularity. Our more habituated eyes might recoil at the sight of such clichés as *20,000 Leagues*, yet from the perspective of 1954 this judgment seems far from fair. Disney's first live-action feature was a blockbuster, costing nearly 9 million dollars, more than any film to that point, and grossing nearly 7 million, the second highest that year.[27] The movie features many respected actors, including star James Mason as Captain Nemo; winner of the Academy Award for Best Actor, Paul Lukas, as Professor Pierre Aronnax; famed James Bond villian, Peter Lorre, as the Professor's apprentice Conseil; and two-time Best Actor nominee Kirk Douglas as Ned Land. The film won two Academy Awards, for Best Art Direction and Best Special Effects, and is today considered a classic. On its release, *New York Times* critic Crowther predicted the movie would be a 'sensation' loved by kids, and in 2007 critic Steve Biodrowski declares the film 'quite an achievement . . . far superior to the majority of genre efforts from the period (or any period, for that matter), with production design and technical effects that have dated hardly at all'.[28]

Why, then, do I describe *20,000 Leagues* as a cliché? First, *20,000 Leagues* presents the typical American Dream narrative. The filmmakers needed a way to adapt the episodic string of events in the original Jules Verne novel into something suitable for the classical mode. The screenwriters reportedly translated the novel into a classic jailbreak plot, with Ned, Conseil and the Professor attempting to escape from Nemo's submarine *Nautilus*.[29] This narrative is a cliché of the classical modes' whole, fitting perfectly into the American Dream's poles of behaviour and milieu. Just before the ship sinks, when the Professor begs Nemo not to blow up his inventions because 'yours was a dream of the future,' even viewers of the time were likely to be ready for the typical suspenseful ending to resolve into another verification of the American Dream, so the movie presents a cliché of the classical mode.

Second, the movie closely follows the techniques of framing and other translocations common to the classical mode, the blatantly obvious direction of attention to the individualised stars standing out from the crowd of types. In fact, in comparison to films today, the translocations seem tame and obtuse; the camera appears intent on orienting the viewer to space, establishing the sensory-motor linkage. Today, films often use the camera as an affective technology with movements, twists, turns, dives and vibrations carnally experienced, abandoning the immediate sensory-motor linkage and expecting audiences to adapt to the dynamism of space. In *20,000 Leagues*, camera movements are slow and clearly directed, mostly maintaining the main characters in centre frame. Besides camera movements, everything in the frame – including the lighting, costumes, props and arrangement – is designed to direct attention baldly to the main characters, to make them stand out, and as we will see, comporting and adorning oneself to stand out is one of the poles of lifestyle consumption.

The best examples of these translocations are action-images introducing the main characters. Ned is introduced first, showing up to a meeting where people are discussing attacks by a sea monster (the submarine *Nautilus*). An establishing long shot is followed by a typical medium-length circular shot, looking down on the crowd from an elevation. The crowd includes nearly indistinguishable sailor types, wearing almost uniform hats with grey suits; they form a 180-degree circle around the spectator. Ned shows up with two women, one on each arm, and forces his way through the crowd to the front and centre of the circle. A transposition moves closer in on Ned and the women, directing attention to the main character, and Ned further stands out from the uniformed sailors by his dress: a tan leather coat, a red striped T-shirt and dark jeans, with the same hat (to signal he is also a sailor). The only other distinct colours are the reds, pinks and light blues on the fancy dresses of the women that flank Ned, helping him stand out vividly. After another transposition cutting into the crowd, Ned whispers to the ladies and cracks jokes about the monster, showing bravado in stark contrast to the fearful sailors. Ned announces that he is a harpooner in the business of hunting monsters. His ego angers, a brawl breaks out, Ned punches some of the men, the police come, and Ned is captured after nearly escaping. In these shots, it is almost impossible to tell what is happening except for Ned's actions, since the camera follows and reframes him, directing spectator attention.

The following scene introduces the Professor and his apprentice. The 'sea monster' has stranded them because no ships will risk travel. Three reporters besiege the Professor and Conseil, lining up around the Professor at the centre of a circle shot. They want to know his opinion on sea monsters. All three journalists, with two on the left and one on the right side, wear similar grey, peaked hats and unicolour coats. They are turned mostly away from the spectator, in slight profile, facing the Professor, and bathed in shadows from the prominent light above the Professor, centring attention. The Professor also wears a hat and coat, but his hat is maroon and his coat is lighter and speckled, with a cape that drapes over his shoulders. Conseil wears the most colourful, maroon coat with a similar cape and blue hat. The reporters trail them outside as they get into a horse-drawn carriage, followed by another circle shot, this time with Conseil in the centre, the Professor to his right, one reporter to the far right, and two to the left. Amazingly, even though they are outside, the sun shines directly on the Professor's seat. He expresses his passion for science, and Conseil warns him about being misquoted. Transposed to the next morning, we discover that the Professor has indeed been misquoted. They have just woken and changed clothes because the Professor wears a brighter blue coat with a red waistcoat underneath and Conseil wears a dark blue suit and tie. Conseil packs his coat from the prior scene. Such changes of outfits are blatant throughout the film, contributing significantly to why the film constitutes a portrayal of lifestyle consumption.

Such classical translocations continue with the introduction of Ned on board the ship hunting the *Nautilus*. Ned is playing a guitar in the planning room when the Captain arrives. We see another circle shot, balanced and saturated with people. The Captain is in the centre and Ned is also pretty much in the centre, just past the Captain's shoulder. Another officer flanks the Captain's right side, parallel to Ned, who stands out because he is the only blond, the only one not in a coat, and because he wears his signature red striped T-shirt. At the right edge, two reporters look down and scribble notes, backs almost turned to the spectator, wearing muted grey and brown coats. Also to the right, but much closer to the Captain, are the Professor and apprentice, wearing the brightest, most distinct brown and green suits respectively. The light and centring indicate that the Captain is the focus of attention, and the light casts on to the Professor, whose face is the only other one directly illuminated. The cut-ins follow an SRS sequence demonstrating that the Professor and Captain are centres of attention. The first shows the Captain from the Professor's point of view, centred and flanked by the other officer and Ned in a medium-close shot. The second is a reverse shot showing the centred Professor, flanked by Conseil and a reporter. The Captain expresses his disbelief in the monster, and the Professor protests because they have not proven anything scientifically. Everyone besides the stars leaves the room, and Ned circles the table, taking up position in the centre between the Professor and Conseil as they discuss the Captain's decision.

The same translocations continue as Ned leaves, going up the stairs and starting to play the guitar on deck. The film transposes, directing attention to Ned as he enters from the stairs. Ned elevates by sitting on the ship's frame; a light shines down on him. The sailors, in the same blue uniforms, circle around Ned, some lower down with their backs to the spectator but most filling the right and left sides of the 180-degree circle. Ned performs the song, 'Whale of a Tale', a guitar ditty 'about the flappin' fish and the girls I've loved' that compares women to fish. Ned, who may be the only blond in the movie, dances, spins the guitar and puts on a show. This section seems obviously staged to feature Ned as a stylish individual, standing out from the typical sailors who circle around him and ham it up, participating in the chorus.

There is one more main character to introduce, Captain Nemo. After the song, the *Nautilus* emerges from the depths and destroys the ship. Somehow, the Professor, his apprentice and Ned all survive and float on to the submarine, which is damaged. The Professor and Conseil go down into the submarine and express their amazement at the interior, which looks like a ritzy, modern house. They see the engine, and add a little commentary. The Professor calls it 'great genius', and Conseil replies, 'Yes, and great evil.' Eventually, they are spotted and captured. Nemo ascends a staircase and walks past the camera to an empty spot in the middle of another circle shot. He wears a blue Navy coat with gold embroidery symbolising his rank and is the only actor with a full, dark beard. Conseil is front left, with his back turned to the spectator, wearing a green coat. On the front right is the Professor, who most directly faces the Captain and whom the Captain engages in conversation. Ned, in his red stripes, is on the back right, close to the Captain and the frame's centre, but guarded on each side by sailors in blue uniforms. Nemo says he respects the Professor's work, but he orders the other two to be drowned. The Professor protests and, in the first of many moments expressing his evil, Nemo retorts, 'I am not what you call a civilised man, Professor.'

Eventually, Nemo changes his mind, has his prisoners confined to quarters, and invites them to dinner. When they appear, they have all changed clothes (again!). Nemo remarks, 'Your clothes are being dried and will be returned to you shortly.' Ned sports a blue uniform, which looks like that of Nemo's sailors but has a dark red trim and flamboyant red pockets, unlike the others. Conseil wears a blue coat with a white silk scarf underneath, and the Professor dons a dark blue coat, with gold embroidery around the sleeves. Nemo has also changed clothes, and is now wearing a bright red lounge coat with black cuffs and collars. He sits on the left side at the head of the table, with the Professor directly across from him. This places Ned and Conseil in the middle of the frame between the Professor and Captain, across from the camera. The table is set with crystal and silverware, and they all comment on Nemo's riches. Nemo is clearly pleased, and he tells them that they eat sea snake and cream from the sperm whale. An SRS sequence shows the three protagonists from Nemo's point of view, and Nemo from the Professor's. Ned and Conseil are sent off to prepare for the next expedition, and the Professor and Captain pontificate while they smoke seaweed cigars. Nemo then offers the Professor an abundance of commodities relevant to the lifestyle consumer, including access to his nicely furnished study and impressive array of books and music.

The rest of the movie explores the conflict between the optimistic Professor and the pessimistic Nemo through a series of mostly action-images, such as the destruction of a slave ship and battle with the squid. In this famous scene, Ned saves Nemo, and the Professor records the events in his diary. Nemo reads the diary and says that the Professor makes Ned into a hero, like the kind in cheap fiction. And this is precisely what we have, cheap fiction, a cliché. Ned, of course, proves to be the hero, the man of the nation who responds to the milieu, acts and saves the Professor and, by extension, his American dream of technological abundance. The narrative whole and the individual shots are cliché, epitomising the classical mode. The transpositions are tame, bluntly and obviously directing attention to the stars, who always stand out as being the centre of the circle, the focus of the lighting or the most stylishly dressed. Their costumes, props and movements delineate them as individual stars from the rest of the characters, who play indistinguishable types. The framing is always balanced, with the supporting types carefully arranged so that attention is repeatedly directed to the stars. The characters, either stars or types, are continually comporting themselves to stand out in the frame or to fit into the background, similarly to the comportments of lifestyle consumers.

It is likely the spark of the fantastic that pleased *20,000 Leagues* viewers of the time, yet I can best describe my affection watching the movie today, as a cliché of the classical mode, as one of cheesiness: that is, the film feels aged and stale. The movie seems to have lost the spark of fascination so many experienced in the early days of the classical mode. Seeing things that cannot be seen, such as a giant squid attacking a ship, no longer really fascinates, at least as presented through the classical mode. I believe it is the classical mode that evokes this cheesy feeling, not simply the content, especially the formulaic translocations that are reliant upon techniques such as framing, centring, frontality, props, lighting, and costumes borrowed from the theatre. Whereas *20,000 Leagues* shies away from the dramatic use of camera movement to shape attention, contemporary viewers are accustomed to more dramatic angles, more rapid cuts, more affective camera techniques, less spatial orientation, less stereotypical characters, and less hand-holding in the direction of attention. In *20,000 Leagues*, the characters are so blatantly individualised or massified, so obviously good or evil, so bluntly the centre of attention that the shots seem cheesy for this contemporary viewer, who is accustomed to blurrier boundaries between stars and supporting roles, protagonists and antagonists, and spectator and viewer. The primary goal of these translocations is to direct attention to the individual stars, making them visible as lifestyle consumers, standing out from the types who consistently fill the background.

Although the focus of this book is not on the affections of contemporary audiences innervated by old movies, a little more reflection on my cheesy feeling can help reveal further how the classical mode contributes to lifestyle consumerism. One could argue that what is happening is that the movie is no longer 'interesting', as conceptualised by Sianne Ngai.

According to Ngai, the interesting emerged as an aesthetic style and affective judgment with the proliferation of mass consumerism. As producers continually make available fresh waves of novel goods, consumers and critics engage in the assessment of 'interesting' as a way to sort through the morass. As such, the interesting works through an economy between the continuous and discontinuous, sameness and difference, or standing out and fitting in similar to both the classical cinematic mode and the lifestyle consumer. As Ngai remarks, 'In other words, the judgement interesting hinges on recognition of its object as being meaningfully different from others of its type.'[30] The interesting designates a sense that an object has some novelty or difference from others around it, just as *20,000 Leagues* and the classical mode employ transpositions and translocations to make the individual stars appear different from the surrounding types.

As such, the interesting has an inherent relation to time. Not only does the interesting constitute a promise to return to the object again, but it also tends to fade over time.[31] 'The objects or persons we find interesting are therefore never stable or permanent.'[32] Following Ngai's lead, then, we could describe my feeling of cheesiness as simply the decline of interest over time; a film that once fascinated no longer does so because it is a clichéd representation lacking novelty. Indeed, a cheesy feeling may be one of the likely results of the waning of affective sparks, as the new creases become worn and habituated.

Yet Ngai contends that the opposite of interest is not cheesiness but boredom – 'The interesting oscillates between interest and boredom' – and my feeling is not best characterised as boredom, or even lack of interest.[33] The action and actors are still interesting; the movie still holds my attention. At the level of information, of content, the movie remains novel since it is one of the few cinematic adaptations of Jules Verne, the most recent movie and only colour version of *20,000 Leagues*, the most expensive special-effects effort of the time, and the first live-action Disney feature. Ngai isolates information as a key concern of the interesting, because the interesting is a judgment of difference and, as in Gregory Bateson's famous formulation, information is a difference which makes a difference.[34] In other words, the interesting is a judgment about difference in information; the interesting 'becomes an aesthetic of difference as information'.[35]

The movie has plenty of difference at the level of information, and would seem therefore potentially to invoke the feeling–judgement of interesting. Yet *20,000 Leagues* has garnered no academic criticism of which I am aware, and Ngai concludes that there is a fundamental connection between the interesting and criticism. Judging something as interesting means justifying it as an object for criticism: 'We tell people we find works interesting when we want to do criticism.'[36] So while *20,000 Leagues* remains potentially interesting, there must be other affections stopping critics from analysing the movie, and it is likely that the feeling of cheesiness is responsible. Cheesiness designates the sense that the object is aged, stale. Similar aged objects are likely to have been covered before in critical analyses, even if this specific text has not; therefore choosing *20,000 Leagues* as a text for criticism remains unlikely.

However, unlike the interesting, this feeling of cheesiness does not come at the level of information but at the level of form. It is the manner of the movie – the mode – that evokes this feeling of cheesiness, the sense that this is just another cliché of the American Dream and an aged interface reliant upon careful translocations. As a result, cheesiness constitutes another opposition to the interesting, one that occurs at the level of form rather than information, and thereby stems from a different economy than the interest–boredom continuum. Cheesiness flows forth from an economy between interesting information and stale mode, giving viewers the unique pleasure of being interested by the content and simultaneously able to laugh at the silly or simplistic manner of its presentation, perhaps chuckling about how previous audiences could be so moved by such cheese. In short, cheesiness is a unique affection that balances interest with a sense of (and pleasure from) recognition of the same, rather than difference.

The significance of this discussion for the shape of consumer culture comes from the fact that this recognition of sameness, expressed by the feeling of cheesiness, is a recognition that what is shared across the classical cinematic mode is a repeated stress upon being different, upon standing out as an individual from the scene. In other words, the cheesiness here flows from a sense that classical Hollywood repeatedly relies upon a mode that instructs in lifestyle consumerism, as represented by the repeated changes of clothing in *20,000 Leagues*. At the level of mode, every classical movie has the same message – one should seek to be different, employing a variety of commodities such as fashion to achieve individuality, like the stars of classical Hollywood. This 'message' of the classical cinematic mode is certainly interesting, especially because it helps isolate cinema's unique contribution to consumerism, and, as such, deserves criticism in its own right.

The Cinematic Lifestyle Consumer

Today we can see in *20,000 Leagues* the visible lifestyle consumer, the one who uses clothing and other commodities either to fit into the crowd (the types) or to stand out (the stars). This lifestyle consumer results in impacts on consumer culture that extend beyond simply advertising consumer goods and selling a boatload of movies. As the classical mode spreads and becomes habitual, a lifestyle consumer becomes visible and articulable. For culture industries, consumers become perceived as social *individuals* with an image to manage and shape. In other words, the classical mode expands perception of the emulationist consumer seeking distinction, attempting either to stand out from or to fit in the social picture. This emulationist consumer participates in a lifestyle mode of consumption. In the lifestyle mode, consumers view *commodities as material signifiers for the expression of their image.* Seeking to express their style through commodities, the lifestyle consumer retains two options, as we saw in the analysis of *20,000 Leagues*. They can either stand out, becoming like the individualised stars, or fit in, becoming like the typified crowds. Thus the lifestyle mode works through an economy of sameness and difference, altering the commodity. At one pole, commodities signal a likeness to similar lifestyles, helping consumers recognise where they fit in the cultural landscape. At the other, commodities aim for difference from other lifestyles, allowing the consumer to stand out.

The lifestyle mode has a long history; it does not originate with cinema but is instead translated anew. Throughout history, people have used commodities to express lifestyle. What remains to be explained is the mechanism whereby the lifestyle mode expanded and multiplied. Why does a perceived lifestyle consumer grow in twentieth-century America, and why does the attribution of lifestyle significance to commodities explode? I contend that classical cinema contributes to the proliferation of a perceived lifestyle consumer. The classical mode manifests through viewers who see the world as a camera, projecting and recording. Such a mode readily translates into a lifestyle mode of consumption, entailing two poles: either fitting in or standing out. As culture industries learn to envision consumers through the classical mode's frame, they perceive consumers comporting to the views of camera-spectators, perfecting (as do actors – the ultimate lifestyle consumers) the moving pose. Culture industries infer that such moving poses can be greatly aided by commodities, including clothing, cars, homes and furniture – the very commodities prominently on display in movies. Thus the classical mode provides robust fertiliser for lifestyle consumerism; every movie serves as visible evidence of a particular consumer, one with a self-image negotiating a milieu replete with camera-subjects.

Prior to the cinema, someone might imagine others looking and hence conceive of themselves as having an image for lifestyle display. The

wealthy and powerful often exhibited their bodies in specifically designated spaces, such as the court or other social events. This was especially
true for women, whose life under patriarchal society led to a self 'split
in two', according to Jon Berger in his work on the male gaze.[37] 'From
earliest childhood she has been taught and persuaded to survey herself
continually. And so she comes to consider the *surveyor* and the *surveyed*
within her as the two constituent yet always distinct elements of her identity as woman.'[38] This split recalls the split between spectator and viewer
of the classical cinematic mode, and indeed the culture industry of the
early twentieth century widely perceived women to be the prototypical
lifestyle consumers and cinemagoers. The association with women indicates that these practices of lifestyle consumption, of projecting an image
and recording others, of surveying and being surveyed, existed before the
advent of cinema.

Yet cinema expands this sense of being looked at and breaks down
the boundaries designating the proper locations for display; it makes the
lifestyle mode of consumption more widely visible. Unlike the court or
stage, with their demarcated spaces for social exhibition, cinema's camera
penetrates the most private interiors and traverses the emptiest expanses.
The transposing spectator reveals that everyone has an image, at all times,
from every angle – not just the rich and powerful, or women, on special
occasions or in designated locales. The viewer is solicited to relate to
this spectator, sometimes seeing as one character, then as another, then
as a witness to the side or as a voyeur peeping through a keyhole. The
spectator envisions the social condition of subjective vision: namely, that
subjects are simultaneously seeing and seen, that we project an image and
those images are recorded by others. Desiring-machines able to record
and project become perceivable, with the camera our 'perceptive organ'
and the projector our 'expressive organ'.[39] As Vivian Sobchack elucidates:

> (T)he cinema mechanically projected and made visible *for the very first time* . . . the
> very structure and process of subjective, embodied vision . . . (T)he novel material-
> ity and techno-logic of the cinema gives us concrete and empirical insight and makes
> objectively visible the reversible, dialectical, and social nature of our own subjec-
> tive vision . . . In sum, the cinema provided . . . *objective insight* into the subjective
> structure of vision and thus into oneself and others as always both viewing subjects
> and visible objects.[40]

Classical Hollywood translates, rather than originates, this lifestyle
mode of consumption, renewing the life of this mode by expanding the
arenas in which the lifestyle consumer is visible. For lifestyle consumption to blossom, a vision of the consumer as a subject with a continuous

self-image and a perception of commodities as expressive objects for their self-image are necessary. The classical cinema represents such consumers, in the form of stars and types, and develops techniques for expression through commodities, as we saw with *20,000 Leagues*. With the proliferation of the classical mode, it becomes possible to envision the entire social world as a series of moving pictures, composed of looking camera–subjects and looked-at self-images. The lifestyle mode of consumption is thereby translated from prior cultural practices, becoming newly perceivable in new arenas.

What are some of these newly visible arenas? First, actors and politicians become perceived as 'celebrities'. Basically, celebrities are lifestyles projected for a socius replete with recording camera-eyes. For politicians and celebrities, their status becomes about style; they are rewarded with popularity when they learn to comport themselves to stand out.[41] Take the Hollywood star. As frequently noted at the time of the classical mode's emergence, the style of Hollywood acting marked a dramatic change from that typical in theatre, as Leo Braudy details.[42] Theatre actors have to project across the fourth wall, necessitating exaggerated gestures and expressive voices. In our terms, the viewer-space and diegetic space cannot be brought into closer relation; therefore it was incumbent on the actor to bridge the divide. The classical cinema generally preferred actors with a cooler, subtler acting style, against the exaggerated gestures and vocal projections of the stage. This style of acting, called the American style, emphasised facial expression and restrained gesture over pantomime, with praise reserved for actors who seemingly play themselves.[43] In Braudy's words, 'The film actor emphasises display, while the stage actor explores disguise.'[44]

Obviously, this altered acting style has a lot to do with the transposability and translocatability discussed previously. Since the spectator can be brought closer to the diegetic space, more subtle and restrained gesticulations became highly expressive, especially due to the screen's size. What occurs is a new perceivability of the actor; their lifestyle rather than their role becomes visible. In the theatre, the actor is visible through the role; actors gain a reputation for excellence by playing roles. Thus an auratic distance remains between actor and role. In the theatre, the audience has little expectation of discovering the true person behind the mask. The theatre, with its space marked off from the viewer, expects masks and demands staging. In fact, the best theatre actors are considered to be those who can play a wide variety of roles. A movie, by mingling viewer and narrative space–time, relies on a little confusion between mask and person. The star becomes perceived as a style, as projected image, and hence expectations emerge that the actor play roles like themselves. Thus the widely prescribed Actor's Studio and Stanislavsky approaches stress 'becoming the character', even to the point of imitating the character's daily routines. Braudy spells out the principle: 'Film actors play their roles the way we play ourselves in the world.'[45]

Perhaps more exactly than Braudy – the classical mode makes visible a particular stylisation of the actor, a lifestyle acting. Lifestyle acting is translated from previous practices of personal display, yet it is not a natural or universal way of acting, either for the everyday person or for the film actor. In fact, stars are not just acting like themselves; they learn to pass the test of the camera, to comport to project their image best. Actress Betty Blythe, for instance, recalls being instructed to practise walking in an expensive gown. She reports walking toward a long mirror: 'And I saw my body. I saw my legs, my torso, my long, long arms. I said, is that I? . . . I had never looked at my body as a piece of statuary . . . I had this marvelous feeling; it was most extraordinary. I can still feel the chills all over my body.'[46] Blythe's response recalls the split between spectator and viewer, that relation of image and self so crucial to the classical mode, and attests to the affections ('chills') and potential desire of such a split, of realising one has an image and learning how to relate to it. For many audience members, identification with the star is likely desirable because it is the star who has seemingly mastered this split, an *in*dividual who has successfully fused their desired self and their camera-image. As Richard Dyer, another scholar of the star, concludes, 'Stars articulate what it is to be a human being in contemporary society; that is, they express the particular notion we hold of the person, of the "individual".'[47]

What occurs, then, is not the rise of a more natural or authentic acting style. Instead, the classical Hollywood mode makes visible the actor as lifestyle consumer. This actor-as-lifestyle-consumer comes with specific criteria; actors are expected to conform to the standards of authenticity consistent with a lifestyle mode. Indeed, authenticity is a crucial criterion for Hollywood acting and lifestyle consumption alike. These acting criteria emerge due to the transposability and translocatability of the cinematic medium; with the role brought closer, the audience tests the images for signs of authenticity. Authenticity is measured, first, by a consistency of style. Audiences expect Hollywood actors not to diverge too far from their established on-screen personality. Thus Hollywood studios tend to type-cast stars into particular roles, and Braudy mentions multiple instances where films were poorly received due to too much divergence from the expected role. Indeed, Braudy notes that movie actors accrue a residual image accumulating from their previous roles.[48] Will Smith's or Angelina

Jolie's image persists with them, with some viewers believing they can get a sense of the 'real' actor through their roles. In turn, the actors are expected to 'play themselves' and criticised for diverging too far.

Second, audiences expect acting to be authentic, genuine, not contradicting the star's 'real' personality. The second criterion asks whether the projected image (the style) is consistent with the actor's actual life. Not only must the actor's roles remain relatively consistent, but the actor is also expected to conform their style to their 'real' personality. Stars whose everyday actions do not match their projected image are considered posers, someone staging for camera-audience. Hence the term *lifestyle* – the style and the life must remain consistent to be deemed authentic. Dyer calls them individuals, whom we can think of as those people undivided between their image and their self. Yet how do viewers think they can determine the star's personality or true self? Here, Hollywood readily provided evidence for the testing audience. The Hollywood studios of the 1920s through the 1950s establish what has been called the 'star system', signing long-term contracts with stars, assigning those stars to typecast roles, and promoting their images across a wide variety of media. The star extends off screen; fans obsess over their personal lives, and media promoters emphasise the consonance between their on-screen and off-screen personalities.

From this particular visibility of the actor – the actor as lifestyle consumer – Hollywood studios became focused on image management, constructing a lifestyle for stars across media outlets. The star system emphasised the creation of a distinct look for the actor. Stars develop signature fashion styles, leisure activities, cars, homes, gestures, voices, mannerisms and postures that help them to stand out as a unique individual. Stars are 'ways of making sense of the body'; stars instruct in image projection for the lifestyle consumer.[49] With actors now visible as lifestyle consumers rather than as theatre's role-players, various styles of comportment are developed, based on the criteria of consistency in image and practice, of an *in-dividual* life and style.

This emphasis on the individual may seem to indicate that the stars are all about standing out, constituting one pole of the lifestyle mode. And surely, in the movies, the stars distinctly stand out from the types, as we saw in *20,000 Leagues*. Yet the star evinces both sides of the economy between sameness and difference. The star is a strange hybrid, an individual but also a type, representing a type but standing out distinctly, like Kirk Douglas representing the sailors (in hat) and an individual (in red-striped shirt). Stars, then, comport themselves to both stand out and fit in, the two inextricably linked sides of the lifestyle mode's economy. Just as a picture's foreground and background can be perceived only in relation, so too does standing out also entail fitting in. A lifestyle image will reflect both alignment with one cultural series and distinction from another.

The criteria for successful lifestyles also rely on this economy between sameness and difference. In order to pass the test, the star's image must be both ordinary and extraordinary, what John Ellis calls a paradox. Ellis argues that desire comes from this paradox, because stars are both ordinary and hence available for desire, and extraordinary and hence unattainable.[50] His explication recalls the split between viewer and narrative in the classical mode, the way the spectator both brings the world closer to the viewer's and also maintains a distance:

> The star is ordinary, and hence leads a life like other people, is close to them, shares their hopes and fears: in short, the star is present in the same social universe as the potential film viewer. At the same time the star is extraordinary, removed from the life of mere mortals . . . separate from the world of the potential film viewer . . . The figure of the star crystallizes the equivocal relationship to the viewer's desire.[51]

In modal theory, this is not so much a paradox as an economy between sameness and difference, or continuity and discontinuity, through which the classical mode operates. The split between viewer and narrative space, and subsequently between actor and role, drives an economy where standing out and fitting in are structural necessities, as well as the limits of the potential options. The star negotiates an economy between the ordinary and extraordinary, between viewer and narrative, between realistic and fantastical.

The classical Hollywood mode expanded the range of the lifestyle consumers' visibility by extending lifestyle consumption from designated social spaces, such as the stage or the court, to the everyday life of leisure. Lifestyle consumption became envisioned, through the classical mode, not as the province of a certain class or locale but as an obligation for all persons living in a social milieu saturated with camera-subjects. Perceiving through the classical mode leads to a widespread awareness that everyone projects an image and that, at any time, someone might be recording your image. This is not a guaranteed result; surely some do not engage the classical mode and others even resist a lifestyle mode of consumption. Nevertheless, the virtual potential becomes available; the lifestyle consumer becomes visible. People become perceivable as subjects of the camera in both senses. They can become the subject acting through the predicate camera, taking motion pictures of the surroundings. They also can become subjects of the camera, those under its watchful eyes. As subjects of the camera, daily habits and the cultural habitus radically transform, demanding comportment *as* and *to* the lens. With photography or theatre, people could pose or avoid capture. With camera-subjects everywhere, one acts all the time. Looking as a camera, people become visualisable as both filmmaker and filmed.

In sum, the classical mode makes visible a lifestyle consumer, represented by stars and translated into multiple practices of the culture industries. Stars 'teach' comportment to a world of camera-subjects, how to become individual through the crafting of lifestyle. We might be tempted to conclude that the same holds true for viewers; they also learn how to engage in lifestyle consumption. Indeed, the consonance between the emergence of the classical cinema and the consumer boom of the 1920s makes such a conclusion tempting, and some such as Larry May have leapt to the conclusion: 'Together the sexes learned from the Hollywood life-style how to find individualism and expressiveness in leisure. As this helped to ease the transition from Victorian to modern life, it also helped to legitimise the consumption economy.'[52] Evaluation of actual consumers is difficult, however, given the cultural, national, gender, racial, class and other differences, not to mention individual eccentricities. It seems likely, and is even supported by audience analysis studies, that some viewers learned lifestyle consumerism from watching classical movies.[53] Yet we must remember that these consumers are not the origin of modern consumerism, any more than are producers or ideological discourse. Consumers are not necessarily dupes but are also not autonomous agents, the drivers of social change. Certain consumers must first become perceivable before their actions can fuel a consumer boom; this is a more complex process of translation involving producers and consumers alike.

While it may be difficult to prove, as in a cause–effect telling of his-story, that cinema generated more lifestyle consumers, our different claim that the classical mode made the lifestyle consumer perceivable has abundant evidence.[54] As the lifestyle consumer became more visible, the culture industry raced to tap into this modal resource. These industries attempted to make lifestyle consumption expressible through a wide variety of commodities. By the end of the 1920s, department stores filled shelves with Hollywood fashions, with Bernard Waldman's Cinema Fashions chain leading the way. With the help of movies, fashion extended to home goods, cars and other commodities. Studios and businesses negotiated agreements for product tie-ins, providing free fashion, furniture and accessories in exchange for the visibility of their commodities to a mass audience.[55] Will Hays, who lent his name to the 'Hays Code' relating to movie censorship, nevertheless remained a stout proponent of film for its business promotion:

Motion pictures perform a service to American business which is greater than the
millions in our direct purchases . . . The motion picture carries to every American at
home, and to millions of potential purchasers abroad, the visual, vivid perception of
American manufactured products.[56]

From the 1920s onward, these industries aggressively attempted to link
their products to this newly visible consumer by portraying their commodities as expressions of lifestyle, worn, used or simply mentioned by
the star.

This is all really just old news – both the role of classical Hollywood
and the connection between consumerism and the lifestyle mode. Critics
from Bourdieu to Veblen, Thomas Frank to Fredric Jameson to Jean
Baudrillard observe the affinity between contemporary capitalism and
the drive for distinction, difference and individuality.[57] The consumer
economy provides materials for individual images and thus thrives in an
environment habituated to a lifestyle mode. Where the modal perspective
offers insights, however, is in tracing the emergence of these consumer
practices to the perceivability of certain consumers and commodities
rather than conceiving consumers as the origin of consumerism. Those
theorists who trace consumerism to practices of distinction often conflate
all consumption under the lifestyle mode and presume some kind of
inherent human instinct for distinction, foregoing the prior questions of
how distinction becomes perceivable, of how people envision themselves
in competition with or relation to social others, of how one articulates
distinction, through what objects or practices. This presumption is by no
means unproblematic. For instance, some critics of consumerism, such as
Adorno or Kalle Lasn, take issue with the claim that the desire for uniqueness and individuality drives consumerism.[58] They see the exact opposite:
a ceaseless push towards standardisation and conformity, motored by the
desire to 'keep up with the Joneses' or by the commodity form. It would
certainly not take long to discover consumers who seem driven more by
conformity than by distinction.

Yet in modal theory, these two explanations are not a contradiction;
both make sense in a perceptual habitus accustomed to the cinematic
mode. In an environment filled with the virtual bodies of the classical
mode, standing out and fitting in are not oppositional causes but mutually
necessary results. Conformity and keeping up with the Joneses require an
active process of looking and comparison, a constant shifting of position
similar to a movie camera. Even fitting in is a desire to blend into the
background that is likely to be encouraged by a world of eagerly peering
camera-subjects. A culture accustomed to projecting and remembering

images will frequently and habitually be both monitoring the Jones and seeking the fashion that will upstage them. Trying to stand out or fit in (both are roles on the screen), consumers project to construct an image. If we want to be a figure, the process prefers the bold and distinct, fuelling fashion cycles. Yet even attempts not to have an image are interpreted as a particular 'look' in a habitus brimming with virtual camera-bodies. Thus the two most predominant explanations of modern consumerism both make sense in a habitus accustomed to the lifestyle mode. The cinematic mode contributes to this perceptual habitus, making the lifestyle consumer and its commodities perceivable in new spaces and ways. Both the obsession with personal image and the consumerism bent on selling such images stem from a prior perceivability.

We can see the advantage of a modal approach when considering the specific reasons why commentators connect cinema and consumerism. These accounts generally attribute cinema's contribution to consumerism to two reasons: cinema fetishises objects and beckons identification with stars. First, the viewer becomes a consumer by imitating stars, particularly their fashion, makeup, hairstyles and gestures.[59] Yet this explanation begins with the consumer, presupposing an existing desire to identify without explaining the mechanics of such desire. What do viewers perceive that might make them desire to be like the star? The explanation assumes the popularity of classical cinema and the stars, whereas a modal approach allows us to explain their desirability, based in the production of affect. Conceiving the classical mode as productive of affections such as astonishment enhances this account by explaining the desirability of the classical mode, a desirability whose actualisation makes newly perceivable the lifestyle consumer.

The second reason why scholars connect cinema and consumerism is that movies bestow allure on the on-screen objects, encouraging commodity fetishism. For instance, Anne Friedberg and Charles Eckert compare the cinema screen to a display window in a department store, 'windows that were occupied by marvelous mannequins and swathed in a fetish-inducing ambiance of music and emotion'.[60] For Beller, cinema represents the very paradigm of post-Fordist economics; capital becomes a cinematic apparatus that extracts value from perceptual labour. This perceptual labour produces commodity fetishism: 'We manufactured the new commodities by intensifying an aspect of the old ones, their image-component. Cinema was to a large extent the hyper-development of commodity fetishism.'[61] Attributing the cause of modern consumerism to fetishism again starts with the consumer, presupposing how the fetishising consumer becomes visualisable and how various commodities become articulable and legible as fetish. In other words, cinematic fetishism is conceived as a version of a pre-existing, often perverted or distorted, desire. Such accounts often presume something about the psychology of individuals, groups or cultures and typically envision the cinema as yet another iteration. The problem with this assumption is that it fails to tell us about the hows of desire. How are these consumers fetishising? How do they plug their desiring-machines in and to where? What objects are articulated as fetish?

A modal account better describes these desiring-machines. As we have seen, this machine operates by perceiving a continuous story from a discontinuous set of images. The classical mode works by relating viewer space–time to narrative space–time, via spectator space–time. The viewer plugs into the image flow, allowing their perceptions to be transposed and translocated through the spectator. The desire of such a machine is the desire of relating to a society of images, the pleasure of seeing the world through other eyes – indeed, of seeing the world as composed of cameras recording and projecting. Classical cinematic desiring-machines engage a Bergsonian account of the world, the world as image, image as matter, image as the only thing that matters. The classical mode makes perceivable virtual bodies engaged in habits of perception such as recording and projecting, the viewing of self as image, and the perception of a world of recording, testing camera-eyes.

With this new mode, a particular form of fetishising objects becomes articulable-objects for lifestyle significance. If we can call this fetishism at all, certain objects become perceivable as 'fetish' because they serve the purpose of passing the camera's test, of standing out and fitting in, of crafting individuality. The objects further the character's images, whether stars or types, as we saw with the multiple costume changes in *20,000 Leagues*. These filmic objects help one's image stand out or fit into the picture. Their meaning comes in relation to character lifestyle, since the classical mode continually translocates attention to human characters. Props and other objects are given significance, but usually a significance charged with personal or psychological meaning. This is not so much fetishism, in the sense of substituting the object for social relations, but deployment of the commodity for social expression, as consistent with the lifestyle mode. Thus Doane correctly recognises that the cinema's promotion of consumption is more accurately narcissism, about self-love rather than the obsessed object-love of a fetishist.[62] In the lifestyle mode, the object is part of the *style*; the *life* rests elsewhere, in the person, not in the object as it does in Marx's take on the commodity fetish.

Doane and Beller deserve credit for pointing to the fundamental connection between media and consumption, a primary conclusion of this book. Consumption involves mediating the self via commodities, generating desirable affect through this folding. Unfortunately, Doane and Beller replicate the conflation of many cinema scholars, equating the impacts of live action and animation on consumer culture. Beller, who confesses that by cinema he really means all moving images, concludes, '(T)he other side of consumerism is to turn all social activity into investment – an investment in an/one's image.'[63] Similarly, Doane states, 'For all consumerism involves the idea of self-image (perhaps this is why the woman is the prototype of the consumer).'[64] Yet the idea of self-image is only one manner of mediating consumption and therefore only one of many desires consumer culture subsequently mines. The perception of a manageable self-image is proper to the lifestyle mode of consumption. Classical Hollywoood spreads the lifestyle mode; via its translation, the lifestyle consumer becomes perceivable in new spaces and articulable with new commodities.

As the quotation from Doane attests and many others such as Friedberg have shown, by the 1920s women became perceived as the prototype moviegoer and consumer.[65] This is probably because women have been trained for some time before cinema to consider their image, to see a split between self and image. Women often are taught to view themselves as a heterosexual man might look at them, as an image. Thus women are historically more associated with and accustomed to the lifestyle mode and its accoutrements such as fashion, makeup and the like. Once again, the cinematic mode is a translation of previous cultural practices, such as the folding of self and image practised by many women. Cinema's new iteration does not originate the lifestyle mode but merely fans the flames of its circulation. As the cinematic mode and its lifestyle consumer become widespread, it 'makes sense' to associate classical Hollywood with women. As Hollywood materialises the lifestyle mode, women become perceived as the demographic actualisation of the virtual bodies of the classical mode and, hence, as a new terrain to be territorialised by consumer industries. These various industries begin to perceive women as their target audiences, due to the mode's connection to lifestyle consumption and the prior cultural association between women and lifestyle modes.

What about Disney?

Before detailing the differences in -abilities and modes between animation and cinema, we should first note how different Disney's perceivable consumers are from those of classical cinema. Rather than women, most conceive children as the target markets for Disney movies, as evidenced in Chapter 6. This is because Disney's mode of animistic mimesis offers different affections from classical Hollywood and, hence, a differently perceivable consumer body – what we will call the daydreaming consumer. Primarily, what is absent in Disney's translation is the emphasis on human comportment, the classical mode's focus on human gesture, adornment and action. Watching Mickey does not offer instruction in lifestyle commodities; nor do the transpositions and translocations of animation reveal the subjective character of vision, since the world we watch is distinctly not a human world, not one in which the astonishment of lifelike movement could be evoked. In short, the virtual body of the lifestyle consumer is distinct from Disney's animistic mimesis, which conceives life not so much as social and externally oriented but as inward life, as affection innervated. Thus Disney's translation does not encourage perceiving the self-as-image. Connecting animistic mimesis to a lifestyle mode is difficult since we do not see individual humans comporting themselves to stand out or fit in. Animistic mimesis differently mediates and thereby contributes to a different consumer engaged in a different mode of consumption, much closer to fetishism than the narcissism of the lifestyle mode.

Full-length Disney animation, in fact, represents one of the first moves away from the classical Hollywood mode, driven by the sense that the fantastic and astonishment were waning and hence so were profits. As we have seen, the classical mode seems too careful, worried that we may not be able to follow rapidly shifting transpositions and translocations. The translocations and transpositions appear young, tentative, unsure, less challenging. The classical mode does everything to make it easy for the viewer to see through the spectator. The camera-spectator is translocated and transposed primarily to witness the individualised stars, rarely severing the sensory-motor link. Today, movement-images and psychological narratives have not disappeared, nor has the American Dream template, but the complexity of transpositions and translocations has dated offerings such as *20,000 Leagues*. As we will see, Disney's translation of the classical mode into animation attests to how the classical mode had become commonplace, assumed to be the only realistic way to present the fantastic. As a result of these translations by Disney and many others, cinema would begin to explore various cinematic modes, some starting not with movement-images but with time-images.

The shift to the time-image was motivated by such clichés, by the decline of cinema's astonishing and fantastic sparks. According to Deleuze, the movement-image was in crisis after World War II, facing inured audiences and a radically transformed sociopolitical landscape.

Time-images emerge in this context, seeking to modulate cinema in ways different from the clichéd movement-image and classical mode. Rather than an indirect image of time presented through the narrative whole, time-images offer a direct image of time, turning films into a temporal experience more than a fantastic portrayal. The cinematic experience, as in Disney, becomes more about *feeling* the rhythms than *witnessing* the attractions. Thus the construction of time-images transforms the transpositions and translocations. Rather than an open whole completed by the film's end, the time-image presents a whole that is outside; the events on screen take place in a whole beyond the film's scope. In other words, the events take place in a human rather than narrative world, a world in which every person is denied access to the whole that extends beyond their own episodic experiences. There is no neatly completed story and few happy endings, only slices of an external and greater, perhaps ungraspable, whole. Instead of an organic circle, the time-image presents a crystalline whole, folded in and reflecting on itself, that blurs the real and imaginary, virtual and actual, subject and object.

In time-images, characters do not stand out as lifestyle consumers but become wanderers or seers, adrift in this ungraspable whole rather than actively saving it. Transpositions, then, do not move the spectator so that they can witness actions composing a narrative; they follow these drifting movements, making the spectator likewise into a wanderer or seer. The sensory–motor linkage is severed or upset; false continuities link shot to shot rather than using transpositions to create a continuous, realistic space. The shots are seemingly delinked, cuts become irrational, and the transpositions and translocations take on a meaning and affectivity of their own. Instead of depicting a narrative whole, the affective, cinematic experience itself becomes the object. By severing sensory–motor links and externalising the whole, viewers experience the movie as a moment of unfolding time, a time-image. Transpositions do not serve to position a spectator for reading a narrative; they become open to interpretation and part of the viewer's, rather than spectator's, temporal experience.

Translocations transform dramatically with the time-image as well. The camera often moves independently of the characters, sometimes drifting away or seemingly refusing to centre them. Translocations become aimed directly at the viewer and not the spectator, attempting to evoke a temporal experience. In Deleuze's terms, they create pure optical or sound images, opsigns and sonsigns, where the viewer experiences seeing and hearing something directly, not seeing and hearing something indirectly as spectator-witness. The aim becomes to affect the viewer directly, to bestow a temporal experience, to make them feel the movie rather than see it. Deleuze contends that the time-image seeks to give the viewer a body and brain, to make them feel and think time instead of seeing movement via their proxy, the spectator. In the movement-image, the spectator was always the mediator between viewer and narrative. In the time-image, the spectator becomes a technique for directly touching and affecting the viewer, for giving them bodies and brains, for making them feel and think about the outside whole called life, called time, in which we all float. The spectator is a 'spiritual automaton', or, more precisely, this was a new spectator, a new 'spiritual automaton', differently modulated from the classical mode. Disney's *20,000 Leagues* may be a cliché of the classical mode, but their earlier, animated features already bear witness to the crisis of the movement-image and the beginnings of time-images. As we will see, Disney's animated features attempt to make viewers feel the transformations of the drawings, blurring the boundaries between real and imaginary, and causing many to experience the wonder of time unfolding and begin to think, '*What is life?*'

CHAPTER 4

Animation's Marvel and the Graphic Narrative Mode

Disney translates both classical cinema and earlier animation into mutual-affection images, an interface for the mode of animistic mimesis, forming a hybrid movement-time-image. Translating both live action and animation should come as no surprise, since the two media have always had an intertwined historical relationship. Cinema began as animation, a descendant of devices like the magic lantern, praxinoscope and Emile Reynaud's Optical Theatre. These devices work similarly to flip books, passing images quickly before the eye to give the perception of movement (what is called apparent movement due to the 'phi effect').[1] How to create apparent movement was known by the time Athanasius Kircher described the process in 1646, and by the 1850s numerous devices existed to create apparent movement.[2] Such devices helped constitute what Nicolas Dulac and André Gaudreault call the 'cultural series of *animated pictures*'.[3] Cinema started as one of these series; in fact, some accounts originally gave the name 'animated photographs' to the images shown by Edison's Vitascope and the Lumière's Cinématographe. Thus tracing Disney's translation into animisitic mimesis requires outlining not just classical cinema but earlier animation as well.

Indeed, Disney's hybridity results from how they translate the -abilities and modes of earlier animation. Animation comes with different -abilities from live-action cinema that we will call *transformability* and *transferability*. Early animation, especially during the 1920s, will relate animation's transformability to the viewer's capacity to perceive form and trajectory, resulting in a mode of *graphic narrative* that, from the viewer's perspective, entails *perceiving moving lines as animated characters*. The graphic narrative mode, like much other early animation that emphasises transformability, illustrates the affective differences with live-action cinema outlined in the previous chapter. Since drawn animation does not offer the lifelike quality of the photograph, its spark is distinct and greeted that way in the historical record. Audiences were not so much astonished at lifelike movement but *marvelled* over the artificial movement and repeatedly distinguished their affections from live action.

Indeed, before the movie camera, the animated screen was associated with magic and mystery, not realism, indicating the different affections of animation. After, promoters stress the realism and lifelike quality of photographic movement, explicitly distinguishing them from the tricks of animation. For instance, the *New York World* was sure to distinguish between live-action film and animation:

> Life size presentations they are and will be . . . You'll sit comfortably and see . . . almost anything, in fact, in which there is action, just as if you were on the spot during the actual events. And you won't see marionettes. You'll see people and things as they are.[4]

From an early date, as the photograph becomes part of screen content, exhibitors delineated its realism from animation's artifice:

> It will be seen that the [stereopticon] exhibition differs from the exhibition of painting [on glass], in that it presents us with a literal transcription of the actual . . . by the combination of optical laws so feebly hinted at in the Magic Lantern. Stereoscopic Pictures are placed before us which are the exquisite shadow of the photograph, freighted with all the minute details of the subject as it really exists, not a flat monochromatic shadow, but a rounded, glowing picture, thrown up in splendid relief with all its marvelous accuracy magnified, all its tints preserved, and the whole character, subtle and sublime of the existing thing itself, reproduced in a splendid shaft of artificial life, so that for the moment, we seem to be looking at bold picturesque facts and not ingenious and shadowy fancies.[5]

Such distinctions emerge because animation and cinema split the viewer differently. With animation, the split does not exclusively occur between the time–space of the viewer and the screen but also between their capacities to infold form and motion. Neuroscience has discovered that the brain processes apparent motion with the same receptors as real motion, so we perceive animation's apparent motion as real motion. Yet the forms of animation illustrate and even, at times, flaunt its artifice; it is readily apparent that these are drawn, painted or otherwise constructed figures, not real things. Thus with live-action film, viewers perceive real motion from lifelike forms. With animation, the viewer perceives real motion from an artificial form, a split not readily available before the advent of animation. Eisenstein describes this split as one between knowledge and sensation:

> We *know* that they are . . . drawings and not living beings.
> We *know* that they are . . . projections of drawings on a screen.

We *know* that they are . . . 'miracles' and tricks of technology, that such beings don't
really exist.
But at the same time:
We *sense* them as alive.
We *sense* them as moving, as active.
We *sense* them as existing and even thinking![6]

With live action, viewers can know the fictional world does not exist but
perceive that the actors do exist and their motions did occur. With animation, in contrast, viewers can know that the characters and motions do not
exist but sense them as moving, even living, nevertheless.[7] Such splitting
occurs as the virtual transformability of animation enters into a relationship
with the viewer's capacities to perceive form and motion, and such splitting
frequently leads people to describe animation as magical, mysterious and
illusory. In fact, many greeted the earliest animation devices like the magic
lantern as evidence of ghosts, magic or spirits, some so strongly perceived as
to spark panic and prompt censorship. We can label this spark the marvellous, especially since the marvellous denotes the 'extraordinary', the 'superb'
and 'admiration'. Such terms indicate an appreciation for the act of artifice,
similar to the way we might marvel over a magic trick, pondering how it was
done. Musser concludes that it was the audience's appreciation that this
was a trick, not the result of spirits, that marks the 'decisive starting point
for screen practice'.[8] Prior to this time, animation apparatuses were used to
fool or manipulate unsuspecting viewers. With an awareness that these were
tricks, the screen becomes demystified and the modern spectator emerges.

In fact, animation often punctured the modes associated with photography and cinema, leading to questions about the 'reality' of the photograph.
For some, the sense of movement was so remarkable that it challenged
the presumed fidelity of photography. Many viewers were sent through
the rabbit hole, questioning their perceptions of spatio-temporal reality,
perceptions that were, in the early twentieth century, heavily shaped
by photography. For instance, the first animator to achieve a semblance
of cinematic realism successfully was Winsor McCay, who drew fully
three-dimensional worlds with rounded, weighty characters that seem to
inhabit those worlds. Upon watching McCay's 1914 *Gertie the Dinosaur*,
a *Chicago Examiner* critic illustrated this spark, stating, 'Thus the camera,
that George Washington of mechanisms, at last is proved a liar.'[9] For this
critic, the sensation of life brought into question the camera's presumed
truth-value. The marvellous spark punctuated the mode of perceiving
photographs as direct captures of reality. Since animation's photographs
did not reveal a *that-has-been*, they called into question the fidelity and
realism upon which Barthes's *punctum* rests.

The marvellous indicates the spark felt by an audience who knows the images are constructed, but who marvels at their movements and transformations nevertheless. In other words, animation splits viewers between what they see and what they know; viewers infold movement that they recognise as illusion. Drawn animation splits the folds between the perception of the form known to be false and the movement we sense to be true, potentially innervating the marvellous spark. To play on Barthes's terminology, if photographs portray a *that-has-been* whose capture can lead to consideration of mortality, animation portrays a *never-has-been* that appears to live and move. The viewer knows the characters are not real, yet they seem to act, speak, emote and even die. If the photograph's *punctum* comes from the characteristics of a bizarre medium, 'false on the level of perception, true on the level of time', animation also fits the formula since the form is patently false but the movement is truly perceived.[10] Barthes's phrase 'temporal hallucination' fits like a glove.[11]

Eisenstein responds to this temporal hallucination, calling Disney a 'marvelous lullaby for the suffering and unfortunate'.[12] Viewers like Eisenstein who sense the marvel, the life in these caricatures they know do not exist, often ponder metaphysical questions such as 'What constitutes life?' Animation's marvellous spark suggests that life can exist in another space–time from the real world, that life can exist in the imagination.[13] Many comments provide evidence for such a spark and the metaphysical questions it provokes. Take art critic Dorothy Grafly in 1933: '[Disney] repudiates representation, but it aims to provoke the poignant reality of the unreal. It, too, goes back to the study of the primitive and the child in its basic realisation that to both, a fairy tale is more real than actual experience.'[14] Or, writer William Kozlenko said in 1936, 'The uniqueness of the animated cartoon lies in the fact that, of all film forms, it is the only one that has freed itself almost entirely from the restrictions of an oppressive reality. Its whole conception of life and of movement is based on fantasy.'[15]

A similar spark struck Benjamin as well. To him, Mickey Mouse films 'disavow experience more radically than ever before', revealing a 'vast and unsuspected field of action' not available to natural human perception.[16] Likewise, Robert Feild, who penned the first academic tome on *The Art of Walt Disney*, also feels the marvel of animation.[17] He describes Disney's animation as the making of miracles, revitalising youth and the imagination, and he finds himself questioning reality:

> This, then, is the Disney world – a timeless, spatially unlimited realm where all is one continuous adventure for those who have retained their youth, one in which whatever laws there may be are in a state of permanent transition; a world where one

is baffled by his inability to decide what is real and what is only imaginary. It is an exciting world in which one can scare himself almost to death for the fun of it, or be so scared in spite of himself that he is only too glad to escape from it.[18]

In sum, animation's transformability relates to the viewer's infoldings of form and motion, splitting the perception of movement from the perception of form. Such splits spark, at times, a marvellous affection that ruptures modes of perception in which the perception of form and movement is unified. This marvellous spark raises metaphysical questions and is often described as animation's magic or mystery. As producers develop animation's transformability in the hopes of innervating this spark, they develop an interface we will call the 'motion-image'. The motion-image plays on the fold between the perception of form and movement, divorcing the movement's trajectory from its motivating force. The result will be, throughout the 1910s and 1920s, affected audiences who laugh hysterically at the motion-images of such characters as Felix the Cat and Mickey Mouse.

The -Abilities of Animation

These different affections stem from the different -abilities of animation, in comparison with live action. Due to their intertwined histories, the similarities and differences between live action and animation remain a frequently discussed subject. Indeed, the appearance of animated photographs was only the beginning of animation and cinema's respective, mutually influenced series of becomings. Photography first became animated, producing live-action cinema, but shortly thereafter, animation became cinema. Once cinema emerged as a standardised technology, animation adopted the projection technology and photograph as basic means, using this technology to reproduce the images for the screen. Thus Donald Crafton, a scholar of early animation, dates the first animated film to 1898 and denies that Reynaud, the praxinoscope and other early devices had much influence on animated film. For Crafton, Méliès, one of the first directors to exploit trick photography, represents a more direct predecessor. Such a denial, however, forces Crafton to conceive live-action film as dominant and to assimilate animation under its sway. Thus he states that animation is 'a minor branch of the history of cinema', calling animation 'a subspecies of film in general'.[19]

Crafton's subordination of animation to film remains the most common gesture in film studies, with most scholars focused on live action and relegating animation as a childish or trivial stepchild.[20] This demeaning relegation is so prevalent that Crafton feels it necessary to state that he 'appreciates that intelligent and mature adults' can enjoy animation, and that 'serious' history can and should be done on 'this not-so-serious subject'.[21] The past twenty years have witnessed some ground being clawed back, with scholars elevating animation studies to its own respected subfield. Yet much of this scholarship simply places animation within the larger category of film, arguing that animation is an important type deserving more focus. As Alan Cholodenko states, 'For the overriding tendency . . . on the part of animation scholars continues to be to treat animation as a genre . . . without going the extra and radical step . . . to see all film as a form of animation.'[22]

This extra, radical step appears to differ dramatically from either ignoring animated film or relegating animation to live-action cinema, instead inversing the privilege given to live action and esteeming animation. As Cholodenko concludes, '(A)ll film is a form of animation . . . It has *never not* been animation.'[23] Likewise, Paul Watson warns against an 'artificial opposition' between animation and cinema due to their entangled histories, technologies and techniques.[24] Since animation was a precursor to live-action cinema, Watson finds it more appropriate to see live action as a form of animation. As reciprocally influencing translations, the relationship between cinema and animation is undoubtedly more complex than a strict opposition. Any consideration of film animation must address the contexts and conditions of live action because of animation's dependence on cinema's theatres, technologies and studios, as I attempt throughout this book.

Yet Cholodenko and Watson's position also downplays the differences by conflating animation and cinema, just reversing the priority traditionally given to live action. The relationship between live action and animation remains more than one of dependence or essential sameness; translation is not simple transference. Sure, animation may borrow from live action, and live action may depend on an animatic apparatus. Yet conflating these media will not suffice any more so than ignoring animation or treating it as a subset of cinema. This is especially true, as we have seen in the section above, from the perspective of affect because live-action cinema and animation generate different affective experiences that are sensed and interpreted differently. Yet why are these affections experienced differently? What makes animation's affections *special*? Answering these questions begins, first, with consideration of the differences in virtual -abilities of animation and cinema, before outlining the differences in mode and image-interface in early animation before its translation into Disney's features.

We will outline two different -abilities of animation: its transform-ability and its transferability. These -abilities stem from the differences in formative substances between live action and animation. The photo-graph constitutes the primary substance of live-action film. Run through a projector, these photographs gain apparent movement and duration; the space captured becomes mobile and temporal. In Deleuze's words, '(T)he cinema is the system which reproduces movement as a function of any-instant-whatever that is, as a function of equidistant instants, selected so as to create an impression of continuity.'[25] Similarly, art historian Erwin Panofsky designates this process as film's '*dynamization of space*'.[26] Projected at a fast enough rate, photographs create apparent movement, adding duration to the static images. Yet even an image without apparent movement has duration once projected on the screen. Thus instead of the dynamisation of space, which implies movement, we can better clarify cinema as the temporalisation of space, a temporalisation that happens in still shots and those bustling with movement alike. In sum, the movie camera captures photographs as its basic substance, and the projection of these photographs makes time the basic content of the movie. Each picture is a duration, exactly and always 1/24th of a second. The content is a moment in time, what Deleuze calls a mobile section of movement. Time/motion goes into the camera, is split up into any-instant-whatevers and then projected back into time/motion. As such, time or duration becomes reproducible and hence part of the content a director can manipulate. As we saw in Chapter 2, duration becomes meaningful content.

What, then, is the primary difference between animation and cinema? Obviously, animation is also reproducible and can employ duration as content, yet animation does not constitute the reproducibility of time because the content of animation is not a mobile section of movement. Photographs do not compose the substance of animation. The photo-graphs take place much later in the process, after the drawings that give *the illusion of motion* are already completed. These drawings never moved; they were never moments in time. Instead, drawn animation creates the illusion of time and motion through the projection of still images. Thus animation's substance is fundamentally different from cinema, as said by animator Alexandre Alexeieff: 'Contrary to live-action cinema, animation draws the elements of its future works from a raw material made exclu-sively of human ideas, those ideas that different animators have about things, living beings and their forms, movements and meanings.'[27] Both may present an indirect representation of time, but animation of the time period does so self-consciously, never quite achieving the astonishment of cinema's lifelike movement.

If animation's content is not time, then what is its content? Rather than capturing a mobile section of time, animation creates image-movement. Animation creates movement where there was none before, from a *never-has-been*. Animation produces the artistic imitation of motion, creating any-instant-whatevers that can be projected into movement from a raw material that was never any-instant. Where cinema's content is movement-in-time, animation's content is drawings (or clay, and so on) that create movement. This is an oft-repeated observation. Philip Brophy compares the cinematographer and animator:

> the former dealing with real-time and the latter trading in artificial time, the former accepting or co-ordinating the inherent and manifest rhythm of the action being photographed and the latter engineering, producing and orchestrating rhythms in order to *make action happen*.[28]

Famed animator Norman McLaren also distinguishes thus: 'Animation is not the art of drawings that move, but rather the art of movements that are drawn. What happens *between* each frame is more important than what happens *on* each frame.'[29]

In contrast to the *that-has-been* movement captured by the movie camera, animation creates the illusion of movement from *never-have-been* figures or graphic lines. Instead of live-action cinema's translation of an instant into an any-instant-whatever, animation transforms a single frame into an any-instant-whatever. Put simply, animation composes apparent motion frame by frame. Animation's basic unit, the level where most filmmaker manipulation takes place, is the frame, the individual image. In contrast, the shot represents the basic unit of cinema. Cinema captures time and movement within the shot; animation creates time and movement between the frames. Another animation scholar, William Schaffer, develops a useful definition from this recognition: 'Animation in the most general sense is this unique art of direct interaction with every interval of the any-instant-whatever generated by film.'[30] Crafton advances a similar definition, and, following this definition, the early trick filmmaker George Méliès is indeed a proper forebear of animation. Even in live-action movies, many tricks – such as as stop-motion where the camera is stopped, things are rearranged, and then the camera is started again – are properly animatic because they compose images at the level of the frame.

The techniques of live action and animation also illustrate the differences. The primary techniques of film are editing and camera work, with the fundamental components being the shot and montage. From what is recorded and edited, the live-action movie is composed. After shooting, the directors sit down with a massive amount of footage and shrink it to the desired length. From hundreds of hours, the film is reduced to a couple. The editor cuts out the bad acting (hopefully), the misplaced objects, and the mechanical apparatuses that might give away the artifice. They then splice together a motion picture of shifting points of view and moving cameras. Thus editing comprises the fundamental creative element of cinema. The editor primarily engages in cutting, slicing, subtracting and splicing, taking the shots and composing the whole.

Animation, in contrast, is an additive art. Editing plays a secondary role, and little is added to the image from camera movements. The camera enters the picture at the final stage, taking a still photograph of a drawn or moulded image. Although animation's multiplane camera (discussed more later) allows for some camera movement into the depth of the image, the room-sized device does not move through space. In fact, one of the challenges of animated photography and the multiplane camera is keeping the camera and images still so that a clear picture develops. The images might simulate camera and other movements but do so by keeping the camera motionless. This lack of camera movement is why, for Thomas Lamarre, animation can be considered primarily an art of compositing where various image layers (background, figure, foreground) are stacked and the gaps between these layers are managed in different ways. He states,

> In sum, with the animation stand, the tendency is toward an open compositing and thus animatism – an 'animetic' rather than cinematic sense of depth and movement. The film apparatus (the camera) is fixed or restricted in its movement and thus loses its privilege in constructing a sense of movement and depth.[31]

As for editing, animation's camera rarely captures the unnecessary, and its world is not full of boom mikes, mistakes and other material inconveniences burdening the filmmaker. The scene and movements can be perfected from the start. Directors can edit out those images not conveying the desired result; this process is not the creative element but more like redacting a paper. Furthermore, editing does not transpose the spectator through the diegetic space. Drawings or models create the motions of camera and montage. As a result of editing and montage, a live-action movie rarely looks like what the crew experiences on site. After editing animation, the differences are much fewer. In fact, animation's lack of live shoots makes the comparison moot. Through the fabrication of framed images, animation additively creates the transposing movements that editing constructs in cinema.

We have uncovered how the substance, content and techniques of animation differ from live action, yet what is the virtual -ability of animation driving these differences? Whereas live-action film captures time, enabling a reproducibility of movement, animation's manipulation frame by frame capacitates a *transformability* of the figure and a *transferability* between cels (cels are transparent film on which animated images are drawn). Many have noted the transformability of animation. Eisenstein calls it animation's 'plasmaticness', that ability to shape form like malleable plasma, resulting in the most astounding and impossible transformations of figure, such as Felix's tail becoming a question mark or Mickey being stretched like a rubber band.[32] Panofsky describes transformability as animation's ability to effect 'metamorphoses', endowing things 'with a different kind of life'.[33] Indeed, many early magic lantern and praxinoscope scenes portrayed transformability as a magic trick, with practitioners claiming they could conjure the dead or suspend laws of nature. Such transformability was also often actualised in early film animation. Emile Cohl, perhaps the first film animator, relished this transformability of animation, presenting scenes such as his 1908 'Phantasmagorie', in which clowns suddenly sprout long hair and then go bald, their heads become detached and bounce across the screen, and threatening police dissipate into atomic particles.

In addition to transformability, animation also comes with a potential for *transferability*: that is, *the ability to layer surfaces and transfer between them*. Transferability comes from two technological preconditions: clear cels, which allow light to transfer between the layers, and the animation stand, which stacks layers and allows their relatability. Composing images frame by frame requires stacking and relating the layers since those layers transfer on to one another, such as the foreground figure casting on to the background cel. Thus animation's transferability is a surface transfer, meaning the conveyance of content from one surface to another, such as tracing and drawing, both key steps in animation. Indeed, Disney animation requires a large number of surface transfers. Typically, the transfer moves from the story to storyboard, a series of preliminary sketches arranged in narrative order. From the storyboard, the animator transfers the narrative into rough drawings. The rough drawings are transferred into 'pencil tests', where the animator projects the drawings in sequence to see if the movement works to their liking. Assistant animators then transfer the rough drawings to the full image, including all the 'in-between' drawings that give the illusion of movement. Tracers then transfer drawings on to celluloid film, and painters then colour the traces. The cels are then transferred to film by shooting photographs. Through the projector, the film is finally transferred to the screen, sometimes composited with sound layers containing music, voices and other noises.

Every new transfer creates new space, composing a single space from the various layers of cels, ink, paint, photos and sound. As animated figures are drawn, stamped, traced, coloured or transferred from one surface to another, that surface becomes a new space because the graphic line functionally creates space. As Benjamin states, 'The graphic line is defined by its contrast with area . . . The graphic line confers an identity on its background.'[34] The graphic line constitutes an area by delineating a background, simultaneously generating a figure and space. If we draw a line on a sheet of paper, the sheet becomes background; after drawing a few more, we see the white of the paper as an ocean wave or the sun's rays. The drawn animation from the 1920s to the 1950s examined here remains primarily an art of the graphic line, of transference that engenders space.

Like transformability, animation's transferability stems from the different substances of animation in comparison with live action. Drawn animation depends on graphic lines whereas live-action cinema rarely employs them and can live without.[35] Live-action cinema depends instead on the mark, which contrasts with graphic lines. Graphic lines are printed on something, whereas marks emerge from space. If we scratch a wall, a mark is left behind, emerging from the surface, yet the mark does not delineate the wall as background. We perceive the mark as part of the wall. Live-action cinema is the art of the mark, of the index or trace that emerges from space rather than creating new space. Cinema's movement-images capture marks of movement instead of birthing space through the transfer of graphic lines. The transposability of cinema merely transforms that space, making it appear to be a narrative place. Yet the original movements remain in their actual space; the space is simply fragmented, snipped and joined to a different whole. This is why Deleuze can call cinema the movement-image. The image captures movement in space, of characters and camera. Live-action cinema creates meaningful places but does not transfer moving figures into another space. In contrast, animation transfers figures into space, from surface to surface. As Mickey is transferred from storyboard to drawing to cel to screen, each surface becomes a new space. Space is created rather than captured.

As a result, if the classical cinema has to manage the split between viewer and spectator, animation has to manage the split between the different layers of animation, with different modes managing these layers in different ways. Each transfer creates new space, transforming the cel or photo or screen into an animated world. In drawn animation, the construction of space begins from the seemingly boundless blank page and cel. Space is not manufactured for the camera, as it is in live action; space is manufactured to make it seem *as if* there is a camera. The challenge is not how to move the camera smoothly through space but how to create space that seems moveable, traversable, inhabitable. Animators face the primary task of how to have characters transferred into the animated space, rather than how to move the camera through physical space. Thus, more than transposability or translocatability, animation relies upon transferability, the ability to transfer space to the cel and screen as well as transfer between the various layers in these spaces.

Such transferability enables the relatability of image layers, creating the potential for relations between layers that can be managed in a number of ways. Transferring the background, centre and foreground on to different cels allows animators to stack them, creating depth that the multiplane camera enhances. Inking the pencil tests creates bolder outlines, making the figures stand out more clearly from the background. Colours and shadows cast from one surface to the next, creating a sense of depth. One way of managing the different layers, employed by Disney, was to create semblances of a cinematic world, of an inhabitable world in which the characters move. And it is only in such a world that Mickey might come alive, might be sensed as possessing the ability to affect and be affected. In other words, Disney's surface transfers are crucial to the mimetic experience of animistic mimesis, the transfer or contagion of affect from characters to viewers. Yet prior to Disney's translation, transferability created many constraints for animators, who downplayed the relation between layers to focus on the transformability of the graphic line, resulting in a mode of graphic narrative dominant in the 1920s.

Graphic Narrative and the Motion-Image

In the early twentieth century, animation became film, borrowing the cinematic apparatus to construct its apparent movements, yet drawing techniques were primarily translated from newspaper comics of the nineteenth century. This was a technological necessity. At the time, animation's capacity for transferability was limited. Animators could not stack many layers of celluloid to form backgrounds and foregrounds without losing image quality, so animation was largely restricted to flat lines drawn for the flat page. Thus Esther Leslie titles her book *Hollywood Flatlands*, demonstrating how the anarchic transformability of these graphic lines captured the imagination of the modernist *avant-garde*. Many themes also present characters struggling with the rapid changes of the modern world, especially adapting to the machinery of industry and consumerism. Norman Klein, the scholar who has done the most to outline the modes of this period, concurs: 'Cartoons are not story trifles; they are folklore about the rituals of daily life, in our case about consumer life.'[36] Klein labels the predominant mode of the period 'graphic narrative', which can be clarified as the *perceiving of moving lines as animated characters*. The mode of graphic narrative actualises in an interface we will call the motion-image, an image that separates the trajectory and motivating force of the motion, splitting the perception of motion and form to produce affection, most often surprise that becomes expressed as laughter.

This humour is the humour of gags, which interrupt the narrative trajectory (typically a chase) and thereby separate the force behind the trajectory from the trajectory on screen. In other words, characters like Felix and Mickey repeatedly confront or make use of invisible forces violating the expectations of progression, speed, direction, shape and acceleration. Due to the transformability of animation, space and bodies bend, stretch, mutate, evolve and unfold in quite unexpected ways. The characters face these unexpected obstacles and, often, turn the transformability into opportunity, as best seen with Felix's handy, metamorphosing tool – his tail. Unsurprisingly, then, these movies were often understood as fables of modernity, consumerism and industrialisation, since these cultural formations engendered a widespread sense that human trajectories were also being shaped in unexpected ways by invisible and unpredictable forces. Felix and Mickey's ability to adapt to and exploit such forces made them among the most popular screen stars at the time, often put in company with the most famous live-action stars, including Buster Keaton and Charlie Chaplin.

Critics frequently fault Disney for abandoning the anarchic transformability of the 1920s, replacing the flatlands with cinematic depth and realism, and thereby sacrificing the modernist impulse. There is some truth to these criticisms, yet we will question the extent to which Disney abandons animation's transformability shortly. For now, however, it suffices to note that this process of becoming more like cinema is a translation, and the synchronisation of sound (the addition of sound layers) provides a crucial step. So, in this section, I outline the features of graphic narrative and the motion-image through reference to Otto Messmer and Pat Sullivan's Felix cartoons. Then I demonstrate how Disney continues this mode and the motion-image in Mickey's first animated shorts, including the first, *Steamboat Willie* (1928). *Steamboat* also begins the translation process towards the imitation of cinematic space by adding sound, drawing on animation's transferability. This addition allows a different folding for viewers, split not only between trajectory and force in the motion-image but also between motion and accompanying sound. Sound contributes both to the perception of an apparent trajectory and to a realisation that a different force is at play in these animated worlds.

Felix and the Motion-Image

Felix the Cat premiered on 9 November 1919 in the short entitled *Feline Follies*. The film was a major hit and Sullivan studios set to work on producing a running series. Although Felix entered an environment with the graphic narrative mode firmly established, Felix proved to be one of the most successful and long-lasting examples, becoming an icon whose image was widespread in films and on merchandise throughout the 1920s, was the first tested for television, and that reappeared periodically as the star of television series and full-length animated movies. Crafton describes Felix as the 'quintessential cartoon of the 1920s and the favorite of a growing number of aficionados of the medium'.[37] Even Mickey's original design owes a great deal to Felix.

In addition, Felix contributed to a trend towards animals as main characters and epitomised the tendency beginning in the late teens to feature recurring characters. Before this time, characters often changed from film to film, and the recurrence of characters such as Felix is, in part, responsible for his immense popularity. Repeated offerings allowed audiences to become familiar with and fond of the characters' personalities. Felix possessed a trademark pace (pensively looking down with hands crossed behind his back), a mischievous, childlike spirit, and a famous, detachable tail that delighted audiences. Felix constantly chases after basic needs, including food, sex and security, needs with which audiences could readily identify.

Felix cartoons epitomise graphic narrative, especially the perception of moving lines drawn for the flat page. Backgrounds were typically limited, featuring mostly the white space of blank pages along with a few lines to indicate general settings because technical limitations precluded much more than a flat, sparse backdrop; a few simple, straight lines were drawn to represent a building, mountain, field or wall in the background. Two other important aspects of Felix's graphic narrative form include the linearity of the drawings and the sharpness of the outlines. Messmer reports that they drew Felix in all-black shapes because it allowed Felix to stand out from the background distinctly, instead of attempting to draw fine outlines for the figure. This was especially crucial due to the limited nature of the backgrounds. Such sharpness allows Felix to remain a coherent, clear figure, distinct from the rest of the environment. Many artists of the time replicated this technique, including for Disney's Oswald and Mickey characters. In addition, the linearity of the drawings limits Felix's transformability, leading Crafton to label it a 'linear metamorphosis, where the lines come to life, as if they were characters in their own right'.[38]

This linearity explains why Felix's tail becomes a central prop because the tail is a simple line that, with a few bends, can become a device for other uses. These devices tend to be linear as well, with the tail turning into exclamation marks, skis, canes, toothbrushes, cranks and swords.

Characters constitute the other important element of the graphic narrative mode. Compared to earlier animation where figures constantly transform, morphing into shapes and sizes completely unlike the original, in graphic narrative the transformability of animation becomes somewhat contained in the character.[39] In *Fantasmagorie*, Cohl's clown becomes a man with an umbrella, and, in *Hasher's Dream*, grapes become a bug-eyed man who morphs into a bell, then a lighthouse, a wine bottle and many other forms. If there are characters here, they are certainly difficult to pin down. In contrast, Felix's form changes shape and function, but Felix remains Felix and the original shape always returns. Such containment of transformability in the character is perfectly represented by Felix's detachable tail, which transforms only to be reattached and become tail again. In sum, in graphic narrative, moving lines constitute fictional characters. These characters have a solidity and consistency all their own and necessary to create a personality; thus the characters limit the extremes of transformation.

Given these two elements, graphic narrative operates through an economy between the moving line and animated character, or between motion and form, enabled by animation's transformability. Graphic narrative offers the form of a character polarised against the motion of the transforming line, producing a field of potential energy and affect. Klein's label, graphic narrative, perfectly encapsulates this economy, since it indicates both moving lines (graphic) and character (narrative). Felix's popularity demands tapping into and balancing the energy of the graphic and the narrative, movement and character, motion and form. Too much semblance of character would make the animation too realistic, draining it of the force of animation's magic – its transformability, which is a major source of Felix's humour. Too much play of the moving line, however, would preclude developing a character with a unique personality, with whom audiences could identify and sympathise. This modal economy was economic in the narrow sense as well, since, as Crafton notes, by 1918 animation was at risk of losing audiences due to over-saturation and stereotypical imagery. Thus animators developed distinct characters 'that audiences would respond to in personal, not stereotypical, ways'.[40]

We can see the energetic tension of this economy in scenes where Felix 'speaks'. I put speak in quotation marks because these are silent films, but on occasion text bubbles form, replicating the technique for indicating speech in newspaper cartoons. During these moments, moments crucial to the narrative, all movement stops as the animators provide time to read. These scenes manifest the tension between movement and character, motion and form. Too much motion during these moments might distract, leading viewers to miss the things said that form the plot and character. Leaving text bubbles up too long or only using text, however, would rob the images of their animation, their movement that was crucial to the special, affective experience.

Two content features result from the mode of graphic narrative. First, other than the brief speech bubbles, motion persists constantly in the images. Felix unceasingly chases, paces, flees, flies, swims, fights, eats, sings, works, whistles and performs nearly every other kinetic action one can imagine. As Crafton remarks about *Steamboat Willie*, a remark that readily applies to Felix, 'Hyperkineticism prevails; everything moves.'[41] Second, the requirements for motion and character dictate a narrative structure largely based around chases and gags.[42] The chases, or other pursuits, drive the motion and narrative forward. For instance, in *Feline Follies*, Felix runs from a housewife who is mad over her destroyed kitchen and from his kittens' mother, and in other episodes Felix chases after girls, mice and fish and runs from bears, storms, Russians, apes, boyfriends and the villian Dan McStew.[43] Such narrative action produces a distinct character with psychological motivations and personality. The gags punctuate this action, providing the humorous attraction. Gags offered an effective vehicle to deliver the novelty of movement, since gags rely on motion for their comedy, such as throwing a pie in someone's face or transforming Felix's tail. The gag and chase, then, also articulate to graphic narrative's economy between motion and form, the moving line and character.

During the gags, the motion-image appears, splitting the trajectory of the apparent movement from the force motivating it. The viewer folds their perception of apparent movement into two, its trajectory and force, with the trajectory revealed to be only perception and the force revealed to be the animator and animation's transformability. Of course, other gags and jokes exist that do not present motion-images; Felix and other characters enact standard gags inherited from places like vaudeville. Yet the gags based in transformability are unique to animation and constitute the motion–image, along with its special affects.

In the motion- image, animation's transformations rupture the perception of the motion's trajectory. In animation before the late teens, this rupture was often found in images featuring the animator's self-figuration. That is, animators most commonly created the motion–image by putting themselves as a visible force in the animated scene, usually by showing their hands drawing. As the animations began to move along a certain trajectory, the animator's hand would apply force to transform this trajectory, often morphing the figure. Many times, the figures would appear to resist or fight back, provoking another unexpected, humorous encounter. Such self-figuration accomplishes the motion-image by splitting the trajectory of the motion from the force behind it, making visible the animator's force. This self-figuration version of the motion-image makes the animator appear as the force behind animation's transformability. Crafton recognises that self-figuration represents a common tendency in early animation, and he connects it to animation's transformability:

> (T)his genesis theme is the result of the animator's presenting himself in the role of life giver – not mysteriously but deliberately and . . . with increasing subtlety until finally we take for granted that the animator can vivify things that could never have otherwise existed. Part of our enjoyment of Felix . . . depends on our vicarious participation in the ritual of incarnation.[44]

As this quotation indicates, self-figuration becomes less common by the time of Felix and the maturation of graphic narrative. The motion-image no longer relies on making the animator visible to illustrate the split between force and trajectory. Instead, the comedy results from the split between the perception of trajectory and an invisible force, despite viewers' knowledge that the characters do not move with their own force. We laugh at the motion-image because the fold between trajectory and force creates a gag, such as when Felix encounters a locked door and flattens himself to slide under it, or when he is sucked into a telegraph line, travels to Russia, arrives with the letters F-E-L-I-X spelled out on the tape, and finally materialises from those letters into cat-like form. These are prototypical motion-images. Felix's movements run into obstacles, and he transforms to overcome these obstacles, revealing the force of the animator. As Felix and Mickey's worldwide popularity illustrates, such motion-images spark some striking affections from the folding, affections that typically result in laughter. The joke is sort of on us: when the semblance of the motion, the vector of its apparent movement, tricks us into not expecting the next movement despite the fact that we *should* know better because everything is constructed by an invisible hand. Nothing should be unexpected, yet we are surprised or at least tickled none the less. 'You got me that time, Felix and Otto!'

Instead of self-figuration, two different types of motion-images exist in Felix and Mickey cartoons. Most often, animators place the force in the character; the main characters are endowed with the magical force of the invisible, unrepresented animator. It is thus little surprise that many accounts describe Felix as a manifestation of Messmer's personality and Mickey as a manifestation of Disney's.[45] At other times, the animator's transformable force acts on the main character, creating obstacles that provoke response. Both types constitute motion-images, splitting the movement of the situation from the force of the animator-in-the-character or splitting the movement of the character from the force of the animator-in-the-world. In motion-images, sometimes the trajectory lies on the character's side and the force on the world's side, and sometimes the world moves and the character enacts the force of animation's transformability. As such, the motion-image constitutes an energetic tension through poles between the situation, which sparks the trajectory of the movements, and the force of those movements, a tension felt affectively as surprise and mostly expressed in laughter.

Felix's humorous encounters with hot dogs provide examples for these two types of motion-images. Most frequently, Felix possesses the animator's force, transforming himself or the environment to address obstacles confronting him. In *Felix Gets the Can*, Felix contemplates how to get to Alaska to catch salmon and two question marks materialise out of his head. Felix grabs the question marks, and turns them into skis for a sled. He then whistles at some hot dogs, with musical notes leaving his lips and striking the meat. The hot dogs come alive and line up to pull the sled; Felix pulls a whip from his pocket and drives the 'dogs' to Alaska. In *Felix Finds Out*, however, the dogs gain the animatic force, motivating Felix's movements. As Felix attempts to split a hot dog with his friend, the dog comes alive, dances mockingly and then runs away. In response, Felix meows at the remaining hot dogs at the food stand, which also come alive, bark angrily at Felix, and chase him, running with dog-like gait. They pursue Felix into a doghouse and a brawl ensues, with the house shaking and contorting. Felix has the last laugh, however, as he wins the brawl and eats the hot dogs.

The early Mickey shorts, such as *Steamboat Willie*, also employ both types of motion-image for comical effect. Mickey possesses the animator's force and also faces the obstacles of a mysteriously transforming world. Yet Disney advances the motion-image through new drawing techniques, and, most importantly, by adding sound to the silent visuals. The addition of sound creates a third type of motion-image, one that splits the trajectory of the motion from the sound, creating another unexpected, comical moment. These different drawing techniques and the addition of sound will be the first steps translating the flat world of graphic narrative to the three-dimensional world present in Disney's full-length features.

Mickey in the Motion-Image

Not the first animated cartoon to be synchronised with sound effects but the first to
attract favorable attention. This one represents a high order of cartoon ingenuity,
cleverly combined with sound effects. The union brought laughs galore. Giggles
came so fast at the Colony they were stumbling over each other.

Variety on the *Steamboat Willie* opening[46]

Steamboat Willie, the first Mickey short, opened on 18 November 1928.
Not only were there giggles and laughs galore, but the movie and its
follow-ups, *Plane Crazy* and *Galloping Gaucho*, almost immediately made
Mickey an international cult star, a hero for the little guy, whose image
would soon be blazoned on countless commodities and become one of
the most recognisable American icons. The laughter was not limited to
this first showing, since many reports detail the affections of Mickey's
audiences. At an early trial of the sound synchronisation, Walt Disney
described the affections thus: 'The effect on our little audience was nothing
less than electric. They responded almost instinctively to this union of
sound and motion.'[47] Likewise, Ub Iwerks, the primary animator, claimed
that after the trial he had 'never been so thrilled in [his] life. Nothing since
has ever equaled it.'[48] Audiences worldwide felt this thrill and electricity,
expressing their admiration for Mickey in song, writing, consumption and
movie attendance. The reviewer for the *Exhibitor's Herald* claimed to be so
affected that *Steamboat* 'knocked me out of my seat'.[49]

Most accounts attribute the success of *Steamboat* to sound synchronisation, and this was certainly its novelty at the time, adding another type
of motion-image. As animation scholar J. P. Telotte shows, these early
Mickey shorts also mark the beginnings of a translation of graphic narrative, especially departing from the linear drawings and flat pages. There
is something more three-dimensional about Mickey, something 'stereoscopic'.[50] In these shorts, Mickey does not just move across a flat world;
he also moves into and out of the depths of this world, as a scene in *Plane
Crazy* perfectly emblematises, where the plane plunges, spinning out of
control, and the images show the landscape getting closer and rotating.
This scene offers a prime example of what Lamarre calls cinema's ballistic
perception, where the spectator is placed on the tip of a vehicle or other
projectile and sent speeding into the depths of the diegetic world.

The addition of sound enables this creation of depth, since noises seem
to emanate from inside characters and sounds provide many techniques
for creating a sense of distance, direction, and on-screen versus off-screen
space – in short, the sense of a three-dimensional world. Such techniques
are called 'sound perspective', the phrase based in a comparison to the

Figure 4.1 Mickey and the rubber-hose technique in *Steamboat Willie*.
(Screenshot from *Mickey in Black and White* DVD)

visual Renaissance perspective that also suggests depth. Most techniques for sound perspective are exploited in the early Mickey cartoons. As Telotte states, 'These and similar sounds essentially function to help construct the traditional reality illusion in a variety of ways: denoting an action, announcing a presence, suggesting contiguous space, and motivating character response.'[51]

As seen in Figure 4.1, the detail of background and foreground far exceeds that of Felix's world and, furthermore, the movements of Mickey and companions differ from the linear metamorphosis of Felix. Disney developed 'rubber-hose' drawing, which adds bends and curves to the flat lines of graphic narrative. Characters move like wet noodles controlled by an invisible hand, by bending and flexing, compressing and stretching. Such rubber-hose techniques added more realism and fluidity to the apparent movement and created more sense of volume and depth. Figure 4.1 presents a common gag that draws on this greater depth. Since the characters look like rubber hoses, the animators often drew gags where the characters stretch, flex, expand and contract as if they are actually made

of rubber, as with this unfortunate duck's neck. This stretching and contracting gives the characters greater volume to fit better into the greater
depths of this more stereoscopic world.

In fact, such rubber-hose gags are the most common way in which
Disney constructs the motion-image in this period. Rather than having
linear parts that detach and reattach, combine and break, the Disney characters have rubber parts that expand and contract, flexing and stretching
well beyond the limits of their outlines. At the beginning of *Steamboat*, for
instance, the steamboat's exhaust pipes contract and then expand like an
accordion, puffing out smoke. Later, when a skinny cow will not fit into
the loading harness, Mickey pushes a shovel full of hay down its throat,
causing its stomach to balloon greatly. Disney repeatedly exploits the
rubber-hose technique to create motion-images; the movement trajectory goes well beyond expected parameters, stretching and contracting,
bending and twisting in ways that reveal the animator's force. Mickey
frequently embodies this force of the animator, pulling, poking and prodding others to give them unexpected shapes. In *Steamboat*, Mickey cranks
on a goat's tail, smashes a cat, pulls a cow's tail, and molests a group of
piglets and mother, who take comical and unexpected forms in response to
Mickey's force. When prodded, each animal emits a synchronised noise.

Animation's frame-by-frame manipulation enables precise sound synchronisation at a level above that of live action. Live action has a difficult
time finding music that precisely matches the rhythm of the actors, yet
animators can draw the characters' movements to match the music.
Disney exploits this potential in all the early Mickey shorts and continues in the series of *Silly Symphonies* that follow, as well as in their
full-length features. Indeed, this synchronisation of music and movement
is so predominant that Crafton describes *Steamboat*'s 'plot' as 'just an
excuse for a minstrel concert'.[52] Synchronisation adds another layer to
the motion-image because the sound not only creates a sense of depth
but also adds to the gag repertoire. Disney uses sound to create another
motion-image that operates through the economy between semblance and
play of graphic narrative. In short, sound creates a greater semblance of
movement into depth, but it also creates the possibility to introduce sound
gags, now a common staple of animation such as Warner Brothers' *Looney
Tunes*.[53] Telotte describes the resultant energetic tension as a 'kind of
sound fantasy, an aural environment in which real and expressive sound
imagery easily merge, where they are constantly in narrative negotiation,
constructing a kind of in-between world that is, I would offer, one of their
key attractions.'[54]

This third kind of motion-image, splitting sound and trajectory, can be seen throughout *Steamboat*. A goat eats Minnie's sheet music, prompting her to twist its tail into a crank and begin turning. Mickey opens the goat's mouth, which transforms into a speaker playing 'Turkey in the Straw'. Mickey then proceeds through a variety of motion-image gags, prodding and pulling on animals that emit sounds synchronised to the music, such as when Mickey plays the xylophone on a cow's teeth. Sometimes the sounds emitted are animal noises yet, at other times, the noises are something else completely. Thus Disney creates a third type of motion-image by the addition of sound layers. The non-realistic or extra-diegetic sounds reveal the split between the trajectory of movement and the animated force. Rather than hearing the sound of an animal, we hear the sounds animators select, usually chosen for humorous purposes. The most common example is the slide whistle, which typically accompanies a motion-image gag. For instance, when Mickey stretches and contorts a car to transform it into a plane in *Plane Crazy*, the slide whistle accompanies the motions, not sounds of crunching metal. Just like the humour of an unexpected force in the other types of motion-image, these sounds provide a surprising punch line to accompany the motion. The realistically synchronised sound we have come to expect is suddenly violated, splitting the perception of sound and image. In response to this splitting between aural and visual infoldings, audience members worldwide were affected; the laughs and giggles abounded.

Towards Disney's Animistic Mimesis

Throughout Disney's history and even today, all three varieties of the motion-image continue as common elements of animation. Yet the dominance of cinema and the changing of audience expectations will constitute new sociocultural forces and necessitate new modes to address those forces. The marvellous magic trick alone will not generate enough capitalisable energy. Indeed, the different substances of animation and cinema presented cinema with a significant economic advantage. Cinema needed only to record motion to produce movement-images; animation had to create image-movement frame by frame. A seven-minute short required over 10,000 drawings, necessitating large, industrial production, especially as technological advances in sound and colour emerged. Unfortunately, seven-minute openings to the film bill received only a small portion of the proceeds. The smaller revenues could not sustain the capital necessary to produce animated shorts. For Disney and other animators, time and money were running out. By the late 1920s, animation was in economic crisis and facing a major decline or even extinction. As

Deleuze states, 'This is the old curse which undermines the cinema: time is money.'[55] Animation's *creation of time* was proving too expensive, especially as the motion-image became mundane, and the marvel and laughter it provoked became muffled.

Despite Mickey's international success, Disney knew it needed a new strategy. As Walt recalled,

> We had money in the bank and security. But we didn't like the looks of the future
> . . . Cartoons had become the shabby Cinderella of the picture industry . . . Some of
> the possibilities in the cartoon medium had begun to dawn on me. And at the same
> time we saw that the medium was dying. You could feel rigor mortis setting in.[56]

Just as the financial crisis of the movement-image sparked the time-image, so too did economics motivate Disney's translation of the classical cinematic mode. In order to compete, Disney pursues a translation of the classical cinematic mode, requiring that they abandon the exclusive reliance on graphic narrative, motion-images and gag-driven content. The laughs will remain but Disney will also aim for a mimetic experience, creating *mutual-affection images* as interfaces that tap into animation's potential for *transferability*.

To achieve this goal, rubber-hose animation and the silly characters of graphic narrative will no longer suffice. To produce full-length movies, Disney began employing many of the same techniques of the classical mode, necessitating a translation of animation from the earlier graphic narrative mode into something closer to the classical cinema. Through certain technical advances in transferability, Disney became more able to imitate the spatial depth, translocatability and transposability of cinema. The organic spatiality and sensory-motor links are enhanced, thereby opening animation to the narrative practices of classical cinema. Yet Disney's full-length movies are a translation, bound not to replicate the cinematic mode faithfully but to transform it. Contrary to protestations from many critics who bemoan Disney's move towards 'realism', Disney's translation also employs the transformability of animation and its transferability between surfaces. By 1937, the transformability and transferability of animation, coupled with the transposability and translocatability of cinema, will enable a mode of animistic mimesis to emerge – a mode in which, for the viewer, synchronised movements and sounds become perceived as living, affectable beings. The resultant mutual affection-images will constitute a hybrid movement- and time-image, marking Disney as one of the first phases in the transition to the time-image regime and constituting a unique contribution to consumer culture by making perceivable daydreaming consumers.

CHAPTER 5

Of Mice and Mimesis:
The Wondrous Spark of Disney

Before its release on 21 December 21 1937, *Snow White* was widely known as 'Disney's folly', both because of mounting costs (nearly 1.5 million dollars) and because many believed animation could never hold the audience's attention for the length of a feature. Sceptics insisted that audiences would never care enough for drawings in order to evoke the full range of emotions commonly experienced in live-action films. The marvel of animation seemed restricted to motion and, hence, the chases, gags, crashes and bangs of graphic narrative. Animation could be an art of motion, many thought, but not of life.

After release, *Snow White* was praised as a wonder, a masterpiece, declared a true breakthrough, something never seen before. Such responses stem from the experience of a different spark – not the marvel of the moving line but the wonder of life, and therefore the full range of emotions such as fear, sadness and joy that accompany life. In this chapter, we will see how this spark results from the mode of animistic mimesis, in which the folding occurs between the viewer's knowledge of non-existence and their sensation of life. In animistic mimesis, viewers perceive synchronised sounds and drawings as expressive, affective life. This perception is more about touch, about feeling, than about sight; hence the term mimesis. And it is the feeling of another life, both human and not; hence animistic.[1]

Disney translated cinema and graphic narrative into animistic mimesis, drawing primarily on animation's transferability to formulate an economy between semblance (cinema) and play (animation). Disney created a world with semblances of 'real', cinematic space in order to feature the transformative play of animation, especially in privileged mutual-affection images that are frequently cited as the most emotional moments of the films. Transferability will be employed throughout Disney's features but most distinctly in these peak moments of animistic transformation, in which puppet becomes boy, maid becomes princess, and elephant becomes star. Transferring light, colour, sound and gesture between the layers enabled viewers to enter into those layers, to be affected via a mimetic communication that felt, in transition, like life (affect) and would be described as wonder (affection). In turn, this mode will result in a newly visible daydreaming consumer, uniquely impacting the course of (post)modern consumer culture.

The Wondrous Spark

There were certain words – 'warm', 'wonderful', 'amazing', 'dream', 'magical' – that attached themselves to Walt Disney's name like parasites in the later years of his life. They are all debased words, words that have lost most of their critical usefulness and, indeed, the power to evoke any emotional response beyond a faint queasiness. They are hucksters words.

Richard Schickel[2]

In a trenchant critique of Disney, Schickel outlines many of the common terms used to describe the spark of Disney's full-length features. We will label this spark wonder, meaning the perceiving of life in an inorganic or inanimate form, like conceiving of the life of the Grand Canyon (which is really a series of rocks, even if parts are living) or the life of the Great Pyramids or the life of a ventriloquist's dummy. The wondrous often makes us wonder, evoking metaphysical questions about life and its mysterious forces, where they come from, what it means to be alive, or what makes me 'me' (my favourite childhood pondering).[3]

The terms 'dream' and 'magical' also bear a close relationship to the affective experience of wonder, since magic often serves to explain how something inanimate becomes alive and since it is often in dreams that one perceives non-living things as living. Both magic and dreams are therefore frequently used to describe Disney, as Schickel indicates. I should remind the reader that these terms serve merely as placeholders, since the terms wonder, the fantastic, astonishment and marvel are basically synonymous and are often used interchangeably as commentators describe their affections in words. Indeed, one could easily replace wonder with the fantastic, especially since audience studies report that Disney is most frequently associated with the terms family and fantasy.[4] Certainly, Disney constructs a fantasy world similar to much live-action film, although from different materials. These different materials, however, oriented into a virtual relation, potentially innervate a different affection we will call wonder.

Wonder is a much different spark than what Barthes finds in photography's *that-has-been*. If the photograph embalms the *that-has-been*, Disney animation vivifies the *never-has-been*, creating the unique prick sending some adventuring into a blind field full of metaphysical puzzles. Although also a *punctum* of time, animation's wondrous spark is about life rather than death. The viewer feels wonder, sensing as alive that which does not live. This sense of life is so powerful, this wound so deep, that even knowledge otherwise sometimes cannot displace the sense that these animations live. For instance, in an oft-repeated anecdote, famous Warner Brothers animator Chuck Jones tells a child that he created Bugs Bunny.[5] The child stubbornly refuses, correcting him by saying, 'No, you draw pictures of Bugs Bunny.' In this child's eyes, Jones is only responsible for drawings and not the living character. Jones might make the character move, but Bugs has his own life. This child experienced animation's wonder, sensing as alive that which only exists as representation.

In response to *Snow White*, most commentators attest to the wondrous spark, insisting that the movie represents a breakthrough unique from the marvel of earlier offerings. As the *Variety* reviewer stated, 'While one marvels at the skill of its producers, "Snow White" permits no mental ramblings in the course of its unreeling.'[6] Instead, 'So perfect is the illusion, so tender the romance and fantasy, so emotional are certain portions when the acting of the character strikes a depth comparable to the sincerity of human players, that the film approaches real greatness.'[7] The *New York Times* critic Frank Nugent concurred – 'You'll not, most of the time, realise you are watching animated cartoons. And if you do, it will be only with a sense of amazement' – concluding, 'It is a classic, as important cinematically as *The Birth of a Nation* or the birth of Mickey Mouse.'[8]

The affective intensity surpassed marvelling over moving lines mostly because audiences felt the characters as alive instead of simply witnessing them move. As such, commentators stress the sense of life as the reason for Disney's uniqueness:

> [Disney] has made the beloved childhood myth a living, inconceivably beautiful film of limitless worth. Certainly the Disney achievement is the most important picture, from a production perspective, that has emerged since the advent of sound . . . Unbelievably beautiful . . . Unutterably charming . . . The beloved fairy tale comes to vivid life.'[9]

Similarly, the *Time* critic exclaimed (emphasis added):

> Technicolor is . . . giving a *vital*, indelible reality to the fairyland locales. Skeptical Hollywood, that had *wondered* whether a fairy story could have enough suspense to hold an audience through seven reels, and whether . . . an audience would care about the fate of characters who were just drawings, was convinced that Walt Disney had done it again . . . A combination of Hollywood, the Grimm Brothers, and the sad, searching fantasy of universal childhood, it is an authentic masterpiece.[10]

Similar testimonials to the wonder of sensing life greeted all of Disney's full-length features in the 1930s and 1940s. *Pinoccho*'s (1940) animation was reportedly 'so smooth' that the 'figures carry [the] impression of real persons . . . rather than drawings.'[11] Many thus consider Pinocchio to be the best Disney movie, due, for Nugent, to its 'charm', that 'pulsating, radiant, winning something that shines through . . . and makes it so captivating'.[12] At the release of *Fantasia* (1940), the *Time* reviewer reported that the movie 'as a whole leaves its audience gasping' because 'strangeness and wonder belong to the show itself.'[13] Describing *Fantasia* 'as terrific as anything that has ever happened on a screen', *New York Times* reviewer Bosley Crowther explains that 'one's senses are captivated by it, one's imagination is deliciously inspired.'[14]

Apparently a short year later, another Disney feature topped *Fantasia* for Crowther, since he called *Dumbo* 'the most genial, the most endearing, the most completely precious cartoon feature film ever to emerge from the magical brushes of Walt Disney's wonder-working artists'.[15] Crowther beckoned audiences to 'see the wonderland you first saw within the pages of story books', because it 'leaves you with the warmest glow'.[16] Crowther further explains that such glowing stemmed from an affective sensation of life (emphasis added): 'Never did we expect to fall in love with an elephant. But after meeting up with Dumbo at the Broadway theater last night we have thoroughly *transferred* our *affections* to this package of pachyderm.' The *Time* reviewer also sensed human (animistic) life in *Dumbo*: 'Dumbo is a most human little fellow, not bright, but willing . . . (T)he charm of *Dumbo* is that it again brings to life that almost human animal kingdom where Walter Elias Disney is king of them all.'[17]

While these quotations are too celebratory, animation's spark, as Barthes says of the *punctum*, both attracts and distresses. This attraction explains the rapid, international success of Disney; an attraction captivated fans. Such attraction distressed critics; the spark was also an enormous source of discomfort and conflict. Disney's translation is reviled as emblematic of the culture industry and consumerism. Critics agonised over the sentimentalism, realism, escapism and sanitisation of animated films. This distress grew out of the sense of wonder as well since, at its root, critics bemoan the transformation in spatio-temporal parameters of the 'real world'. Critics feared that Disney offered audiences a delusional escape from everyday existence, leaving audiences resigned to the inevitable pangs of actuality.[18] The spark of animation did not strike everyone but it wounded many, attracting the highest acclaims and harshest rebukes from those attracted and distressed by their adventure through the rabbit hole.

Most often, viewers felt this wondrous affection in the films' peak moments, the mutual affection-images analysed shortly. These include the moments of animistic transformation, such as the maid Snow White becoming a fugitive and then becoming princess, or Pinocchio becoming moving puppet, then donkey, then boy. These scenes reportedly resonated with viewers emotionally, causing tears, fears and a whole range of emotions. For instance, animator Art Babbitt reports watching the scene where Dumbo visits his mother in a cage 'in several places around the world and each time people in the audience weep'.[19] Historian Leonard Maltin felt fear from the scene in *Pinocchio* where he becomes a donkey, surmising, 'That any film, let alone an animated cartoon, could elicit such a remarkable range of responses from adults and children alike was astonishing.'[20] Disney's folly had become a shared affection; emotion, as we will see, was in the process of capture.

Although the artists intend to evoke emotional identification, emotions do not constitute Disney animation's wonder. Crying for Snow White does not represent the spark; crying or sadness is the emotional, subjective response to this pre-subjective affect. The mode is mimetic; one feels the transfer from animated bodies to one's own. The affect is the variation, the transition, felt pre-consciously, from moving into or being transferred on to another body. The affection is wonder; the interfacing of these two bodies makes one feel life despite our knowledge otherwise. We might say that this spark is the sting or prick someone experiences from the very idea that they could cry over the death of a *never-has-been* character, although this idea probably does not enter consciousness but is instead affectively experienced, a kind of tingle or wound that set Barthes on a quest for meaning, as did American culture in the wake of Disney animation. We are focused here on affect, not the emotional translation and capture that occurs afterwards. Crying is the conscious sealing of the affective experience, its registration at the level of subjectivity. Once it is registered, Disney knows it has a success and, as we will see, proceeds to capture that emotion in the form of profit.

Since it is the result of a pre-subjective mode, this sense of wonder may never strike some viewers. As Deleuze and Guattari remark, desiring-machines are constantly breaking down, usually when they approach the limits of its economy. The spark, like the *punctum*, is non-intentional and hence not guaranteed. Yet the mode makes such sparks possible (it is pre-subjective) and this spark was undoubtedly widely experienced in American culture. Viewers who sensed life in these caricatures they knew did not exist tried to make sense. They often pondered metaphysical questions such as 'What constitutes life?' As we will see, the mode of animistic mimesis would redefine life before and through our very bodies.

Animistic Mimesis

What do these commentators mean by life? How was Disney more 'real' than previous animation? In other words, what is the latitude of animistic mimesis, the relationship of capacities forming a plane of potential within which these affective intensities might flow? Basically, animistic mimesis relates animation's transferability to the viewer's capacity for mimesis, establishing an economy between semblance and play. Mimesis describes a bodily form of communication, the infolding of another's manner, the transfer of affect from one body to another. In Anna Gibbs's definition, mimesis means 'the corporeally based forms of imitation, both voluntary and involuntary . . . At their most primitive, these involve the visceral level of affect contagion.'[21] Gibbs refers to Tomkins's notion of affect contagion, a notion called transmission by Teresa Brennan.[22] We will call it a *transfer* since mimesis involves the transfer of characteristics from one surface to another. This transferability designates affect's potential to rebound or resonate, as one body becomes attuned to another. Affective transfer occurs through a sort of contagion, the passing of manner from one to another, like being affected by a rhythm, gesture, posture or mood. Although Tomkins and Brennan focus on the transfer of affect from person to person, Disney animation reveals that such a transfer can occur between animated bodies and human ones, crossing the gap between screen and viewer, directly affecting viewers as might time-images.

Examples of mimetic communication include when a person unconsciously smiles in response to the smile of another, or when the rhythm of mother's voice becomes the rhythm of baby's movement, or when a dancer becomes attuned to music, moving in synchronic harmony.[23] For Benjamin, mimesis is the oldest human faculty, a faculty behind the development of art and language alike but one that is waning in the modern world, except in children: 'Children's play is everywhere permeated by mimetic modes of behaviour, and its realm is by no means limited to what one person can imitate in another. The child plays at being not only a shopkeeper or teacher but also a windmill and a train.'[24] Children are the most able to see with 'pure eyes', often noticing similarities in objects and then projecting themselves into that world to play.[25] As all of these examples illustrate, mimesis is crucial for human development. Michael Taussig, in his masterful work on Cuna Indians' mimetic modes, makes this development part of his definition and further testifies to the wonder of mimetic modes. Mimesis is

the nature that culture uses to create second nature, the faculty to copy, imitate, make models, explore difference, yield into and become Other. The wonder of mimesis lies in the copy drawing on the character and power of the original, to the point whereby the representation may even assume that character and that power.[26]

There are many different neurological explanations for mimetic communication, many based upon the existence of neurons that mirror the pacing, rhythms and gesture of others. Regardless of the neurological mechanism, we should stress that despite its similarities to the term 'imitation', mimesis is not a visual mode in which one views and then copies another. Mimesis, instead, is a direct bodily transfer, often occurring without conscious knowledge, such as when, in conversation, we adjust our tone, rhythm and body position to those of another. As such, mimesis is a non-representational mode, closer to touch than to vision. In Gibbs's terms, '(A)t the heart of mimesis is the immediacy of what passes between bodies and which subtends cognitively mediated representation . . . Mimicry is not a representation of the other, but a *rendering*.'[27] Such rendering is felt more than seen and then imitated, helping clarify a perplexing claim made by McLuhan that 'touch' is not contact with skin but 'the interplay of the senses, and keeping in touch or getting in touch is a matter of a fruitful meeting of the senses, of sight translated into sound and sound into movement, and taste and smell'.[28] Although not necessarily a physical touch, touch is a useful metaphor for mimesis because even physical touching is a dual transfer; touching is always also to be touched, affecting and affected.

Of course, McLuhan is not denying the existence of a sense of touch produced by skin touching surface. He is pointing to another experience of being touched, a mimetic experience, and, importantly, he connects this experience to synaesthetic transfer. As he proposes, 'It may very well be that in our conscious inner lives the interplay among our senses is what constitutes the sense of touch. Perhaps *touch* is not just skin contact with *things*, but the very life of things in the *mind*?'[29] Most commentators on mimesis note its cross-sensory or synaesthetic character. Sounds become the rhythmic movements of dancers or of the happy baby; energetic gestures transfer and transform into louder voices or wider smiles. Taussig thus describes the mimetic experience of the Cuna Indians as essentially synaesthetic:

> (T)he senses cross over and translate into each other. You feel redness. You see music . . . You may also see your body as you feel yourself leaving it, and one can even see oneself seeing oneself – but above all this seeing is felt in a nonvisual way. You move into the interior of images, just as images move into you.[30]

Although at times triggered by visual inputs, the experience of mimesis is fundamentally non-visual, more a haptic seeing in which the eye becomes a tool for touching the body rather than for representing an object.

Since mimesis is synaesthetic or cross-sensory, relying on haptic vision and the perception of rhythm and movement in many sensory registers, its economy cannot only be about representation, about producing a semblance of the other. Instead, in a mimetic mode, semblances become the substance of communication but the content transforms as it becomes part of a new surface. For example, one might hear someone singing, and as that rhythm passes to their body, it becomes transformed into gestures, dancing feet and snapping fingers. Thus Benjamin describes semblance and play as the two polarities of any mimetic mode. The mime both 'presents his subject as a semblance' and also 'plays his subject . . . In mimesis, tightly interfolded like cotyledons, slumber the two aspects of art: semblance and play.'[31] This economy constitutes the limits of mimetic perception. Imitating a model is the limit of semblance, the point at which mimesis does not take place because there is no play, no cross-modal transfer from body to body but instead a representation of another body, which can occur without the presence of that body. Complete play without semblance, without some element of imitating another, represents the other limit.

Although cinema might tap into mimetic capacities, especially through the facial expressions and gestures of actors, the mimetic mode of animation remains different from the classical mode, primarily by reversing direction. Rather than the images coming out into the viewer space for their recording, in a mimetic mode, the viewer enters into the diegetic world. The rhythms and movements of the diegetic world become the rhythms and movements of the viewer, unlike in cinema whose transposings and translocations can be said to belong to the viewer, altering the relation between viewer space and spectator space, but are distinctly *not* the movements of the diegetic world. The transposings and translocations give a dynamic view on the diegetic world but are not the movements of that world, which are mostly movements (mobile sections) of humans, vehicles and animals on screen. Noting this reversal, Benjamin gives an example from children's books:

> The objects do not come to meet the picturing child from the pages of the book; instead, the gazing child enters into those pages, becoming suffused, like a cloud, with the riotous colors of the world of pictures. Sitting before his painted book, . . . he overcomes the illusory barrier of the book's surface and passes through colored textures and brightly painted partitions to enter a stage on which fairy tales spring to life.[32]

Rather than projecting diegetic space into viewer space, rather than using viewers as surfaces for recording, viewers become writers, projecting themselves into the space so that they might inscribe. As Benjamin says, 'The child inhabits them . . . Children fill them with a poetry of their own. This is how it comes about that children *in*scribe the pictures with their ideas in a more literal sense: they scribble on them.'[33] A similar process occurs with the Disney animated image. The viewer fills in the (non-existent) movements and rhythms between the frames with their own rhythms and movements, experiencing a form of mimetic synchronicity. Indeed, the low level of detail in the cartoon image demands that viewers become a part of the image. The viewer fills in so much detail that they feel they are participating in the image-world; in fact, they do participate by seeing image-movement between the frames that does not exist.[34] Animation thus materialises a mimetic mode. Viewers see lifelike semblances and then play with those semblances by mimetically rendering similar affections. Whereas the cinematic mode potentially reminds us of the images we project, animation potentially reminds us of our childhood; it shows anew how to give life to objects, how to animate the inanimate through daydreams, how to turn couch pillows into forts or mud into pies or mice into men.[35] Rather than witnessing the reproduced movement of living beings, viewers perceive image-objects as animated. This is a different experience from the cinematic mode's relating of camera-subject to other camera-subjects. It is a relationship of camera-subject and image-object.

Conceiving Disney as a mimetic mode, then, explains the commentators' references to life. This was an affective life, rather than a realistic one, a life felt more than seen, as indicated by the quotations above that stress the transfer of affection, the impression of real persons, and the captivation of senses. Indeed, Crowther seems to depict the economy of mimesis when he says that 'one's senses are captivated by it' (semblance), 'one's imagination is deliciously inspired' (play).[36] Disney animators Frank Thomas and Ollie Johnston similarly describe this reversed direction of animistic mimesis, this entrance of viewers into the work: '(O)ne might find a better concept in the word "captivating". Audiences have to be impressed, absorbed, involved, taken out of themselves, made to forget their own worlds and lose themselves in ours for cartoons to succeed.'[37]

This mimetic transfer reportedly affected not only the viewers but the animators as well. Animators mimetically become-cartoon; they feel-as Mickey in order to draw Mickey. As such, Disney's best animators were called the 'best actors', those who could imbibe the character's internal dynamics. Many portray Bill Tytla as the master. Donald Graham, an instructor at Disney, describes Tytla's approach: 'He does not animate forms but symbols of forces . . . this is a revolutionary conception . . . instead of seeing a character as a round body, beautifully modeled in drawing, he sees the animating forces inherent in it.'[38] Drawing these forces often requires mimesis; Tytla and other great animators experience a transfer from character to animator's body. Rather than standing off 'removed' and 'directing him', as Warner Brothers animator Bob Clampett expresses it,

> I get inside of Porky and I think like Porky. I talk like Porky. I have a s-s-s-s-speech ppp-problem. I walk like Porky, and I feel like Porky . . . I'm helpful, trusting, concerned, kindly and sometimes a trifle pu-pu-pu-put out. S-s-s-s-shucks I am Porky.[39]

Through this affective transfer, animators become-cartoon.

Walt Disney offered similar advice to struggling animators, imploring them to become-cartoon: 'You know what's wrong with this? . . . It's feeling. You've got to really be Minnie, you've got to be pulling for Mickey to beat that big lunkhead. You've got to hit that mat hard, you've got to stretch.'[40] As reported by many colleagues, this becoming-cartoon was Walt Disney's true talent. He was not the best director nor did he draw, but he could act as cartoon characters in a manner invaluable for artists. Thomas and Johnston describe an incident where Disney attempted to act out Pluto for animator Norm Ferguson. Disney remembers a dog he had seen on a farm and then raises his eyebrows one by one, imitating this particularly inquisitive (and hence animatable) dog. He begins acting out Pluto, sniffing around, scrunching his face, and eventually his antics have the animators in stitches. Ferguson finds the acting very helpful for visualising the drawings, but not drawings of Walt – 'they were drawings of a dog with personality . . . Somehow [Walt] had the ability to make you see what was funny about the character itself.'[41] Disney experienced mimesis, the affective transfer, had become-cartoon.

Before turning to how Disney employs the transferability of animation in relation to the viewers' mimetic capacity, the split responsible for the wondrous spark can now be explained. Although Disney maintains classical cinema's split between viewer and spectator and (at times, although restrained) graphic narrative's split between motion and form, animistic mimesis folds the body differently. In the previous chapter, Eisenstein described a split in animation between the 'we know' of the artifice and the 'we sense' of movement and life. Our analysis helps clarify these as two different modes, articulating to the two definitions of animation. Whereas graphic narrative split the knowledge of form from the sense of movement, the wondrous spark of animistic mimesis splits knowledge of form from a mimetic perception of life. Graphic narrative remains mostly about movement, animation's first definition. This movement is diachronic, in between the frames, and hence transforming (from form to form, as in the pose-to-pose drawing method). Hence their images emphasise motion, with all the crashing, colliding and chasing of the gag. Animistic mimesis, instead, remains mostly about the mimetic sensation of life, the ability of affect's rhythmic variations to transfer from body to body, animation's second definition. Rather than marvel over the moving line, then, viewers experienced a wondrous spark, generated from the split between knowing the characters do not exist but sensing them as alive nevertheless. The characters become alive through the viewer's mimetic transfer, potentially touching viewers directly as they notice the semblances and enter into the diegetic world to play.

Disney's Management of Transferability

How could Disney's images spark a mimetic experience? How could they overcome the 'we know' enough to have viewers sense life? Essentially, Disney achieves an interface for relating to the viewer's mimetic capacities through managing animation's second -ability, transferability, the capacity downplayed in graphic narrative. Disney manages transferability to articulate the poles of semblance and play, which, in the formal context, can be considered the poles of classical cinema and earlier animation. The animation pole contributes to the play, to the knowledge of artifice. The cinematic pole contributes to the sensation of realism, to the sense that these movements occur in a three-dimensional world. The resultant split is between knowledge and sensation, a split between what conscious minds tell and what the sensing body receives. The knowledge that these movements and lives do not exist allows one to perceive animation as play, to enjoy the transformation of the graphic line, to let our guards down, to open perceptions to the magical, the impossible possibilities of artificial space. The sensation of life allows us to experience and enjoy the animation anyway, to forget or to stop caring, if only for a moment, that what we see are illusions, to feel those illusions as living, to be affected nonetheless.

In short, Disney draws on the force of cinema's astonishing realism and on the force of animation's marvellous transformations. Disney animation becomes more cinematic in order to articulate to the pole of semblance, yet it maintains the playful transformations to express a view of life as animistic becoming. As such, Disney's animation can neither be too realistic, too close to photographic cinema, nor be too far, completely unrealistic or non-lifelike. These poles mark the extremes, the limits of perception in animistic mimesis. The perception and pleasures of Disney animation come from this tension between semblance and play, from the ability to seem real while remaining artificial. It is not one or the other but the energy of their contrasts from which pleasures derive. These are economic forces in the narrow sense as well, since animation's transformability is at the heart of its consumer attraction and because classical cinema was dominating, forcing competitors like Disney to adapt to its marketplace. Tracing this translation from modal economy to social economy is precisely the task of *Special Affects*.

Many denounce Disney's translation from the gag-driven shorts to full-length, cinematic features. Critics like Panofsky, Eisenstein, Adorno and Kracauer fault Disney for pursuing realism, abandoning the anarchic creative freedoms that, they believed, held more liberatory potential.[42] For Kracauer, the animated cartoon 'strives not after the fixing but the dissolution of conventional reality'.[43] By pursuing realism, then, Disney abandoned animation's essence, resulting in staid conformism and submission to a bleak reality: 'They subordinate themselves in terms of content submissively to social convention . . . instead of flying with his mother to an unknown paradise, Dumbo ends up as a highly paid star for the same circus director who beat his mother.'[44] Such criticism continues today, with some indicting Disney for abandoning early animation's 'flat-lands' for the stifling depths of live-action narrative, thereby betraying the original modernist impulse.[45] As Leslie insists, 'From the 1930s onwards the Disney studio had been taming the cartoon, displacing its original avant-gardish anarchy and formal inconstancy . . . Disney produced an animated imitation of realist cinema . . . romantically realist, an idealized real.'[46]

Although Disney did pursue increased realism as defined by the cinematic mode, this translation needs to be more exactly outlined because such criticism often conflates Disney and classical cinema. Critiquing animated movies featuring flying elephants and talking puppets for being too realistic certainly misses some of the experience. Rather than a rote imitation, Disney's translation merges aspects of the cinematic mode with elements drawn from graphic narrative. In short, Disney simulates the cinematic mode, particularly its representation of space, in order to achieve the semblance pole. Yet, they also must address the play pole. Therefore, their aim is not to 'draw a reality which can better be photographed', as Kracauer maintains.[47] If Disney was simply an imitation of photographable reality, then it is unlikely that its animation would ever be popular since it falls so short of cinema's reality-effect. The 'we know' aspect of the perceptual economy that Eisenstein references could never be eclipsed. Instead, the special affects of animation come from the energy, the tension, between the poles of knowledge and sensation, semblance and play. Disney simulated the cinematic mode to achieve a semblance of space, but that semblance allows it to feature the play, 'the magic', the *time* of animation. Hence Walt Disney often describes the company's style as an 'illusion of life' or a caricature of realism. As he explained in a memo to animators:

> Our most important aim is to develop definite personalities in our cartoon characters. We don't want them to be just shadows, for merely as moving figures they would provoke no emotional response . . . Nor do we want them to parallel or assume the aspects of human beings or human actions. We invest them with life by endowing them with human weaknesses which we exaggerate in a humorous way. Rather than a caricature of individuals, our work is a caricature of life.[48]

How, then, did Disney employ animation's transferability to achieve a caricature of life? Transferability denotes the transfer between layers in a single frame, not the transformation between frames. These layers include layers of cels, ink or line, colour, light and sound. Disney's management (mostly synchronisation) of these layers contributes to both semblance and play. We will trace how Disney manages these layers by detailing some techniques, mostly through reference to the primary source for insider insight into Disney's practices, Thomas and Johnston's *The Illusion of Life*, and also by using *Fantasia* as a specific example. *Fantasia* may seem a strange choice to illustrate the aesthetic features of animistic mimesis since many critics of Disney's 'realism' exclude *Fantasia*. They believe *Fantasia* offers something different from the other full-length features. Although the differences are stark at one level, I find a more basic consistency of aesthetic technique and mode across all of Disney's full-length features.

To illustrate, *Fantasia* offers a good starting point mostly because the movie relies primarily on animation techniques. Most scenes do not depend on the cinematic mode, employing little montage and oscillation of viewpoint. Fantasia is a musical term referring to free-form music, and *Fantasia* is more free-form than the Disney movies with plots and characters. *Fantasia* lacks dialogue, featuring images synchronised with orchestra pieces such as Stravinsky's 'The Rite of Spring', Tchaikovsky's 'Nutcracker Suite' and Beethoven's 'Pastoral Symphony'. A couple of sections include an identifiable story, such as 'The Sorcerer's Apprentice'. Yet the lack of dialogue, episodic organisation and minimal transpositions all indicate the difference between *Fantasia* and other Disney movies. By relying less on cinematic devices, *Fantasia* comes closest to fully expressing Disney's actualisation of animation's transformability and transferability.

The economy of semblance and play becomes modulated through some aesthetic techniques at each image layer – the cel, ink, colour, light and sound layers. *Fantasia* exemplifies each of these techniques, presenting them in their non-cinematic glory, yet the other movies also employ these techniques, particularly by constructing mutual-affection images. In the chapter following, then, I turn to the other Disney features, illustrating how the mutual affection-images constitute an interface for animistic mimesis, and thereby serve as the peak moments in which emotion most often flows forth. These crowning moments embody the becoming-other, the animism, of the character infused with the viewer's life, who is becoming daydreamer, becoming consumer.

According to Thomas and Johnston, Disney's search for more cinematic realism is due to the desire to give the fantasy worlds a level of plausibility or semblance. The animated character must appear to inhabit space and to be driven by internal motivations, two conventions borrowed from classical cinema. To do so, Disney translates the classical cinematic mode, imitating its techniques for constructing space by managing cel layers. First, space no longer transforms for the purpose of gags, without narrative justification. Similar to classical cinema, the construction of space is hidden, made invisible. Snow White's world is existent and stable, not constructed and ever-shifting. Disney's worlds are made subject to organic laws. Characters become heavier, denser, rounder and self-contained. The figures morph less often, losing plasmaticness. Space becomes more limiting; the play with boundary is minimised, if not completely absent. Second, Disney draws the scenes from different angles, thereby relating viewer space to diegetic space, transposing in order to establish a sensory-motor linkage and create a continuous and organic narrative world. In addition to drawing different 'camera angles', the improvement of cel transparency allowed Disney to construct more detailed foregrounds and backgrounds for depth, beginning with the *Silly Symphonies* and the early Mickey shorts. Indeed, the history of animation space is much more complex, including a longer transition than this simple opposition between graphic narrative and illusion of life implies.[49] Such a contrast serves an analytic purpose none the less.

The cel layering was also managed, and space made more cinematic, through the multiplane camera. Animated cartoons are projected on film, so each drawing had to be photographed and spliced on to a reel. This required holding the camera steady; the panning, tracking and other movements were impossible for photography. Disney developed a way to simulate some movements by improving on the multiplane camera invented by Ub Iwerks. The multiplane camera placed the different layers on spatially separated planes that were vertically arranged. This allowed the camera to move into the scene, getting closer to the figures and passing by the foreground while maintaining perspectival consistency. Prior to the multiplane, if a camera zoomed in on a flat drawing, the foreground and background would grow larger at the same rate, betraying their flatness. The multiplane camera allowed the background to remain distant, growing at a slower rate than the foreground, emulating natural depth. With the multiplane camera, Disney manufactured the appearance of camera movements while using still images. To achieve cinematic space, Disney had to manage the layers between images through devices such as the multiplane camera.

At the layer of inking, improvements were also necessary for cinematic semblance. Disney had to create characters that appear to inhabit this 'realistic' space naturally. This meant developing more weight, depth, roundness and fluidity of movement; characters had to register gravity and other forces similar to physical bodies on earth. So, Disney animators sought techniques capable of producing a better semblance. Over time, the animators developed a technique called 'squash and stretch'. Thomas and Johnston call 'squash and stretch' the 'most important discovery' because it solved the rigidity of movement while providing the figures with a sense of three-dimensionality.[50] Squash and stretch describes two things: the range of character shapes and the principle of movement. Characters range from a squashed position, as if being flattened by a heavy object, to a stretched position, as if trying to reach the tallest branch. The characters move by oscillating between squash and stretch, keeping a constant volume but shifting under gravity and weight. Squash and stretch led to a rounded transformation of the characters' shapes, such as Mickey's familiar pear-shape in *Fantasia* (Figure 5.1). These three-dimensional characters pushing and pulling against space and gravity greatly enhanced the semblance of life.

Squash and stretch allowed the animators to manage the transfer of a character's body, as the surfaces change shape under the forces of movement and gravity. A squashed position transfers some of the force and weight downwards on to lower surfaces, whereas a stretch position expands the surface area itself. Not only did the oscillation between squash and stretch give a more three-dimensional and weighty semblance of movement, but the technique also enabled playful uses, mostly for comedic purposes. The squash and stretch capacities maintain a certain bodily range that, under the force of an outside body, could become distorted, such as a crushed face resulting from an encounter with a frying pan. Most importantly, however, squash and stretch enabled a semblance of cinematic space by allowing the inked lines to belong to the three-dimensional world, rather than resting on top of it.

Figure 5.1 Mickey squashed and stretched.
(Screenshot from *Fantasia* / *Fantasia 2000* DVD)

Also at the layer of line, the middle layer in the stack, another drawing technique contributes to both the semblance and play of animistic mimesis. These are the techniques called anticipation and follow-through. As the bookends of a pose-to-pose movement, anticipation visually prefigures a coming movement, and follow-through culminates the movement. Each technique exaggerates movements in order to make them highly expressive. *Fantasia*'s 'Sorcerer's Apprentice' scene portrays a narrative through such typified gestures (Figure 5.2). The scene begins with the sorcerer raising his arms upwards, as if lifting a heavy object; as he does, smoke rises up and transforms into a butterfly. Then, the sorcerer tickles the smoke downwards, cramming it back into the skull from which it emerged. When the sorcerer leaves, Mickey pulls his arms to his chest (anticipation) and thrusts them forwards rapidly (follow-through). As he does so, the broom comes alive. Then, Mickey mimes picking up two buckets and walking, and the broom performs his command. Satisfied, Mickey falls asleep, only to awake suddenly to a flooding lodge. Unfortunately, he does not know the gesture to make the broom stop. Arms extended as if to say halt does not work. He decides to chop up the broom with an axe, and after splintering it into many pieces, he leans against the door and exhales

Figure 5.2 The Sorcerer in an anticipation pose.
(Screenshot from Fantasia/Fantasia 2000 DVD)

in relief. The splintering creates an army of brooms, however, and we see his face switch from satisfaction to horror. Luckily, the sorcerer returns to save the day, gesturing to stop the brooms and then scolding his apprentice with a finger wag.

In anticipation and follow-through, animators hold the anticipatory and anterior movements for a few frames, just a fraction long enough to ensure bodily reception of the gesture but not long enough for audiences to think, 'The character is about to do X.' The response is a mimetic, affective transfer, where the viewer does not imitate the character's gesture but their body (perhaps imperceptibly) shifts to account for the upcoming movement, just as one might shift in response to someone raising a fist. As a whole, the series of anticipation and follow-through, combined with the squash and stretch technique, creates a bouncing rhythm to the animation that is registered mimetically and described as life, wonder. Indeed, David Abram explains the importance of such expressive gestures for the magician, reminding us of the animator's similar becoming-cartoon:

> The magician, for instance, may make the magic palatable for the audience by following the invisible coin's journey with the focus of his own eyes, and by imaginatively

'feeling' the coin depart from the one hand and arrive in the palm of the other; the audience's senses, responding to subtle shifts in the magician's body as well as to the coin, will then find the effect irresistible. In other words, it is when the magician lets *himself* be captured by the magic that his audience will be most willing to join them.[51]

With such magical gestures as anticipation and follow-through we once again find a dual transfer and the economy of semblance and play. From the semblance of the coin's movement, magical play happens in space, potentially coming alive through audience affection. They 'know' coins cannot move but 'sense' their actual movement, with bodies affectively registering the movement without imitating it. Such techniques are similar to what Brecht describes as the theatrical *gestus*. Often translated as gest, the gestus refers to both 'gist' and 'gesture'; in short, the gest is a series of performed actions that express the gist of an attitude. To accomplish the gest, Brecht prescribes simplification through aesthetically significant and repeatable movements. Brecht describes it as feeling one's way 'into their characters' skins', and notes that people often perform such mimesis in ordinary life, such as when a person imitates a friend's gait or mannerisms.[52] Similar to the magician, the gest is an attempt to make the gesture quotable and therefore imitable or transferable to the viewer. Brecht hoped to use the gestus to produce an epic theatre spearheading the revolution against cinematic, consumerist reality, and therefore would be likely to take offence at the comparison to Disney. Yet this is precisely why the specification of modes is important, against the conflation of media. Disney's animistic mimesis employs a version of gest for consumerist aims that are anathema to Brecht. Yet the comparison remains apt because the gest is a similar dual transfer, an affective transfer actualised through a surface transfer of imitable gestures.

During anticipation and follow-through frames, Disney employs one final technique called moving holds that adds semblance. Moving holds mean never having characters completely still. A completely still pose looks lifeless, whereas slightly moving holds enhance realism. Through these techniques, Disney was able to convey the image-movement as *life* by transferring from layer to layer, from the 'realistic' space, complete with gravity, air and force, to character movement and back again. For the audience, this sensed transfer was a sense of life, not only the characters' ability to affect and be affected by one another but their ability to affect the audience as well, who imbibes the rhythms of their squashes, stretches, anticipations and follow-throughs. A popular short during the Depression, *Three Little Pigs* was one of the first to employ these techniques successfully, amazing audiences with the rounded characters and individual personalities. Animator Chuck Jones remarks about the *Three Little Pigs*,

> That was the first time that anybody ever brought characters to life. There were three characters who *looked* alike and *acted* differently; the way they moved is what made them what they were. Before that, in things like STEAMBOAT WILLIE, the villain was a big heavy guy and the hero was a little guy; everybody moved the same way.[53]

At the layer of colour, we again find the economy of semblance and play and this dual transfer, between the animation layers and mimetically to viewers. Colour moves on the screen, through a sort of synaesthetic transfer. In fact, synaesthesia is often known as 'coloured hearing'. The 'Rite of Spring' episode exemplifies Disney's use of colour (Figure 5.3). The scene visually tells the story of earth's natural history, from the expanding universe forming the stars to the volcanic primal soup to the dinosaur age. Colour does not simply fill the lines of figures but instead spills over and leaves traces; colour transfers from surface to surface. Comets leave trails of sparkling light in the dark universe. Radioactive purple clouds hover over the atmosphere, infecting their surroundings through their radiance.

Figure 5.3 Light and colour in 'The Rite of Spring'.
(Screenshot from *Fantasia / Fantasia 2000* DVD

Bubbling and exploding lava splashes light on the surrounding rocks, filling the screen with a red tint. Swirling grey gasses lighten the scene, exploding in bursts of orange and yellow. Water bubbles and mutating amoebas create shifting blue–greens in their liquid milieu. Dinosaurs change colour as they cover with dirt or when rain bounces off their skin. Lightning fills the scene with a flash of white.

These examples illustrate the interplay between light and colour. Darkness casts an ominous shadow over the colours, muting them in grey, whereas lights bring brightness. Light and dark enable the transfer of colour between figures. As new lights, like lightning, or new refractions, like bubbles, occur, the colours change. Water and fire have a privileged role, moving the light and hence transferring the colours from surface to surface. Water, smoke and fire exist in every scene in *Fantasia*. As fire flickers and cracks, as water ripples and drips, the light sources are refracted and reflected differently, making the colours of figures bleed, blend and transform. Drawing tiny effervescent sparks emanating from magical objects comprises another common technique for colour transfer through light. The Sorcerer's hat glows and sparkles when Mickey thinks about donning it. The fairies' wands emit similar sparks that transfer the magic from figure to figure. Colour continually transfers through the medium of light, and the experience of this constantly moving and shifting colour is sensed mimetically, especially given the synchronisation of the images to the sounds.

Disney's colour is living, fully animated. Colours affect and are affected, participating in a transfer; they do not segregate but instead blend and mix. For instance, in the 'Pastoral Symphony', the rainbow goddess streaks across the sky and colours drip on to the ground, further colouring the landscape. This colour lives, outside the boundaries of the rainbow, visualising the surface transfer between figure and environment. Colour moves, bleeds, seeps and stains; it transfers from surface to surface, as when Pegasus and Cupid fly through the rainbow and become orange. In addition, the contrast between light and dark, reflected in the colours, further conveys an emotional tone, adding to the possibility for mimetic contagion. Darkness always accompanies sadness or fear while brightness, like the colours of the rainbow, accompanies happiness.

Such use of colour actualises transferability between the layers, as well as modulating the economy of semblance and play. First, colour allows Disney to address the lack of depth in animation. The shifting colours suggest depth through shading and shadowing, thereby enabling a higher semblance of space.[54] Second, the colour paints scenes with emotional hue. The colours become purely affective; they reflect the narrative conflict and cooperation between figures. The red glare of lava conveys an angry and violent tenor, and the ominous shadow of Chernabog fills the screen with a dark grey fear. This colour is not so much seen as it is felt – *like music*. Like music, *Fantasia*'s sections were colour-keyed, matching the action's emotion and sound. In sum, the colour creates a better depth illusion while enabling a fantasy world where affections appear distinctly, in living colour. Both functions articulate to the economy between semblance and play.

Disney's use of colour compares to Benjamin's theory about children's mimetic perceptions. Children have to be taught to colour within the lines; their colourings spill over and mix with others. According to Benjamin, they see colour as animated, not as a deceptive cloak or artificial addition: 'Color is single, not as a lifeless thing and a rigid individuality but as a winged creature that flits from one form to the next. Children make soap bubbles.'[55] Many children are attracted to soap bubbles, magic lanterns, fire and water because the colours shimmer and change intensity under the light or refraction. Colours bleed and blend, transferring from one figure to another. Colour is thus pure mood, expressing a child's mimetic receptivity. In Disney, colour is this total sensory experience, constituting a surface transfer aimed at achieving mimetic transfer.

Disney was one of the first studios to use colour in this manner. In fact, animating colour was the crucial development leading to public acceptance of colour pictures. Many 1930s movies that attempted the new Technicolor process were a box-office and critical failure. The public seemed to prefer black-and-white movies, and the huge expense of Technicolor significantly limited colour's emergence.[56] Some critics even claimed that colour was destroying cinema's ability to be an art form. In a 1938 *New York Times* article, Robert Edmond Jones correctly diagnosed the problem. He argued, 'Black-and-white thinking still dominates the screen' because movies lacked colour composition as artists understand it.[57] Rather than attempt to use colour for artistic purposes, directors were judging Technicolor a success if the audience simply did not notice it. The basic problem was that Hollywood was not making colour pictures 'but colored pictures'.[58] Movies added colour after the fact, like filling within the lines of a colouring book. This relies upon a static notion of colour, one inappropriate for the *moving* picture.

Disney's use of colour would change Hollywood practice. Disney signed an exclusive rights agreement with Technicolor and premiered their first colour short entitled 'Flowers and Trees' in 1932. The film was a success, and Disney was hailed as one of the first studios to use colour effectively. Disney's colours moved and, hence, helped move the audience. Later, Jiminy Cricket would feature twenty-seven shades to match the changing light and moods.[59] Jones concludes, 'This movement, this progression of colour on the screen is in itself an utterly new visual experience, full of wonder. The colour flows from sequence to sequence like a kind of visual music and it affects our emotions precisely as music affects them.'[60] Today, Disney continues to be cited as a model for the use of colour.[61] It pioneered a way to turn colour into a mimetic experience instead of a secondary attribution to the primary substance.

Although physical touch, taste and smell are not present, the other sensory inputs, including sight, sound, space, motion and colour, synaesthetically fuse, becoming rhythmically synchronised. 'Walt gave it to you with all your senses involved, except smell, and he was always working on that,' remarks animation historian John Culhane.[62] Indeed, Disney did consider piping in smells during *Fantasia*. We can only wonder what they might have chosen, but even the fact that they were considering smell points to their aim for a mimetic, synaesthetic experience. Smell touches and affects us to repulsive disgust or pheromone-lust. In fact, many scholars argue that smell is one of the most powerful sensory channels for mimesis. Brennan connects the transmission of affect to the sense of smell, especially due to the transfer of pheromones.[63] Horkheimer and Adorno concur:

> Of all the senses, that of smell . . . bears clearest witness to the urge to lose oneself in and become 'the other' . . . When we see we remain what we are; but when we smell we are taken over by otherness.[64]

Disney's aim, then, to encourage the viewer's transfer would be well served by including smells. Although never realised, the fact that they considered using smells illustrates their intent to fulfil a synaesthetic experience. The more complete the sensory experience, the more likely audiences are to experience a mimetic touching.

Two final, crucial layers complete Disney's actualisation of transferability, enabling an interface for animistic mimesis. The first is the layer of light and relates to Disney's use of shadows. Throughout the feature films, every character and object casts a shadow. Furthermore, in *Fantasia*, shadows are repeatedly featured, not just added to figures. In 'Toccata and Fugue', the orchestra transmutes into shadowy silhouettes that then merge into shifting images of notes and instruments. Disney described the effect as 'like something you see with your eyes half-closed' or something you see on a shadowy night.[65] Likewise, the scene where Mickey cuts the broom into pieces is shown only in shadow. Such scenes feature shadows as a way of showing off Disney's technical advances.

Indeed, featuring shadows throughout the layers was quite an accomplishment because shadows presented a major problem for earlier animation, since flat characters cast no shadow. Animators would draw shadows under characters, but these were usually too dark and were simple blobs that came nowhere near looking as if they really transferred from character to ground. Disney established a shadow team in the 1930s and developed two improvements, both based on adding a layer of light (with the help of cameras). The first techniques painted a black shadow on a foreground layer, then would shoot the background and mid-layer together without foreground at high exposure. The foreground shadow was then layered and shot at low exposure, producing a double exposure in which the shadow looks more translucent. The result was, in Crafton's words, a 'more photorealistic effect . . . that subtly articulated a believable performance space by better defining characters' volume and their place in the environment'.[66]

The second shadow technique was even more complex and time-consuming. The first technique worked fine for shadows that fell on flat surfaces, but ones that fell on curved or irregular surfaces presented a problem. Disney developed a device called Shadowgraph to compensate. They would build three-dimensional models of the background, then take a transparent cel with the character, position it vertically in the scene, and cast a bright light through it. As a result, the character's outline would cast a real shadow on to the set, which was then photographed and drawn into the scene to match. In this instance, the animated character actually casts the shadow, making a perfect perspectival match. Crafton depicts a scene using the technique: 'When Snow White ascends from the cottage staircase, for example, the candlelight throws shadows onto the stairs and floors in perfect perspective.'[67] As a result, 'it is no longer meaningful to speak of the shot's foreground and background, since now the entire scene is camera space.'[68]

In other words, such use of shadows actualises transferability, contributing to the economy of semblance and play. Shadows fuse the foreground and background, and thus help imitate a realistic world inhabited by rounded characters. In addition, the play of shadows allows figures to morph from shape to shape. Shadows that appear to be one thing often turn out to be another, a perceptual experience responsible for many children's nightmares. At times, the shadows themselves even come to life. Take the example of Mickey chopping the broom. After Mickey splinters the broom, the world of shadows comes to life. In shadow, the splinters grow to full size and come alive, unleashing an uncontrollable army of labouring brooms. In short, shadows transfer from one figure to another, enabling a semblance of depth, and their amorphousness allows an abundance of opportunities for the playful imagination in these shadowy worlds.

The final layer is the layer of sound, the most crucial aspect of the mimetic experience. Working frame by frame, Disney animation can achieve a synchronisation of movement with sound that is difficult if not impossible in live-action cinema. Such synchronisation contributes to the poles of semblance and play. As discussed in the previous chapter, the synchronisation of sound and image, begun with *Steamboat Willie*, creates depth since characters have voices that seem to come from inside their bodies and worlds have sounds coming from the depths. By making distant objects quieter and closer ones louder, Disney replicated the sound perspective common in live-action films. Yet unexpected sounds also add some play to the aural texture, creating the jokes of the motion-image outlined previously. For Disney, the sounds may be playfully unexpected but they are always synchronised, most often to music, creating a fusion that is experienced synaesthetically and potentially transfers mimetically to viewers' bodies.

Fantasia exemplifies this transfer of sound and image layers into a synchronised whole, demonstrating that animistic mimesis is more a synaesthetic fusion of sight and sound than either independently. The music is not simply heard but also seen; images seem compelled and sometimes created by the music itself, as in 'Tocatta' when the orchestra's silhouettes transform into abstract bands of colour, rolling hills and violin clouds. Everything moves in rhythm to the music, until suddenly this is flipped and a character's actions (a stumble, a crash) in turn cause musical sounds to emit or the rhythm to alter. Characters move to the music and at times move the music. Separating this fusion of sight and sound is impossible; one transfers into another repeatedly.

In *Fantasia*, this synaesthetic fusion is represented by the character Sound Wave, who appears after the intermission. Conductor Deems Taylor, the narrator, introduces the audience to Sound Wave, a white line shimmering nervously. Taylor claims he 'ran into' Sound Wave around the studio, a kind of 'shy' fellow, but he soon realised Sound Wave is someone 'very important' to *Fantasia*. This is because every beautiful sound creates an equally beautiful picture. Taylor then proceeds to use Sound Wave for an audience tutorial. Sound Wave visualises some sounds from high to low pitches, each with different colours for brass, string and percussion. Sound Wave turns yellow–green, with wide loopy waves for the harp. The violin makes him fuzzy, like TV static, with sustained and vibrating yellow–red lines. Sound Wave embodies *Fantasia*'s fusion of sight and sound, and Deems insists on its importance in order to instruct the audience in the preferred mode. The opening scene, 'Toccata and Fugue', also illustrates the synaesthetic fusion of sight and sound. In the scene, shadowy silhouettes of the orchestra are cast on a white dome wall above and behind the orchestra. The orchestra's silhouettes slowly bleed into and blend with the new images forming on the wall. The musicians transform into abstract, rolling bands of colour and cloudy formations. Eventually, some images begin to resemble the music, with cloud-violin bows stroking to the music. Each change in music produces changes in images. 'Toccata and Fugue' is the opening act, and Sound Wave is the introduction after the intermission. Each launches a kind of tutorial, instructing viewers to experience the synaesthetic blending through a mimetic mode.

Yet there is more to the synaesthetic transfer of animistic mimesis than the representation embodied by Sound Wave. Disney pursued a synaes-thetic experience, not simply a caricature of sound–image transfers. One key to this experience was developing a more complete sound experience. Disney realised that the orchestra would not sound as full coming out of mono-speakers, since mono lacks the left-to-right range of a live orches-tra. Thus Disney engineers developed stereophonic sound that they called Fantasound, working out the basic principles of stereo sound commonly used today. Disney spent a reported $85,000 per theatre to equip them with Fantasound, and therefore *Fantasia* only debuted in twelve thea-tres.[69] Fantasound envelops the audience, producing sound that moves from front to back and left to right. With dimmed lights and enveloping sound, the audience was in for a fully sensory experience, furthering the fusion of sight and sound.

The total-sensory experience helps evoke an affective touching by enabling a profound sense of connectedness, a mutual affection of char-acter and audience often described as life. In Disney animation, physical touch is noticeably lacking, but the fusion of other senses helps simulate the embodied experience of life. Psychical life never experiences sight or hearing in isolation; all senses exist in relationship, and simulating this relationship encourages the viewer's mimetic transfer. In almost every aspect, *Fantasia* is aimed at producing this affective touching through a synaesthetic experience. The music selections convey an emotional tone, moving the audience from the edge of their seats to floating in the air with flittering flutes. Scenes move from dusk to dawn, from Autumn to Summer, and from the beginning of time to the present, all common vehi-cles of emotional metaphor. Visually, the characters are ominous or reas-suring, graceful or gangly, playful or mischievous, curious and naïve, wise and vengeful. Each signals clearly the emotion with which the audience is supposed to greet their presence. Viewers sympathise with the curious and naïve apprentice, Mickey. They shrink in fear at the sight of the giant stone demon, Chernabog. They pity the shy, neglected and nervous Sound Wave, and they are in awe of the violent power of Tyrannosaurus Rex and Stegosaurus.

Such synaesthetic synchronisation of sounds and movement remains the central principle of how Disney manages transferability. They harmonise the moving characters, colours and light perfectly with the sounds, creating a fusion across the layers. Such fusion registers affectively, as viewers' bodies become attuned to the rhythms of the synchronised movements and sounds. This is why I have depicted animistic mimesis, from the viewers' perspective, as the perception of synchronised sounds and images as an expressive life. With the synchronisation, the characters seem affected by the music and voices of others; their surfaces resonate and harmonise with sound layers. Likewise, the audience hears the same sounds, which potentially transfer mimetically to their bodies. Again, this transfer does not imitate the character's gestures and occurs pre-cognitively, as when we find ourselves swaying in rhythm without realising. When a character squashes and stretches to music, for instance, we do not likewise squash and stretch but instead transfer this rhythmic affection to other, even at times cross-sensory, gestures, such as feet-tapping or whistling. As viewer bodies become rhythmically attuned to the synchronised movements and sounds, the characters and viewer seem to share the same affections, a shared affection many describe as a sense of life.

A Living Daydream

Despite those who believe that *Fantasia* is radically different, these features persist in Disney's classical films. Their combination into a mutual-affection image is consistently presented as the privileged, peak moments – the moments of animistic transformation of characters. Thus this analysis of animistic mimesis helps clarify what commentators refer to as Disney's sense of life, as well as addressing the criticisms for pursuing cinematic realism from Kracauer and others. When these critics charge Disney with realism, what they really mean is that Disney has made space more real. And by real, they mean cinematic. Disney emulates the classical mode's 'realism' of space. Thus Disney's translation demonstrates that live-action cinema has come of age; the classical mode is so established that audiences accept the cinematic presentation of space–time as reality. Only such a perception, habituated to classical cinema, allows commentators to portray Disney as a simulation of reality. Disney's translation marks the maturation of the classical mode, its age of parentage, as Benjamin remarks about translations.

Yet Disney's translation, rather than a strict imitation of cinematic realism, produces the distinct mode of *animistic mimesis*, a mode that renews animation by sprouting new growth for future unfolding. Disney imitates the cinematic mode to achieve semblance, a realism of space, but also addresses the play pole, employing the transformability and transferability of animation to portray these 'realistic' figures as magically becoming-alive. Disney translates cinematic space in order to feature the playful transformation of animation. Disney limits the play of space and line compared to graphic narrative, but the characters still play, still transform. Disney does not eliminate gags (just see Thumper in *Bambi* or Dopey in *Snow White*) or metamorphosis. Disney simply restricts the metamorphosis, making it centre on the character's development. The play pole remains. Indeed, these transformative scenes are the privileged moments in the films when the elephant becomes a bird, the puppet becomes a boy, the sleeping beauty becomes princess. The cinematic space achieves semblance, providing a platform to feature these privileged moments of animistic transformation.

In Disney, this play is mostly animistic; characters become-human. Eisenstein even attributes Disney's appeal to the attractiveness of a pre-logical animism. He follows A. N. Veselovsky's definition of animism: 'We involuntarily transfer onto nature our own experience of life, which is expressed in movement, in the manifestation of a force directed by a will.'[70] Yet this is not only a transferral of human qualities to animals, but a dual transfer from animal to human, and human to animal, 'the substitution of man by animal, and of animal by man'.[71] Eisenstein compares this dual transfer to the Borro Indians, who believe that they are simultaneously human and parrot.[72] Such merging of self and other is sensed via the perception of motion and a metaphoric comparison to human life. Viewers see movement as the expression of human life. Thus in animism there is no differentiation between subject and object; the two, as with the Borro Indians, are seen as indivisible.

Disney's hybrid characters embody this indivisibility. In *Fantasia*, centaurs, fairies, demons, unicorns, flying horses, cherubs, sun gods and rainbow goddesses express both human and supernatural characteristics. Fish, leaves, amoebas and fungi move in a human manner, with apparent purpose. Mickey perfectly represents this animism. We might ask, 'Is Mickey a Mouse?' The earlier, flatter Mickey was recognisably mouse but still featured many human characteristics. He walks upright on two legs, speaks, fixes engines and flies planes. Yet the animism of animistic mimesis indicates that Mickey remains mouse *and* human, indivisibly so. His mouse-like body provides the surface and his human-like movements provide the metaphoric vehicle for the audience to see expressive human life.

This is not animism in the sense of attributing human characteristics to animals. In Disney animation, audiences do not attribute; the characters *possess* human characteristics. They move and sound like humans while looking like animals; they maintain semblance and play. The human becomes mouse as much as the mouse becomes human. This is why Disney animators preferred animal characters and why animators still struggle with humans. *Homo sapiens* has been practising a non-verbal language of gesture and faciality for millennia, and so we tend to recognise human presence, as occurs in live-action film. Cartoons never quite match up to the familiar expressions of actual humans, stripping the artifice bare. Again, the affections of animation remain distinct from those of live-action cinema. Animation's different affections caused Disney to struggle mightily with human characters, resorting to rotoscoping a live actress to make Snow White, who still appears hollow and artificial. There is less magic in seeing a human character move like a human than there is seeing a mouse mischievously disobey its Sorcerer master.

As the next chapter will illustrate, Disney constrains the transform-ability of animation, yet in the privileged mutual affection-images, the transformability actualises through an animistic metamorphosis. As such, Disney transforms the graphic narrative mode as well. Graphic narrative created a relation between viewer and creator, with the motion image repeatedly and humorously reminding us that animators were the true force behind trajectories. Animistic mimesis, instead, hides the animator and establishes a direct relationship between image-object and viewer. Disney's surface transfers create a three-dimensional world the characters inhabit, and the viewer's affective transfers give the characters a sense of life. Rather than the animator, animistic mimesis suggests that the viewer is the life-source, bestowing life by being affected by the character. Thus Disney redefines life before and through our very eyes. Life becomes mutual affection, a shared attunement or harmonisation not reserved for two subjects but possible between an image-object and subject. In Disney's mode, viewers sense life, even experience it, when the semblances of expression become registered affectively, when the affective transfer takes place. It is a view of life as expression that affects, which, as we shall see, makes newly visible a daydreaming consumer, often equated with the child. As people increasingly feel wonder over these scenes, the habituated mode makes visible a consumer body, distinct from cinema's lifestyle consumer, which becomes translated into industry practices.

CHAPTER 6

Mutual Affection-Images and Daydreaming Consumers

Disney's full-length features of the 1930s and 1940s create an interface for animistic mimesis by actualising animation's potential for transfer and transformation in *mutual affection-images*. Although Disney's features follow much of the movement-image regime, mutual affection-images mark Disney as one of the first to begin the transition to time-images, enabling a direct experience of time, of affection, of life. As such, Disney's translation will have a unique impact on consumer culture, one that extends into the affect economy and controls society today. This unique impact occurs because the mutual-affection images offer an interface for the innervations of wonder, and the mode of animistic mimesis makes visible a daydreaming consumer bent on the pleasures of self-affection much closer to commodity fetishism than cinema's lifestyle consumers. How, then, does Disney employ the formal features described in the previous chapter to create an interface for animistic mimesis?

It would be easy to show that, despite their cinematic features, *Snow White*, *Pinocchio* and *Dumbo* employ the characteristics of animistic mimesis described in the previous chapter, from the use of colour and shadows to the synchronisation of sound and movement, from the drawing of gestures to the squashing and stretching rhythms. Each story features hybrid characters, including the dwarfs in *Snow White*, the boy–puppet Pinocchio, the flying elephant Dumbo, talking animals, and numerous mythical and mysterious characters practising magic. In almost every scene, water, fire, smoke, bubbles, rain or lightning transfer(s) colours from surface to surface, forming a musical play of colour. Music, in particular, is an essential element. Lest anyone doubt the constant fusion of sound and movements, they need only learn that, at Disney, the conductor and director planned the entire movie *together* before any animator ever began to draw.[1] Each movie has multiple musical numbers where the characters move rhythmically to the music. In fact, the bulk of the viewing time consists of musical numbers, and each feature produced a hit song.

Characters move to the music and then, at times, the direction reverses and their crashes, bangs or pranks move the music as well. The music and characters experience a mutual affection, in nearly every moment on the screen, so much so that the movies are practically musicals.

As musicals, these movies create what Deleuze calls pure sound-images, where the characters' 'actions and movements are transformed by dance into movement of the world which goes beyond the motor situation'.[2] For Deleuze, music represents one of the most powerful mechanisms of experiencing time directly in the time-image, rather than indirectly in the movement-image. Just as the music unfolds in time, so do the characters' movements in animation, giving them a sense of becoming, a sense of life. As Thomas and Johnston remark, 'Music is undoubtedly the most important addition that will be made to the picture. It can do more to bring a production to life . . . than any other single ingredient.'[3] After all, the rhythms transfer to the characters and likewise transmit to audience members, striking their ears and sometimes moving their bodies.

More importantly, however, Disney blends many of these characteristics in privileged scenes, creating mutual affection-images. 'Mutual' signals the transfer of affect from character to character, not the affective transfer to audiences. Disney's mutual affection-images exhibit affection through the intensive movements of one character reflected on the facialised surface of another. However, these mutual affection-images are most often responsible for sparking a viewer's affective transfer. In short, it is in these privileged moments that people frequently find life in a Disney film – life redefined as the ability to affect, to affect and be affected mutually, the meeting of expression and emotion. It is in these images that the audience is most likely to be affected, to experience wonder and thereby to sense life. Semblances of daring, danger, defeat and victory become emotions like courage, fear, sadness, happiness and especially wonder. A few of these privileged moments have been mentioned previously in relation to the wondrous spark of animation. Audiences report crying when the dwarfs mourn Snow White and when Dumbo and mother embrace trunks. Audiences have gasped in joy when Pinocchio becomes a boy, and shrieked in fear when he transforms into a donkey, or when Dumbo accidentally gets drunk, or when the Queen turns into the wicked witch, or when Snow White flees through the forest.

Thomas and Johnston confess, 'That golden moment is our goal,' acknowledging that they measure the picture's success by whether the audience 'feels' the emotion.[4] For them, the biggest worry at the release of *Snow White* was whether the affective transfer would become personalised emotion. Employees reported that they knew they had a hit when the audience was 'bursting into spontaneous applause',[5] 'bouncing up and down'[6] in their seats, and even crying with the dwarfs as they mourn Snow White's poisoning. Importantly, such golden moments constitute the moments in which affection becomes translated into emotion and hence becomes subject to capture in regimes of (capitalist and person-alised) value. In these moments, viewers acknowledge their affection as a source of pleasure; the pre-personal intensity potentially becomes the 'I am happy' or 'I enjoyed that' of the conscious subject. Once this is personalised and introduced into the realms of conscious emotion, Disney can capture that emotion in regimes of significance and value. Thus Walt concluded, 'The most important aim of any of the fine arts is to get a purely emotional response from the beholder.'[7]

The mutual affection-images register these transformations in a unique way, blending the techniques described previously to display transforma-tive becomings visibly. Specifically, these scenes modulate Deleuze's affection-images, modifying the close-up to create a mutual affection-image. As described previously, cinema's movement-images are com-posed of perception-, affection- and action-images. We are shown a blade (perception), a close-up on the victim's registering face (affection), and then a medium shot of the victim and attacker struggling (action). Disney borrows all three types of images, given their translation of the cinematic mode. But Disney privileges affection-images, putting them in class with the directors Dreyer and Bresson, who epitomise the affection-image for Deleuze. The affection-image works through the force of two poles: power and quality, or 'reflecting surface and intensive micro-movements'.[8] We see affection when the image shows intensive movements (like a grimace or tear) on an immobile face (or any 'faceified' surface).[9] For instance, an actor stands shocked, body paralysed, eyes staring, while their mouth slowly opens. 'The moving body has lost its movement of extension, and movement has become movement of expression. It is this combination of a reflecting, immobile unity and of intensive expressive movements which constitutes the affect.'[10]

These poles are why the close-up represents the affection-image *par excellence*; the close-up shows a face as surface backdrop for the expressive movements of eyes, mouth, brow. The close-up rips the view out of the narrative space–time to present an Entity, affection as expression. The face is detached from the scene, shown in larger-than-life dimension, abstracted from space and time. We see an entity, an affect, a 'feeling-thing', not a scene of action.[11] We see shock, fear, surprise, elation. Thus affection-images are not limited to close-ups or faces. Directors can show affect by focusing on hands or objects, by using medium or long shots.

This is why Deleuze offers 'qualities' and 'forces' as another name for the two poles of the affection-image. The quality is shown by a static, reflective surface contrasted with the movement, force, *animation*. One part of the image becomes quality, becomes-face, becomes-surface and another part becomes-power, becomes-expression, becomes-movement. Powers and qualities can also be actualised in action or perception. That is, we might interpret excitement or dynamism in an action-image. But the affection-image presents the viewer with 'power or quality considered for themselves, as expressed'.[12] Thus the affection-image creates a kind of felt or tactile space, recalling synaesthesia's affective touching.

Disney uses a few close-ups, but typically creates affection-images in a different manner. Animation's surface transferability allows Disney to play with the poles of face and intensive movement, of quality and power. In fact, in the animistic becomings, we witness the characters transfer from face or quality to movement or power. To explain, let us begin with Snow White. The first mutual affection-image accompanies her transformation from maiden to prey. The Queen orders her Huntsman to kill Snow White. The affection-image begins with a close-up of the Huntsman's knife, his body shown in shadow sneaking up behind a nearly motionless maiden. His hand quivers nervously against the backdrop of a solid boulder. Snow White turns and screams, and the Huntsman drops his knife. He cannot bring himself to kill her, and he tells her of the Queen's plans, urging her to hide. As the Huntsman speaks, the scene shows Snow White from the side. Her face is immobile, her mouth wide in shock and eyes staring. Yet she frantically turns her head to look back to the forest and ahead to the Huntsman repeatedly, before fleeing. We have just witnessed the affection of the Huntsman by Snow White, and, in turn, the affection of Snow White by the Huntsman, both featuring intensive movement (quivering hands, frantic turns) against immobile surfaces (the boulder, Snow White). Snow White flees, now become prey. This is mutual affection because one character reflects the intensive movements of another, often in a mutual circuit.

Fleeing through the forest, the spectator and Snow White both see various animals, plants and debris transform into frightening creatures and shapes. Snow White has become prey and, through her eyes, the world has become a scary place. The spectator sees first what the figure is supposed, in fact, to be and then what Snow White perceives, as a tree tranforms into a monster's face, leaves turn into bats, logs turn into alligators, and branches turn into hands. As it transforms, each thing changes colour and becomes animated, moving and living (grabbing, opening eyes). In each shot, the 'camera' begins further away when showing the actual thing, and then zooms in as the objects transform in Snow White's fearful eyes. The difference from the typical close-up is that the contrast between immobility or faciality and intensive movement occurs between the two views. The immobile trees, leaves and logs become faces and then move intensively, opening their eyes and reaching out their hands. This, then, is a mutual affection-image. The images do not just present Snow White being affected; they present a simulated experience of her becoming affected. The spectator becomes Snow White and experiences her affection, represented through the transforming animations. Again, this is a mutual affection-image because, rather than showing the affection by contrasting immobile surface and intensive movements, the images show mutual affection through the contrast of two movements, here the 'real' view and Snow White's fear-tinged one. This is precisely the moment of likely affective transfer, the moment where Snow White becomes alive. Indeed, animators reported that, during a preview of the scene, they wondered out loud whether Snow White could survive a fall that far.[13] The affective transfer struck even the animators; despite their knowledge that she did not exist, they perceived her as alive.

Now prey, Snow White becomes stalked by the Queen. She is duped into eating the poisonous apple and passes into a deep sleep that the dwarfs mistake for death. As noted, many people reported crying in response to the following scenes. Here, the mutual affection-image is created via the contrast between the dwarfs and Snow White, each switching places between reflective surface and intensive movement. The scene begins with dim lighting from candles; the view is foggy, the candles casting their light over the scene. The light grows brighter, revealing the immobile Snow White on her bed, then the heads of the dwarfs crowded around and kneeling, hats off (Figure 6.1). We cut to a medium-close shot of Happy, whose face slowly quivers, followed by a couple of tears before he buries his head and sobs. This shot is repeated for a few other dwarfs before we get a close-up of Grumpy, the dwarf most resistant to Snow White but who has recently revealed his deep affection for her. Grumpy's face also begins to quiver, tears fall, and then he turns away.

These are similar to typical affection-images, but the animators' descriptions of what made this scene so difficult are instructive.[14] Animation's technological differences required that they modulate the typical affection-image into a mutual affection-image. First, close-ups pose a problem for animation. Animators wanted to limit close-ups because showing tense emotions with only facial expression were difficult; animated characters seem lifeless in the stillness of the close-up, deprived of their moving holds and overlapping action that added more semblance. Furthermore,

Figure 6.1 The mutual affection of Snow White and the dwarfs.
(Screenshot from *Snow White and the Seven Dwarfs* DVD)

the dwarfs presented a dilemma. The audience had been conditioned to
laugh when they appear due to what Ngai calls their 'animatedness' –
their exaggerated, frantic displays of emotion and action – but now the
animators wanted sadness.[15] Too much movement would give the wrong
impression; the dwarfs had to be overcome with grief from the beginning.
Yet expressions in animation generally require movement; the caricature
of realism requires exaggeration. The naturalistic acting style common
in Hollywood live action is too subtle for drawing. Thus the dilemma: to
show affect, the animators needed stillness, the reflective face, but stillness
often drained the characters of their animation – movement and life. So
finally, after trying and failing to capture the expression, the animators
discovered that 'sad eyes, slow blinks, and a few tears were all that was
needed'.[16] Such slow blinks and tears, then, serve as the intensive micromovements contrasted with the immobility of Snow White, as well as the
near-immobility of the dwarfs.

In another sense, these images are mutual affection because immobilisation reflects immobilisation and intensive micromovements reflect other
micromovements. These shots work by nearly immobilising the dwarfs,
stripping them of the qualities that so animated them, and then showing

this immobilisation as their affection. The dwarfs become immobile faces, the qualities, on which the force of Snow White's passing is registered, with a single tear. We feel her passing through the immobilisation of the dwarfs. Snow White serves as the reflective surface against which the near-immobilisation of the dwarfs registers. The dwarfs are not completely still, so the image gains some intensive movements in their shrugs and tears. But the affection-image's poles are modified, with the characters' immobilisation registered against one another. The quality of the dwarfs' stillness reflects the power of Snow White's passing; two faces or surfaces reflect one another, and their mutual affection produces intensive movements in the form of slow blinks and a few tears.

Even more in the scene that follows, the mutual affection-image proceeds through the contrast of dwarfs and Snow White. The scene is one of almost complete stillness, a whole scene becoming face. Snow White is asleep, and the dwarfs slowly approach the glass coffin, hats off, placing flowers at her grave and kneeling in prayer. The dwarfs are shown from behind; this time their faces will not serve as the surface for the mutual affection-image. Instead, Snow White's lack of movement – her death as quality– registers as the stillness and slowness of the dwarfs. The Prince approaches and kisses her, then kneels passively with the dwarfs, shown from behind. We see Snow White in medium close shot. Her eyes flicker, she stretches out her arm as if awakening from sleep. These intensive movements register against the stillness of the Prince and the dwarfs. As the dwarfs see her move, they slowly raise their heads, open their mouths wide, and smile. Snow White has come to life, and they begin the kind of animated dance expected from the dwarfs. The image shows the mutual affection of dwarfs and Snow White, her immobility becoming their immobility, her motion becoming their animation, her life becoming their joy. It is here that viewers often saw life. Snow White becomes transformed into princess. Audiences register their mutual affection, and in so doing often complete the affective transfer. 'The audience cried for the first time during an animated cartoon.'[17] Undoubtedly tears of joy, because Snow White lives!

Disney repeatedly uses the contrast between characters to create a mutual affection-image, displaying nearly immobile characters as the reflecting surfaces for the intensive movements of another. Especially if both characters are alive, then having a completely immobilised face becomes impossible. The characters must move or we no longer have animation, so by creating a mutual affection-image, characters can move and switch poles, sometimes intensively expressing and sometimes reflecting the expressions. A prime example comes from the famous scene where

Pinocchio and Lampwick become donkeys. Lampwick's transformation is registered on Pinocchio, such as when he takes a drink of beer and sprouts donkey ears. Cut to Pinocchio, whose eyes widen and mouth drops agape; he then looks at his own beer and shoves it away. Lampwick smokes a cigar and out pops a tail. Pinocchio expresses shock and discards his cigar. After Lampwick's face transforms to a donkey, he asks Pinocchio, 'Do I look like a jackass?' Pinocchio answers, 'You sure do,' laughing, but his laugh suddenly mutates into a donkey's 'hee-haw'. Lampwick looks in the mirror – briefly creating a new reflective surface – then runs screaming to Pinocchio. We see Pinocchio's face in medium close shot, with Lampwick grasping his collar, only to witness the hands transform into hooves, changing colour and casting their glow on Pinocchio. The scene cuts to a medium shot, shown in shadow, with Lampwick screaming 'Mama' and completing the metamorphosis into donkey. We then see Pinocchio responding with fear as donkey ears and tail spring out of his body. By this time, Jiminy Cricket has arrived and becomes the reflective surface registering the affection of Pinocchio's transformation. Pinocchio shifts from reflective face to intensive movement.

In the shift, we have two mutual affection-images, from Lampwick to Pinocchio and Pinocchio to Jiminy. Rather than completely immobile figures, the back-and-forth movements of two characters mutually affect, an image enhanced through the visual techniques described previously. Their status as reflective surface is not expressed through immobility but through minor actions, like changes in expression or pushing away a beer. Even when Pinocchio moves, however, the tendency is towards the pole of immobility. His actions are to *stop* acting. The dwarfs signal their immobilisation with a tear, and Pinocchio does so by getting rid of his beer and cigar. They stop acting and become face, even though they continue to move, remaining animated. Reportedly, audiences were struck with fear during the becoming-donkey scene. Historian Leonard Maltin claims that Pinocchio's scenes 'rank among the most terrifying moments in screen history'.[18]

Pinocchio's becoming-boy scene provides another illuminating example, specifically demonstrating how Disney blends aesthetic techniques such as sparkles, transformation and colour into mutual affection-images. In a scene of less than one minute in length, Disney constructs a mutual affec-tion-image including the transfer of colours, hybrid characters, magic, sparkles and, most importantly, the animism of character, the becoming-boy transformation of Pinocchio, evident in his changed appearance. The scene begins with a medium shot of a motionless Pinocchio on the bed and Geppetto, his father, also motionless, face-down at the end of the bed.

Pinocchio has just drowned in the escape from the whale. Pinocchio's immobility registers in the immobility of Geppetto, whose face is not shown. The scene cuts to Jiminy Cricket by a candle, also hunched over, sobbing and muttering about the loss. One could see Jiminy as the intensive movement on the reflecting surface of Pinocchio, but it is Jiminy's immobilisation that strikes here. Shown from behind, we cannot see his face and gone is his energised personality. He simply hunches over the candle, sniffles and cries. Once again, Pinocchio's immobilisation is registered as the immobility of other characters; all become-surface, reflecting shared grief.

We cut to a medium shot of Pinocchio and hear the Blue Fairy speak. As she does, the screen takes on a grey then blue hue, transforming the colours of Pinocchio and his bed (Figure 6.2). Magical sparkles emanate from Pinocchio's chest in radiating circles expanding outwards. The sparkles are white and transfer their colour to the scene. As the sparkles fade, the original colours return but something has changed. Pinocchio's donkey ears have evaporated, his nose has become shorter and less like a twig, his skin colour has changed, his face takes on a rosy blush, his wooden joints disappear and his eyes morph. In order to make Pinocchio look like a puppet, the animators drew his eyes large and wide, giving him a glassy stare similar to dolls. Now, his eyes are rounder, smaller,

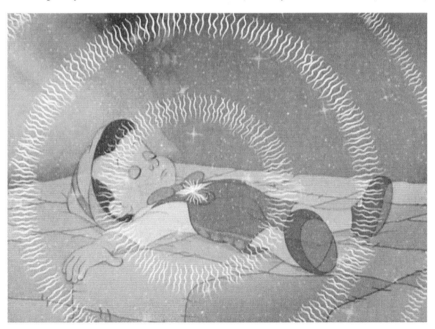

Figure 6.2 Pinocchio becomes boy. (Screenshot from *Pinocchio 70th Anniversary* DVD)

more expressive and human. Pinocchio wakes up, rubs his eyes, feels himself and begins to speak: 'I'm alive, see, and I'm, I'm real.' Once again, Pinocchio's movements register on the surface of Geppetto, Jiminy and the pets. They look up in wonder and go quickly back to their animated selves in a celebratory dance.

This scene is exemplary because Disney employs many techniques described in the previous chapter to form a mutual affection-image. Magic effects the transformation of a hybrid character, the puppet's becoming-boy, accompanied by sparkles and the play of colour, and ending with the fusion of movement and music. Yet even more exemplary is the sequence of mutual affection-images in *Dumbo*. Dumbo, an elephant with enormous ears, becomes clown, then becomes bird and finally star. After his mother fights to protect his honour and is locked up, Dumbo tries to perform with the circus elephants but, after tripping on his ears, he causes a massive crash. The elephants hear that the circus has punished Dumbo by making him a clown. The head elephant responds, 'From now on, he is no longer an elephant.' The other clowns subsequently humiliate Dumbo, and to cheer him up, his friend, Timothy Q. Mouse, arranges a meeting with his mother. Their meeting constitutes a prime mutual affection-image. Dumbo's arrival causes his mother to perk up, but she cannot get close enough to see due to her shackles. She reaches out through the bars and uses her trunk to feel his face. The two then express mutual affection through touch, embracing trunks. Dumbo responds affectively to this touch, becoming the intensive movements and letting a few tears slip. Then Dumbo's mother cradles Dumbo with her trunk, swinging him gently. His expressive smiles contrast with his mother's motions. They are mutually affecting, each becoming the reflexive face for the other's intensive movements. As noted earlier, this is a scene that has moved many to tears.

Commonly, however, the mutual affection-images result from the contrast of the intense Timothy and the immobile Dumbo (Figure 6.3). A mouse and an elephant, an odd couple to say the least, must often be shown in a sort of hybrid close-up, where we see only parts of Dumbo's face as the backdrop for Timothy, who stands between his eyes or on his trunk. Timothy exhibits animatedness, excited and passionate, serving as the intensive movements on Dumbo's forlorn face. The final scenes present a series of three becomings, where we witness mutual-affection through the contrast of Timothy and Dumbo. The first begins when Dumbo and Timothy accidentally drink alcohol they mistake for water. The two become drunk and then become reflexive face. Dumbo hiccups some bubbles, which transform into fluorescent elephants performing a dance.

Figure 6.3 Timothy's intensive movements on Dumbo's immobile face.
(Screenshot from *Dumbo* DVD)

The scene continually cuts between Dumbo and Timothy staring in awe at the hallucination, practically immobile. One cut, for instance, shows Dumbo hiding beneath his ears and slowly peeking out one eye, while another shows Dumbo's ears furl out in shock over what he sees. Once again, slight movements faceify Dumbo. Timothy and Dumbo's faces reflect the intensive movements of the hallucinatory elephant-bubbles. In a couple of cuts, this is shown directly when Dumbo's on-looking face fills the backdrop and the marching elephants cross the foreground. Dumbo becomes the reflexive face on which the elephants engage in intensive movements registering the (drunken) affection of Dumbo and Timothy.

As intensive movement, the elephants' performance looks like something out of *Fantasia*, and, since it lasts several minutes, it makes one wonder how Kracauer ignored this scene in his condemnation for mimicking photographable reality. There is nothing close to a photograph here. The elephants dance and play instruments, moving to the music. Their trunks become trumpets and horns, their bodies emit musical noises when smashed, kicked or stomped. They frequently change from one fluorescent colour to another, casting their hues on to each other and the black backdrop. Two striped elephants merge and blend colours. The elephants constantly morph, at one time dividing into multiple small elephants and then swelling into giant floating heads. The eyes become pyramids and another elephant transforms into a camel. Others become cars, trains, sleds and boats. We see the transference of colour through light, as the elephants dance with a lightning bolt, play in the snow, skate on the water, and even dissolve into abstract forms or whirlpools of colour. We see the play of shadows, as the neon colours transfer from figure to background, casting the elephants in silhouette. Finally, the elephants fade into clouds and we see the sun rise on a tree.

It is the next morning, and this scene shows the becoming-bird of Dumbo. It begins with some birds commenting on an astonishing sight: an elephant high in a tree. Dumbo and Timothy have passed out, and one bird wakes up the mouse, showing him their elevated location. Timothy scrambles up Dumbo's face, waking him up, and we see his face, eyes closed, as the backdrop for Timothy's frantic grasping and fearful gulping. Timothy is the intensive movement contrasted with the reflective face of Dumbo, whose eyes slowly open. When Dumbo looks down, he becomes animated and promptly crashes into a pool of water. Timothy deduces that Dumbo must have flown them up there, but the birds make fun of him relentlessly, dancing to the song 'When I See an Elephant Fly'. Dumbo is still clown. He begins to head back to the circus, but Timothy decides to guilt-trip the birds. Timothy gives a passionate speech about Dumbo losing his mother and being an outcast because of his ears. One cut shows Timothy's shadow projected on Dumbo's unfurled ear, which fills the background. Once again, Timothy becomes the expressive movement on Dumbo's reflective face, this time expressing power through a heart-warming speech.

The mutual affection is also shown in the response of the birds, who now want to make up. They huddle, trying to decide how to persuade Dumbo to fly, and they come up with the solution – a magic feather. Timothy rushes to Dumbo and presents the feather. We then see the birds trying fruitlessly to shove Dumbo off a cliff, a scene that demonstrates how an elephant character ideally represents an immobile surface. Many cuts show Timothy on Dumbo's nose, passionately cheering, once again becoming intensive movement on the immobile face. Dumbo pumps his ears, the screen fills with a dirt cloud, and they disappear. When they emerge, we see Timothy on Dumbo's hat, saying, 'It's no use.' Then, we look through Timothy's eyes to the ground below, which shows Dumbo flying in shadow. Now Dumbo is animated, smiling, curling his trunk, flapping his wings, circling with the birds, gliding down and landing on some wires. Dumbo has become-bird.

There is one more becoming yet for Dumbo – becoming star. The scene changes and we see Dumbo in clown make-up, ready to perform his fall from a burning building on to a trampoline. As Dumbo begins to fall, he drops the magic feather and becomes motionless, plummeting like a rock. Timothy scrambles on to Dumbo's nose, which fills half of the background, and frantically pleads for Dumbo to fly, confessing that the magic feather is a hoax. The camera pans out, and we see Dumbo's face, eyes wide and staring, mouth open, frozen, with Timothy still frantic. The point of view transposes to the clowns with the trampoline, who stare upwards with mouths agape. They become frozen faces on which the intensive movement, this time the shadow of a plummeting Dumbo, is marked. They are being mutually affected as well. At the last moment, Dumbo flies and proceeds to pull pranks on the deserving clowns.

The movie ends with Dumbo signing a Hollywood contract and then flying above a personal train compartment with his freed mother smiling approvingly. Kracauer faults the ending because he believes Dumbo has gone to work for the circus slave-master, proving his claim that Disney has sacrificed animation's transformability to the strictures of the (cinematic) real. Yet such an interpretation focuses on the narrative content and misses the animistic transformation so central to the movie. The mutual affection-images express the magic, the transformation, the animistic becomings. Through the contrast between the intensive Timothy and the immobile Dumbo, the movie shows mutual affection. How could such images ever be photographed? Certainly, Dumbo becomes part of the culture industry loathed by Kracauer, but the message is about self-transformation, about how one's expressions can affect others, about how figures can transform from being immobilised object to animate life. Criticising Disney for photographic realism misses these privileged moments, the very moments that visibly display the differences between live action and animation. In these moments, some viewers feel the wondrous spark of animistic mimesis, sensing never-have-been images as living beings. The ending is simply a way to conclude, not the moral lesson. The 'happily ever-after' endings that so many Disney critics bemoan are not the primary point of the film; the endings simply signal the cessation of the animated-becoming, the stopping of time in these hybrid movement–time images. The story presents a time-image of becoming that concludes with the void of 'ever-after'.

As noted previously, Disney pursued full-length features mostly for economic reasons. Disney's animated features respond to the same crisis that sparks the time-image, the crisis of money. Just as the movement-image's repetitive clichés drained audiences and reduced profits, encouraging the shift to time-images, the formulaic graphic narratives of early animation were growing mundane, prompting Disney's pursuit of full-length features and their translation of cinematic realism. Yet Disney borrows from live-action cinema without fully imitating it and without abandoning the uniqueness of animation, despite the arguments of critics. Disney did not mimic strict realism; it employs cinematic realism as a platform to feature the animated becomings. Critics like Kracauer overlook Disney's mutual affection-images and thereby cannot fathom the popular attraction. Instead, recognising these mutual affection-images helps illuminate the attraction of Disney animation, that wondrous spark of life innervated by the mode of animistic mimesis.

The pleasures of the mode come from the viewer's splitting between knowledge and sensation, in being affected by the transformative becomings despite recognising that the characters do not exist. The mode enables desirable affective transfers despite the unreality. These virtual bodies sense life, and thus viewers sometimes wonder about its meaning. If something can affect me, is it not alive? Could life possibly be mutual affection, the meeting of expression and emotion? The unique attraction, then, of Disney's animation is the same one for the time-image, despite imitating many features of movement-images. In addition to a viewer whose sensory-motor systems are linked to movement-images, the viewer also becomes the focus of a mind–body machine. In addition to presenting an indirect image of narrative time, the film becomes a temporal experience. In addition to the attraction from witnessing the fantastical, the attraction becomes one of feeling, of being given a body and being touched, of plugging into a spiritual automaton, into a circuit between image-object and self. Viewers are potentially affected by the transformation, despite knowing that a puppet cannot become a boy, that elephants cannot fly. Animistic mimesis gives the viewer a body and targets it for affective transfer, for the contagion of mimesis and the animism of transformation. Its mutual affection-images are time-images, those images that give a body, evoking wonder that thinks life. As Deleuze states (italics mine):

> Not that the body thinks, but, obstinate and stubborn, it forces us to think, and forces us to think what is concealed from thought, life. Life will no longer be made to appear before the categories of thought; thought will be thrown into the categories of life. The categories of life are precisely the attitudes of the body, its postures . . . To think is to learn what *a non-thinking body is capable of, its capacity, its postures*. It is through the body . . . that cinema forms its alliance with the spirit, with thought.[19]

Much earlier in these books, in a single sentence, Deleuze conflates animation and live-action cinema by describing both as movement-images.[20]

Disney certainly translates the movement-images of classical cinema, yet it also creates time-images, especially through mutual affection–images. The time-image aspect in Disney extends well beyond Keith Broadfoot and Rex Butler's claim that all animation is a time-image because it is always an unfolding and dissolving, a becoming in time, whose movements appear only between frames.[21] In fact, Disney constrains and masks this constant unfolding by imitating the classical cinema, by creating a sensory-motor linkage and organic spatiality. Yet Disney combines this imitation of classical cinema with privileged moments constructing a hybrid movement- and time-image. Movement-images constitute a (realistic) platform for featuring the (playful) mutual affection–images. Deleuze hints that affection-images pave the way for time-images, since affection-images constitute their own space, outside the realistic strictures of action-movement space. Disney's mutual affection–images also transcend the realities of cinematic space, presenting an impossible becoming, a temporal experience rather than an indirect image of time since time (life) is constituted in and through the transformation. The character becomes alive; time unfolds before and through our newly virtualised eyes.

When mutual affection–images leap from the screen, when viewers sense life through an affective transfer, we are well on the path to the time-image. Deleuze's definition of time is, indeed, mutual affection: 'the affection of self by self'.[22] Time, the affection of self by self, takes place through a mode that puts the self into relation with other bodies and, especially, with the self. When animistic mimesis enables viewers to experience a split between their conscious knowledge of non-existence and sensation of life, they experience time directly; they feel a becoming and think life, even if not quite or always consciously. As their popularity demonstrates, Disney's mutual affection–images often spark the leap, marking one of the first moments of transition from movement-images and demonstrating that plenty of time remains for cinema to make money, especially if studios can sell audiences a renewable experience of time and life. In short, Disney translated the cinematic mode in a way that moved beyond its staid clichés. Through privileged mutual affection–images, Disney created the potential for audience affection, cueing them to give life, to feel the mutual affections, to set aside the doubting 'we know' for the pleasurable 'we sense'. This is the 'message' of Disney animation, in McLuhan's sense. And, as we shall see, this 'message' – namely, that consumers can enjoy affective experiences with image-objects – is one learned by the culture industry as animistic mimesis makes perceivable a new childlike consumer.

Daydreaming Consumers and Commodity Fetishism

As with the classical cinema, many note the connection between Disney
and consumerism. Mickey was one of the first and most successful film
stars to expand into product merchandising, and today synergistic integration of characters and commodities has become standard practice.
Disney remains one of the most successful examples, selling countless
movies and expanding into seemingly every realm of culture through an
integrated, brand-based synergy across a wide variety of commodities
and media. As such, Baudrillard takes Disney as emblematic of American
consumer culture and its regimes of simulation; Disney is 'the precursor,
the grand initiator of the imaginary as virtual reality'.[23] Likewise, Bryman
coins the term Disneyisation to distinguish post-Fordist, consumer-
oriented corporate strategies 'associated with the conviction among many
consumers that goods bestow meaning and are a source of identity'.[24]
For critical pedagogue Henry Giroux, Disney promotes an ideology of
consumerism responsible for changing childhood, displacing the child's
identity as public citizen for a market-based one.[25]

These depictions seem borne out by empirics, and their positions are
versions of manipulationist or emulationist theory, beginning with either a
duped or a distinguishing consumer as the origin of modern consumerism.
Bryman describes Disneyisation as 'a set of strategies for "manipulating"
consumers', and Giroux, Baudrillard and Crawford are also concerned
with how industry practices generate desires to consume.[26] Bryman and
Giroux also relate Disney to the emulationist position, seeing Disney as
offering materials for the expression of identity and meaning. When seen
in the light of producer and lifestyle-based contributions to modern consumerism, conflating Disney with the entire culture industry and animation with live action makes perfect sense. Disney certainly contributes to
consumerism in both of these manners.

Such contributions to consumer culture are significant, yet conflating
Disney with consumerism generally or with cinema specifically misses
many important differences. Specifically, conflating Disney and lifestyle
consumption erases the differences in affection and perception across
many different consumer modes as well as the distinct, virtual bodies on
which they are based. Instead, a modal perspective directs attention to the
differences in embodiment, affection and desire, enhancing understanding of the wide variety of practices constituting consumer culture. In this
understanding, Disney contributes to consumerism through more than
advertising products, promoting consumerist ideology, or selling gobs of
commodities. Disney animation and live-action Hollywood entail distinct

affective and perceptual experiences; thus Disney's unique contribution comes from making perceivable a different consumer from the lifestyle consumer, for whom new types of commodities become articulable. Disney helps make visible a daydreaming consumer, one who is more of a fetishist than an emulator, one who seeks out commodities for affection rather than distinction.

This daydreaming consumer becomes perceivable because the mode of animistic mimesis constitutes a body that engages less in the self-display of the lifestyle mode and more in the self-affection of a fetishistic mode. Animistic mimesis makes visible a consumer body that daydreams through image-objects, achieving a desirable emotional experience through their affective investment. Just as the lifestyle consumer operates according to poles similar to the classical cinematic mode, this daydreaming mode operates according to an economy of semblance and play, seeking semblances in image-objects that afford the play of the imagination. Campbell's work helps elucidate this daydreaming and its economy, when read as one mode of consumerism rather than the singular cause. The daydreamer achieves pleasure by triggering feelings via the imagination; imaginations stimulate affects that bring pleasure. Thus in the daydream, real and imaginary feelings are blurred, just as we might feel real affections from a fictional movie. Real and imaginary spaces are blurred; the daydream begins from the viewer's space and is projected in enjoyable directions. These directions unfold through self-conscious editing. When a person daydreams about experiences with a new commodity, for instance, editing is crucial to the fantasy. The connection with cinematic modes is evident in Campbell's words: '[Daydreaming] may take place in a more or less "directed" fashion . . . Just as in romantic novels and films, heroes and heroines rarely have hiccups, headaches or indigestion . . . so too are our dreams purged of life's little inconveniences.'[27]

Like classical film, the daydream relates the real viewer space–time to a fantastical space–time. Yet Campbell's description most recalls the folding in animistic mimesis between knowing and sensing spelled out by Eisenstein; the daydreamer knows this is a dream but enjoys the sensations none the less. Campbell's own words seem to spell out this economy, making the daydreaming consumer sound more like the animated film viewer than the live-action one:

> This is the distinctive modern faculty, the ability to create an illusion that is known to be false but felt to be true. The individual is both actor and audience in his own drama, 'his own' in the sense that he constructed it, stars in it, and constitutes the sum total of the audience.[28]

With the mode of the lifestyle consumer, it is less accurate to assume that this body is the sole constructor, star and audience of the daydream. Given the economy between similarity and difference, the lifestyle mode demands others as stars, types and audiences; the consumer must be able to model the stars and fit in with other 'types', and needs an audience to recognise how they stand out. Further, the lifestyle consumer links to a milieu that is not wholly their own. The lifestyle mode (and classical cinema) is an externally oriented desiring-machine, comporting to a world of camera-subjects engaged in image management. Desiring-machines plugged into Disney's animation do not rely on the presence of other (camera-)eyes. These are inwardly directed desires, sparked by self-affection from image-objects. Bodies can experience the pleasures of affective transfer despite knowing that this other for whom they feel is non-existent. They become the star, because they fill in motion and life where none is present, and the sole audience, because their affective response becomes the purpose.

As such, the classical mode and animistic mimesis result in different criteria for judging experience. Cinema and the lifestyle mode lead to questions about authenticity. Does the image match the self? Are they genuine or acting? With animistic mimesis, these questions are made moot. Everything we see is acting, posed; someone might think they see the 'real' Will Smith in his roles but witnessing the 'real' Mickey is nonsensical. Instead, authenticity comes from an affective touch; consumers enjoy the experience and perceive it as genuine if it triggers an affective transfer that feels real. Again, the standards for life change; viewers perceive life existing when expression meets emotion, when the affective transfer is achieved and personalised. With live action, we, of course, often are affected, but this is the affection of self by other. Bodies comport to another; the transpositions of the camera might evoke empathy because they put us in someone else's shoes. Life is measured by the genuineness of the other's feelings, by the realism of their response. In animistic mimesis, life is measured by the genuineness of our own feelings, by the affectivity of our own response. This is a notion of life based in emotional authenticity that is very similar to the Romantic's position that strong emotion validates aesthetic experience. For the Romantic, a lifestyle mode, due to its attempts to fit in, is always conformism, blunting genuine experience. Genuine experience requires personal involvement, the uniqueness of an affective touching.

The Romantics sought this experience in nature's sublimity, which might remind the reader of Benjamin's auratic mountain range and therefore disqualify the comparison with animistic mimesis. However,

Benjamin reserves the possibility of perceiving aura in certain reproducible objects like photographs.[29] The age of mechanical reproduction decreases the auratic mode because, watching a film, viewers are unlikely to peruse the images for signs of the actor's here-and-now; they focus on the unfolding role, which, as a mass product, has no uniqueness. Yet it remains possible to watch a movie through an auratic mode by gazing at the actor, not the role. Those viewers who think they see the real Will Smith are engaged in an auratic mode, looking for the actor's unique here-and-now. They divorce actor and role, and bestow on the actor the capability of *looking back*; as the role draws nearer in space, the actor, seen through an auratic mode, gains distance in time, a unique temporal existence evidenced by their ability to gaze back. As Benjamin concludes, 'Inherent in the gaze, however, is the expectation that it will be returned by that on which it is bestowed. Where this expectation is met . . . there is an experience . . . of the aura in all its fullness.'[30]

Here is a major difference between the experience of live action and animation because, with animation, there is no split between actor and role and any expectation that Mickey might look back seems unlikely. In other words, animation does not make visible the structure of subjective vision, as Sobchack says about live-action film. Modal bodies do not see humans looking and being looked at; it is difficult to imagine the dwarfs returning our gaze. Does this mean that animation, being sheer technological production, lacks any possibility of an auratic mode? Certainly, it makes no sense for viewers to envision the accretion of other eyes looking on Dumbo's face, as they might 'see' with the Mona Lisa. When I look at my copy of *Fantasia*, it is difficult to believe that other people have seen that very same movie. My DVD is a copy, one without much of a singular history or enduring temporal existence. In fact, it seems highly unlikely that anyone would look auratically at animation, would look for a spark of the here-and-now within its indirect image of time. Animation seems to confess from the start that it is an indirect image of time, that no actual here-and-now is present.

Yet this is precisely the wondrous spark of animation and why I call Disney's mutual-affection images a hybrid time-image. The drawings, being an indirect image of time, lack a unique here-and-now, but they can evoke a singular temporal experience. The cartoon becomes alive through the viewer's affective transfer. The viewer becomes cartoon, filling in its motion and life. They experience time unfolding, life becoming, registered through their affections. The animated characters become alive and begin to look back; their expressions and movements rebound, becoming affective experience, becoming mutual affection, becoming life.

The successful affective transfer occurs when individual bodies experience animation through an auratic mode that endows the character with the ability to look back. Thus animistic mimesis is not completely devoid of aura but depends fundamentally on it. Only when viewers perceive the character as alive, only when they see the character looking back, is the desire activated. As Benjamin explains,

> Experience of the aura thus arises from the fact that a response characteristic of human relationships is transposed to the relationship between humans and inanimate or natural objects . . . To experience the aura of an object we look at means to invest it with the ability to look back at us.[31]

Animistic mimesis invests image-objects with the ability to look back, creating a unique temporal experience common to an auratic mode and the time-image alike. Contrary to many interpretations of Benjamin, then, Disney demonstrates that technological reproducibility and mass culture are not devoid of auratic modes. Instead, animistic mimesis offers a manner through which bodies can experience the here-and-now from an object that lacks uniqueness or history. Observers of the time might have thought it impossible to experience aura through such reproducible images, especially since movement-images dominated. In the classical cinema, people enjoyed witnessing the action but the separation between viewer space–time and narrative space–time remained. Viewers saw a fantastical there-and-then, not a unique here-and-now. With Disney, the characters' becoming-alive occurs only through bodily affection: only, that is, in the here-and-now of the affective transfer. This affective transfer depends upon bestowing life on the image-objects, on feeling in them a unique existence extending well beyond the screen. In short, animistic mimesis relies upon perceiving the characters through an auratic mode; this distributed body gives the objects on screen the ability to gaze back.

Benjamin compares auratic perception to *perception in dreams* because in dreams things seem to look back at us as much as we see them.[32] The comparison is apt; this newly perceivable consumer is one who daydreams through objects. Although many note that both live-action and animated cinema are similar to daydreams, how desiring-machines daydream in these modes is different. Classical cinema constitutes a movement-focused daydreaming based on an economy of recording and projecting. Animation enables an image-focused daydreaming based on an economy of semblance and play. In the classical cinematic mode, bodies record moments of time; in animation, bodies create time. In live action, people see existent life; in animation, they feel life. Thus Disney animation makes perceivable a consumer engaged in daydreaming through image-objects, i.e. pure commodities. To garner pleasure in this desiring machine, there is no need to comport one's body to others, forming a lifestyle; instead, all one needs is to engage a mode to experience pleasures accrued through image-objects.

Once again, this virtual consumer does not originate from animistic mimesis but becomes newly perceivable, expanding into new spaces and times. Indeed, children had practised a similar mode of daydreaming for quite some time before the advent of Disney, and Marx long ago criticised imagining life in objects as commodity fetishism. Perhaps reminding us of Disney's 'magic', Marx begins describing the commodity fetish by commenting on the 'mysterious' nature of the commodity, 'abounding in metaphysical subtleties and theological niceties'.[33] For Marx, the commodity takes on the 'mystical character' of a fetish when it comes to represent spiritual values and cultural meanings beyond its use-value.[34] Consumers fail to see the conditions of production, the labour and human relations that go into making the product, and fetishise the commodity. Consumers subjectify the commodity instead of valuing its objective qualities, what Marx calls its use-value. His description of a commodity table seems ripped straight from a Disney movie:

> But as soon as [a table] emerges as a commodity, it changes into a thing which transcends sensuousness. It not only stands with its feet on the ground, but, in relation to all other commodities, it stands on its head, and evolves out of its wooden brain grotesque ideas, far more wonderful than if it were to begin dancing of its own free will.[35]

Marx's example of a table with a wooden brain, standing on its head and dancing, seems to presage the coming of Disney animation. In fact, Marx makes the connection to a mode of *communicative transfer* explicit:

> Through this substitution, the products of labor become commodities, sensuous things which are at the same time supra-sensible or social. In the same way, the impression made by a thing on the optic nerve is perceived not as a subjective excitation of the nerve but as the objective form of a thing outside the eye. In the act of seeing, of course, light is really transmitted from one thing, the external object, to another thing, the eye. It is a physical relation between physical things. As against this, the commodity-form and the value-relation . . . have absolutely no connection with the physical nature of the commodity.[36]

In a sense, Marx distinguishes between use-value and commodity fetishism based on a difference between two forms of transfer. Use-value, like vision, is an objective relationship, an *impression* transferred from object to the surface of the eye. The commodity fetish, on the other hand, is an affective relationship, whereby the consumer transfers fantasies on to the commodity. Marx describes the commodity fetish as an appearance, supra-sensuous, imaginary, the 'fantastic form of a relation between things'.[37] The commodity fetish is an affective or spiritual transfer, the 'conversion of things into persons'.[38] Thus he proposes that the most apt analogy comes from the realm of religion.

> There the products of the human brain appear as autonomous figures endowed with a life of their own, which enter into relations both with each other and with the human race. So it is in the world of commodities with the products of men's hands.[39]

In this description, the commodity fetish can be readily compared with animistic mimesis. Both involve a dual transfer that endows objects with an imaginary life. Yet animation is not merely another iteration of a prior fetishism but its translation and hence growth into newly perceivable spaces and forms. Take Disney movies. Seeing a Disney movie is partially a physical relationship between physical things, but it is also a supra-sensible experience in the imagination. So, are movies a fetish or a real physical connection? The pleasure and affections derived from movies are real, existent. Does this make movies' use-value equivalent to their exchange value? If I paid eight dollars for a movie and it made me laugh hysterically, did I get my use-value? What if I was bored to tears but it helped me avoid an unwanted guest? Disney movies are fantastic forms *and* real experiences. Yet we cannot deny that their movies are also commodities that actively edit out the production process and hide the exploitation of labour evident from the numerous strikes in Hollywood during the 1930s and 1940s, including a particularly nasty one at Disney.

Animistic mimesis, the sensation of life in image-objects, is certainly a type of fetishism but one translated and hence expanded beyond the ways Marx depicted. For Marx, commodity fetishism was an objective condition of nineteenth-century capitalism, one inherently accompanying the product's entrance into exchange markets. In other words, the simple fact of being a commodity makes the object a fetish. 'As soon as they are produced as commodities', objects of labour obtain an exchange-value, which is the source of their fetish.[40] This objective view, held by some like Horkheimer and Adorno, contends that fetishism is an inevitable, structural result of capitalism.[41] Commodities take on the appearance of life as soon as they are exchanged because they then objectively have a relation to one another, relations such as exchange value.

A modal perspective recognises objective fetishism as a product of a particular distribution of virtual bodies but also acknowledges that various modes contribute to the perceivability of life in commodities, thereby expanding fetishism to different consumers and commodities. As Sean Cubitt acknowledges, the commodity form evolves over time, especially through the emergence of different cinematic modes. As a result, 'Discovering the temporalities of film is as close as we get to understanding the why and wherefore of commodity fetishism as it has developed over the last hundred years.'[42] In contrast, attributing the fetish to exchange alone, as in the objective view, or conflating all cinematic modes with a general fetishism does not provide a compelling reason for social change, for the proliferation and vast expansion of consumerism in the twentieth century. How can we explain the voracious and encompassing nature of modern fetishism? What accounts for the persistent, insatiable desire to consume that marks consumerism? The answer is at least partially related to the spread of commodity fetishism, but the spread of fetishism requires enabling modes of perception. The commodity fetish appears only through exchange but exchange occurs only because people perceive value. Marx's comparison to religion drives home this conclusion. Religious fetishism does not spread simply due to the existence of religious institutions, any more than commodity fetishism can be said to spread simply because of exchange. Religion requires training in modes of perceiving, through ritual practices that serve as persistent reminders. Consumer insatiability also requires training and constant reminders. Consumerism needs sources that provide instruction, opportunity and actualisation of various modal possibilities.

Disney animation provides one such source, offering both a reminder of the possibility of daydreaming through objects and training for the extension from one commodity (animated movies) to others (like daydreams experienced with all variety of Disney commodities). Thus, animistic mimesis translates earlier commodity fetishism, thereby expanding beyond the realm of objective exchange into new practices of daydreaming through image-objects. Both these earlier and later iterations are translations of a mode of daydreaming through objects. With nineteenth-century fetishism, one could see commodities having a life of their own in the market. With animation, one can see commodities having a life of their own on the silver screen, or even beyond, as did the girl with Bugs Bunny. Animistic mimesis is thus another translation of commodity fetishism. The consumer who envisions commodities as alive because of their exchange, the child who imagines a stick in their back garden as Mickey, and the one who plays in Disney's commodified world are illustrating, through the translations, both the kinship and difference in modes.

That animistic mimesis made such daydreaming consumers perceivable has abundant evidence. As daydreaming consumers became visible, Disney sought to mine this modal resource; they attempted to provide numerous surfaces for the daydreaming consumer's experience of an affective transfer. These attempts were very different from cinema's product tie-ins. Indeed, the articulable commodites were not tie-ins; Disney did not sell what Mickey wears or buys but instead the character image (usually face) itself transferred to a plethora of commodities. With the facialisation of the characters in mutual-affection images, the character's faces in turn become sources of value and significance. Disney's characters become entities of affection, what Deleuze calls *icons*, icons that represent living qualities or powers. Mickey's face emerges as an icon of pleasurable affection, impressed or affixed on to a variety of commodities to enhance their exchange value through the transfer of spiritual value. In short, the characters directly become the commodity, rather than indirectly as with tie-ins, where viewers identify with stars and thereby desire the commodity accoutrements of their individual images. Although Disney's character-images could be appropriated for a lifestyle mode of consumption, using Mickey's face on a T-shirt, for instance, to stand out or fit in, the commodities Disney most frequently articulated to the daydreaming consumer were not objects for consumer lifestyles. Instead of commodities for distinction, Disney mostly pursues commodities for affection, commodities that offer an enjoyable experience such as rides, plays, games, books, comics and toys. Disney's articulable commodities were most often *directly* fetishes crafted with their own semblance of life for this consumer's self-affection, not crafted for the lifestyle consumer's social orientation.

Once Disney envisioned a daydreaming consumer who enjoys self-affection through image-objects, they quickly capitalised by transferring their icons of affection to a plethora of commodity surfaces. Hence Disney became a pioneer in merchandising, transferring images to a countless number of surfaces. Soon, Disney recognises that its movies serve as just one of many platforms for the life of its characters and begins to use its movies in synergy with other merchandising campaigns. By the time of the full-length features, every new Disney movie was an occasion for a line of toys, clothing, books, games, and on and on. In fact, Ben Crawford contends that understanding animation demands attention to this 'paradigm' of synergy, 'which conceives of cartoons as one of a multitude of vehicles for capitalizing on character properties'.[43] Because it is 'more cost-efficient to transfer an image from one product category to another', synergy drives the culture industry and results in aggressive protection of intellectual property.[44] Indeed, animated characters with an aura constitute the ultimate commodities, the commodity as sheer dematerialised image, ready for surface transfer. Mickey's plastic nature allows him to cross national and cultural boundaries rapidly, carried along in the forms of movies, shirts, watches, bags, costumes, toys, games, music, radio, television and even tattoos. The plasmaticness and iconicity of Disney's animated images make their transfer to other media easier, getting rid of the stubborn material resistances of stars and fashion objects that age. These qualities also make Disney's images susceptible to reappropriation, compelling the zealous suing of anyone who infringes on its copyright. Since these animated characters cannot die despite their perceived life, Disney can profit repeatedly (and indefinitely if Congress continues to extend copyright) from the same animated characters but only if it does not allow others to replicate the images, only if it exerts control via trademark lawsuits. Reproducibility must be constrained for the aura to sustain, as Benjamin suspected.

Some, including Beller and Cubitt, describe cinema as the dematerialisation of the commodity. From a certain angle, this is undeniable; if we conceive of images as dematerialised, all movies, whether animation or live action, offer image-commodities. Yet the classical mode places much more emphasis on materiality than animation. The lifestyle mode is primarily social and relational, fundamentally about embodied behaviours and material milieus. The desires generated are corporeal and the 'messages' learned are primarily about comportment of the body-image, the lifestyle. Both stars and objects express through their materiality and garner their meaning through social relations. Animation, in contrast, paves the way for the dematerialisation of the commodity, or, to put it more precisely since all commodities come in material packages, the iconisation of the commodity. Just as with religious icons, where the image becomes a means for the viewer to achieve a transcendent experience, the perceivable daydreaming consumer can achieve pleasure solely through images, not by relating to others. Their self-affection becomes the purpose of their daydreams; they become the sole audience. Today, consumer culture features many such iconic commodities, with character faces transferred from surface to surface as emblems of affection in order to enhance exchange value. The widespread practice of branding follows a similar template, most often selling an affective experience as the very essence of the corporation, which becomes marked by their corporate icons. By illustrating the affective pleasures of daydreaming, Disney helped pioneer this practice of branding, articulating iconic commodities to the newly visible daydreaming consumers. The mode was indeed the 'message'.

In short, Disney's translation, much like cinema's translation into time-images, teaches that there are new ways to modulate reproducible image media, ways that can produce distinct and renewable affective experiences generating consumer desire. This emphasis on the modulation of desire marks Disney as a predecessor to the affect economy. In an affect economy, capitalists see affect as having exchange value and therefore, unlike prior social orders, seek to unleash flows of desire, deterritorialising the limitations on their free range. Corporations then brutally reterritorialise the opened territories, subjecting desire to capture through the mechanisms of control. For instance, modes like animistic mimesis are monopolised and marketed back to us, with consumers made to pay surplus-value for the privilege to plug into commodities and sued for copyright infringement when they do not. These are the indices of an affect economy, with Disney's tactics its epitomisation (as discussed in the final chapter) and the daydreaming consumer its prototype.

At this point, it may be tempting to conclude, along with many Disney critics, that Disney created these consumers, manipulating a pre-existing fetishistic desire. And certainly, it would not take long to discover certain collectors or children who fetishise Disney, filling their imaginations and rooms with Disney products. Yet again, this causal account presupposes the existence of a consumer with inherent desires, rather than conceiving subjects as desiring-machines whose modes make visible certain consumers and articulable certain commodities. Such an account begins with the consumer as the origin of modern consumerism and asserts the motivations of desire rather than asking the 'how' questions of desiring-machines. How do these consumers become perceivable? How do they daydream? How does the desiring-machine work? Armed with an understanding of animistic mimesis, the answers to these questions become much clearer. Animistic mimesis is the software of a desiring-machine, a daydreaming consumer body, that feels life in image-objects. These image-objects operate through an economy between semblance and play, necessitating surfaces with some representational fidelity but with room left for the play of imaginations. The desire is generated through this tension between semblance and play, the folding between knowledge and sensation. Instead of positing some deeper psychological motivation, a modal analysis helps us understand the experience itself as desirous, and helps us see what new consumers and commodities become perceivable through Disney's translation.

More evidence for the perceivability of this daydreaming consumer comes from Disney's subsequent corporate practices. With the spread of animistic mimesis, Disney begins to perceive children as a valuable market. Just as women are perceived as the appropriate target audience for the lifestyle mode, children 'make sense' as the primary demographic for daydreaming consumers. Indeed, many scholars have associated Disney with the emergence of a new notion of the child, which Nicholas Sammond describes as a 'discursive operation'.[45] Yet a modal analysis helps answer the question that lies just under the surface throughout Sammond's insightful work: why did these rhetorical shifts take place? Although Sammond illustrates that the notion of the child changes, how can we explain these changes?

A modal analysis explains these changes as the result of the strong connection between animistic mimesis and children. Children are often accustomed to the mimetic mode; kids imagine entire worlds surrounding their favourite stuffed animal or action figure. In a child's eyes, seat cushions become forts and sticks become swords. No wonder that such strong love for Disney is exhibited by children, or such a strong connection exists between Disney and a childish fetishism in the eyes of many critics. As the software of a desiring-machine, the desires of animistic mimesis are similar to the desires of childhood, the desires of animistic perception and mimetic play. Indeed, much of the subsequent debate over Disney revolves around the child and childishness, with proponents promoting the wonder and innocence of animation and critics fearing childishness and escapism. Disney's daydreaming consumer becomes translated as the child, with proponents and critics alike offering transformed understandings of what 'child' means.

In short, Disney's animation pleases by allowing desiring-machines to perceive life through mimesis, to achieve the affection of wonder via a transferability from imaginary worlds. Disney, in this sense, is a direct commercial appeal: it demonstrates that one can have desirable experiences through commodities. Disney creates image animism for an actual experience of mimesis – the crossing of senses, the entering of the screen, the becoming-cartoon. Thus animistic mimesis constitutes bodies that can achieve affective experiences through an image-object. These virtual bodies turn into consumer habits, as viewers learn that their own affective investments can turn the commodity into a pleasurable experience. It may be a single tear, a hearty laugh or a shriek of terror but it is at those moments of affection that the animated characters come to life, the daydreaming consumer becomes visible, and the desire to daydream through image-objects (commodities) is potentially bred. Affect becomes emotion and then becomes subject to capture in regimes of value.

In addition, Disney learns that it is selling the experience of animistic mimesis, of daydreaming, and hence seeks to offer this experience in other ways. Disney thus translates animistic mimesis to other media, such as the development of the Disneyland theme park. Today, Disney operates multiple theme parks but also stages plays, hosts cruises, owns theme-park–modelled stores and offers holiday packages, all with a similar aim – to encourage the consumer to daydream, to enjoy an affective transfer. Discussing a Disney play, Maria Wickstrom concurs that the provision of mimetic experience is crucial to Disney's success. The commodity becomes fetish through such mimesis:

> By creating environments and narratives through which spectators/consumers are interpellated into fictions . . . , entertainment and retail based corporations allow bodies to inhabit commodities and so suggest that commodities, in turn, can be brought to life . . . In this scenario, it is not through the commodity, but *as* the commodity that experience apparently takes place. Animated when a consumer steps into the as yet unembodied costume, the commodity then appears to take on a life of its own.[46]

Once the daydreaming consumer becomes visible, Disney seeks to proffer multiple avenues for that consumer to project into the image and envision the commodity as fully alive. In short, Disney learns an important 'message' from animisitic mimesis and the daydreaming consumer it makes visible. Disney learns that it is selling modes – experiences not products – and seeks to translate its mode into a wide variety of media. Each shares a kinship, through translation, with animistic mimesis, but each also transforms this daydreaming consumer. Today, such daydreaming experiences have become so prevalent, with many of Disney's techniques for constructing consumer-spaces so widespread, that a critic like Baudrillard can fear that reality has been exterminated, displaced with daydream simulations. Baudrillard's fear is the result of numerous consumer industries, including Hollywood, eventually deciphering a similar 'message' as well. The culture industries realise that they are selling not only toys or fashion, a movie or a star. They learn that they are also selling modes, modes that enable pleasurable affective experiences. Selling modes, rather than commodities, becomes the name of the game. By selling modes, they can sell renewable, potentially inexhaustible experiences. This renewability is perfect for the insatiable and rapid pace necessary for modern consumer culture. Thus Disney, along with many other Hollywood giants, began racing to expand its offerings in a variety of media, illustrating the fundamental connection between media and consumerism that today seems so evident. As Disney translates its animation into new media, it pioneers the future for culture industries – the selling of modes. Selling modes in a variety of consumer media allows the selling of renewable, desirable experiences necessary to keep pace with the rapidity and insatiability of consumerism.

Animistic mimesis also offers an extremely ripe 'message' for the American Dream, that old stand-by ideology of consumerism. Animistic mimesis suggests that one can achieve one's dreams via the imagination, by wishing upon a star rather than engaging in the right actions to transform the milieu. A more perfect 'message' for the consumerist ideology of the American Dream can hardly be imagined, since it erases the labour necessary to make such consumer dreams come true. The following chapter traces the translation of animistic mimesis into a version of the American Dream. This translation provides further evidence of the newly perceivable daydreaming consumer. Of course, the translations are far from uniform; animistic mimesis evokes some contradictory evaluations. Proponents defend Disney as the work of an Uncle genius, full of harmless play appropriate for children. Opponents fear, instead, a watering down of true artistic genius and the spread of childishness. As we shall see, Disney's daydreaming consumers are heaven to some but hell to others. Yet across these translations, a distinct Disney version of the American Dream, with poles different from those of classical Hollywood's American Dream, remains. Critics and proponents alike 'make sense' of animistic mimesis in remarkably similar ways.

CHAPTER 7

The Disney Version of the American Dream

As noted in the Introduction, Massumi and Grossberg each contend that affect is the 'origin' of ideology, both the source from which ideology is translated and the reason that ideology sticks or persists.[1] This is a position similar to Benjamin's idea that ideology is a collective expression of the conditions of existence, and a position that this chapter elucidates in relation to the modes of classical Hollywood and Disney animation.[2] Massumi also depicts ideology as expression, as the translation of empirical events into another process – the processes of cognition and language. He does so, in one essay, through an example with remarkable resonances to the notion of sparks advanced throughout *Special Affects*, a lightning strike. The lightning strike is an event, an actualisation or expression resultant from a virtual, charged field of electricity. Once the strike occurs, it becomes material for expression in other processes, such as evidence of Zeus' anger and therefore support for myths of the gods. The lightning strike, as expression of a virtual field, becomes translated into rhetoric and myth, in short, into ideology. As Massumi writes:

> Creative to the last: so generously creative is expression that it agrees to its own conversion. It allows its process to be prolonged into a qualitatively different mode of operation. It flows into rhetorical captivity . . . The flash doesn't disappear into the black of night. It continues. Its pick-up by a different process is the price of its continuing. Its culmination, the effect of its playing out (in this case a strikingly optical effect), feeds forward into another productive process for which it provides a content.[3]

As cultural lightning strikes, then, the special affects of astonishment, marvel, the fantastic and wonder likewise provide material for ideological expression, for the translation of these affects and modes into rhetoric about consumer culture. It is no surprise, then, that an abundant stream of rhetoric about consumption accompanies the consumer boom of the early to middle twentieth century. People recognise the dramatic changes of modern consumerism and seek to make sense of those changes. As the lifestyle and daydreaming consumers become newly visible, rhetorical translations of the consumer and consumerism emerge.

Unfortunately, most of the scholarship on consumer ideology sees a striking similarity in these expressions, replicating the error of conflation critiqued throughout this book. In other words, consumer ideology is often described as the continual reproduction of sameness, the perpetual repetition of specific, limited codes such as the American Dream. Indeed, the conflation of media and modes enables this conflation of ideological analysis that can recognise only sameness rather than difference in emergence. Many critics have performed such conflating analysis in relation to Disney, with Adorno perhaps the most representative.[4] Adorno perfectly illustrates the conflation of media and modes and the resultant discovery of sameness in ideological expression. He conflates film, sport, music, television and radio together under the moniker of the culture industries because for him only one medium matters – the commodity. As he states, 'For all contemporary musical life is dominated by the commodity form.'[5] For Adorno, commodification turns all art into simplistic and repeatable formulas fitting for a childish audience.[6] The commodity's impact on film or music ensures a single, static and regressive mode common to all media. The fact that cultural products have become commodities, that they are made for and shaped by the market, is the determining factor. The commodity form dominates communication media, transferring its presence to all cultural fare. Thus the 'messages' Adorno consistently garners from his analysis are related to the alienated consumer and capitalist ideology. The message is always the same old American Dream:

> The customary reference to 'dream factory', nowadays employed by the representa-
> tives of the movie industry themselves, contains only a half truth – it pertains only
> to the overt 'dream content'. The message of the dream, however, the 'latent dream
> idea' as promoted by motion pictures and television reverses that of actual dreams.
> It is an appeal to agencies of psychological control rather than an attempt to unfetter
> the unconscious. The idea of the successful, conforming, well-adjusted 'average'
> citizen lurks even behind the fanciest technicolor fairy tale.[7]

Daily, the culture industries broadcast abundant evidence for Adorno's claim; tales spun in American Dream yarn permeate the airwaves, and millions of screens flicker with images oozing childishness. Yet Adorno's conclusions are belied by a perspective focusing on affect and modes that both denies the conflation of media and understands (ideological) emergence as the expression of these differences in mode and affect, expressions that also differ. Rather than media commodities conforming to their means of production, the theory of expression or translation advanced here is

> a theory of change . . . the insistence that what emerges does not conform or correspond to anything outside it, nor to its own conditions of emergence . . . Determination is a differing. Emergence is always of the different: every genesis a heterogenesis. A thing's form does not reflect its formation. It inflects it.[8]

We can expect, then, that the American Dream, as our representative of consumerist ideology, becomes differently inflected when translated through the frames of cinema and animation, as illustrated in this chapter. A long-standing ideograph, the American Dream continually suggests that dreams are real possibilities; change can occur for anyone who follows the right course.[9] Yet the American Dream becomes translated into different versions in classical Hollywood and Disney features, transforming from the success myth of earlier American lore, into the classical Hollwyood version evidenced in *20,000 Leagues*, and again into a magical theory of social change represented by Disney. The Hollywood and Disney versions are underwritten by different *models of communication* that offer various explanations for how such change occurs. The Hollywood version suggests dreams come true for those who engage in the correct behaviours or the appropriate social comportments. In contrast, the Disney version claims that dreams come true for those who engage in the proper imaginings; the individual experiences a transformative becoming when they pursue a dream or wish upon a star.

As the previous sentences hint, these versions of the American Dream and their basic models of communication articulate to the economies and -abilities of the classical Hollywood mode and animistic mimesis. They are ideological translations of these modes, the making sense of consumer practice in another practice – language. In other words, the medium is the message in a literal sense; media structure experience in such ways as to help constitute specific linguistic messages. This is not a new premise; scholars such as Walter Ong, James Carey and John Durham Peters have illustrated how media alter understandings of communication. Peters, for instance, argues that the spread of radio encourages the conceptualisation of communication as dissemination rather than dialogue.[10] Carey argues that the telegraph leads to a model of communication as the linear transmission of information, just as the telegraph transmits dots and clicks along lines of electricity.[11] While the erudite work of Carey and Peters serves as a model for this chapter, few scholars have advanced this line of research, seeking to articulate other models of communication accompanying other media. This chapter pursues such a development through the examination of cinema and animation. In so doing, I show how the modes of Disney and classical cinema are translated ideologically, resulting in models of communication evidenced in different versions of the American Dream.

A Brief History of the American Dream

Of course, such translations do not begin from a blank slate but emerge in a culture with an ideological and rhetorical history from which the translations depart and to which the translations respond. As Massumi remarks, expression 'takes place in a cluttered world. Its field of emergence is strewn with the after-effects of events past, already-formed subjects and objects.'[12] Therefore we should begin by elucidating the history of the American Dream metaphor. Whence came the American Dream? Is it just another nebulous metaphor, a favourite trope for the crafters of rhetoric? At first glance, the latter seems likely; the openness and plurality of the metaphor seem necessary to admit from the beginning. For instance, Americans are familiar with politicians of all stripes painting the dream in different strokes, from Franklin Roosevelt and Bill Clinton to Richard Nixon and Ronald Reagan.[13] The content of the American Dream also lacks singularity. A few scholars have ostensibly studied the 'American Dream', treating the phrase as a placeholder for any public goal or longing. Hence, their analyses result in a smorgasbord of ideals weaving throughout the course of the nation – from puritan asceticism to democratic populism to consumer abundance.[14]

Few of these studies, however, examine the uses of the actual phrase 'American Dream'. For instance, Jim Cullen's *American Dream: A Short History of an Idea that Shaped a Nation* may appear to follow the metaphor's life.[15] Cullen divides his work into six chapters representing different versions of the dream, covering the Puritan's dream of religious freedom, the dream of universal rights, Benjamin Franklin's dream of upward mobility, King's dream of equality, the suburban dream of home ownership, and the Hollywood dream of glamour. Yet the first three chapters do not provide any historical evidence of the phrase 'American Dream'. This is because during the eighteenth and nineteenth centuries, the phrase had not entered common parlance. Cullen's approach may be valuable for understanding the various goals of Americans across history, but they do little to tell us about how the metaphor operates in rhetorical circulation. For example, why express goals, ideals or longings as *dreams*? What makes the Dream *American*?

The phrase 'American Dream' first emerged in the early twentieth century and usually refers to a public desire or longing. Nevertheless, what desire or goal seems quite variable, even subjective. For instance, rhetorical scholar Walter Fisher contends that the American Dream denotes two narratives– the rags to riches story of individual success and the egalitarian myth of national brotherhood.[16] Yet these two myths do not exhaust the various articulations of the American Dream. Just to list a few, the American Dream is: the rags-to-riches tale, the middle-class lifestyle, becoming a celebrity, another melting-pot metaphor, a true democracy, a classless society, racial equality, universal education, westward expansionism, capitalism over communism, and the illusions peddled by the entertainment industry.[17]

When a concept represents such a diversity of ideas, we can also expect both praise and criticism to follow. The writer often credited with first penning the phrase 'American Dream' was James Truslow Adams in his 1931 *The Epic of America*.[18] Adams saw the American Dream as the idea that any person of any class or any background could climb the social ladder. He lauded the American Dream as 'the greatest contribution we have as yet made to the thought and the welfare of the world'.[19] For Adams, writing during the Great Depression, the biggest threats to the dream were monopolisation by profiteers and the reduction of men and women to selfish consumers. He believed the American Dream could never be brought into a reality by 'keeping up with the Joneses' and thus proposed a more equal distribution of wealth.[20]

Despite Adams's insistence that it was 'not a dream of motor cars and high wages merely', most detractors see the American Dream as precisely this – an expression of consumerism.[21] In this take, chasing the dream car, job and house results in a meaningless life of rote labour and escapist leisure. Critic after critic of consumerism equates the American Dream with the fantasies of the culture industry. As Daniel Boorstin writes in *The Image or, What Happened to the American Dream*, 'We risk being the first people in history to have been able to make their illusions so vivid, so persuasive, so "realistic" that they can live in them. We are the most illusioned people on earth.'[22]

Through all this diversity of speakers, meanings, associations and evaluations, the American Dream metaphor lives. Some may disagree on how to define it, but like most ideographs, the metaphor stays alive through its ambiguity and flexibility in use.[23] Nevertheless the metaphor emerges at a specific time, and some similarities remain across this flexibility in translation, similarities that point to the economy of the metaphor, the poles of the American Dream. First, what might account for the time period of the metaphor's emergence? The historical record is full of 'images of possibility' that do not refer to dreaming as a primary metaphor. Why does the American Dream metaphor make sense in the early twentieth century? Including Freud, dreams were certainly on the public mind at the time. Everyone from the Surrealists to advertisers, Hollywood executives to staunch socialists, Benjamin to Carl Jung insisted on the import of dreams. In my estimation, dreams grew to such a stature in public discourse because they seemed manifest in the features of consumer culture. Consumerism provided evidence for the reality of fantasy and proof of the American Dream. Dreams had become reality. In addition, cinema and animation seemed to encourage the indulgence of dreams. Thus shortly after the metaphor's first usage, Horace Kallen wrote in 1936, '"The American Dream" is a vision of men as consumers, and the American story is the story of an inveterate struggle to embody this dream in the institutions of American life.'[24] In fact, we can envision the American Dream as the ideological expression of consumerism, functioning, as does all ideology, to promise the possibility of social progress and often to mask power and the relations of production. The prospects of achieving your fantasies are not equally distributed or accessible; suggesting anyone can become famous or wealthy, can become a Henry Ford or Walt Disney, is much closer to deceit than description, even given the few exceptions.

This emphasis on the link between the American Dream and consumer culture is not to suggest that there are no other uses of the phrase. The qualification of early American consumer culture simply serves to limit my analysis and is based in a historical justification since the phrase first emerges in the second decade of the twentieth century, concomitant with the emergence of many features of modern consumerism. The question remains, however, what does the American Dream metaphor express that allows it to articulate to consumer experience? In all its historical uses, the American Dream is a metaphor portraying fantasy as a real possibility. Metaphor is a perspectival figure whereby one term (dream) is seen through the frame of another (America); the American Dream metaphor envisions dreams through the frame of America. Due to the contrasting relationship of *American* and *Dream*, the metaphor creates a perspective that sees fantasy as a real possibility.

Typically, the Dream element stands for some kind of envisioned desire or longing. This sounds akin to Freud's theory, popular at the time of the metaphor's emergence, whereby dreams express wishes; they are wish fulfilment in elusive, imagistic code.[25] The Dream represents a fantasy or an idealised vision. Yet if the American Dream were just a fantasy, it seems unlikely that it would have attracted such widespread use during the twentieth century. Fantasies have been part of human culture from time immemorial; thus there must be more to this metaphor. Metaphors operate through contrast; the comparison births a new perspective. So, what comparative contrast is represented in the American Dream? If the Dream represents fantasy, then the *American* element stands for possibility. What makes the Dream uniquely *American* is the connection to a long-held myth – the idea that America is the land of possibility. As chronicler of the American frontier Frederick Jackson Turner liked to say, 'America has been another name for opportunity.'[26] America was dubbed the 'land of opportunity' precisely because many saw it as a place without history. In popular understanding, America is a place of the future, which stands for possibility. As Cullen adduces from his study, 'At the core of many American Dreams . . . is an insistence that history doesn't matter, that the future matters far more than the past.'[27] Of course, the details vary but the story of possibility and opportunity remains.

The contrasting economy embodied in the American Dream metaphor, then, is fundamentally between fantasy and reality. The American Dream indicates that fantasies are real possibilities, materialised in our waking lives. In this sense, the American Dream sets up a unique relationship between dreams and reality with specific obligations. The stress on possibility means that the American Dream will only continue to attract and circulate if evidence of its possibility seems to exist. The American Dream continues to circulate through its perceived actualisation, when certain features of the socioeconomic landscape become interpreted as proof of the dream's possibility. The American Dream metaphor lives through the renewal of popular recognition that dreams have become reality. Throughout the twentieth century, the lives of the people responsible for modern consumerism and the products they produce are translated into evidence of the American Dream. Through such figures as John Wanamaker, Henry Ford, Walt Disney and William Levitt, people 'saw' the reality of fantasy. The public acceptance of these as indexical icons is indicated by the countless number of books, articles, speeches and broadcasts that refer to these people and their products through the metaphor. The continued circulation of the American Dream feeds upon such icons.

When told in narrative form, American Dream stories employ a basic template, each depicting what scholars call a rhetorical situation. Lloyd Bitzer, who coined the concept, describes the rhetorical situation as 'a complex of persons, events, objects, and relations presenting an actual or potential exigence'.[28] Bitzer's realist and instrumentalist interpretation of the rhetorical situation has been heavily critiqued, but understood differently, we can simply envision the rhetorical situation as a portrayal or representation of a speaker, audience and exigence. American Dream narratives readily fit this template, depicting a person (dreamer) who faces an exigence, negotiates the constraints, and communicates their dream to society, making the dream a reality. For instance, Walt Disney (an Uncle genius) transfers his dream to audiences (the child in all of us) by developing an illusion of lifestyle and overcoming the competition.

For most critics, the American Dream constitutes consumerist ideology and is envisioned as a response to the emergence of mass consumerism. According to this take, an ideology of consumerism becomes necessary in the face of consumer capitalism's widespread inequalities and uprooting of tradition. Keeping the public subservient demands that they believe consumerism offers the opportunity for their dreams to come true. The American Dream responds to this call, in the interests of the powerful. The problem with such an interpretation is that it ignores the various contradictions and changes in meaning of the American Dream, as well as the variety of consumer modes and the diverse understandings of consumerism. Such a view conflates all versions of the American Dream and conflates all potential exigencies under a single one. As evidenced throughout this chapter, the metaphor is employed by many different rhetors in numerous variable contexts with widely divergent evaluations. In short, top-down ideology theory ignores the prior question of how such personas, exigencies and situations become perceivable.

Furthermore, this ideological position entails an instrumental model of communication that envisions discourse as a transparent means of portraying reality. That is, the situation clearly presents an exigence to which (powerful) rhetors respond. Once again, the history of the American Dream and consumer culture deny such instrumentalism. The interpretations and evaluations of exigencies vary widely, such as the extremely divergent conclusions about the effects of consumerism. In sum, just as there is a multiplicity of consumer modes, there are also numerous translations of the American Dream metaphor. What, then, are some of the versions? How has the American Dream been translated in the context of classical Hollywood and Disney?

Versions of the American Dream: From Alger to Hollywood

Many historians trace the proto-versions of the American Dream to the late nineteenth century. They label these early versions the 'success myth' – the belief that a hard-working individual can and will succeed, traced to Puritan roots.[29] Horatio Alger did the most to popularise this myth. Alger wrote in the late nineteenth century, producing over one hundred novels as 'undoubtedly the most widely read author in the world'.[30] Every Alger story follows the outlines of the American Dream template, telling of a gritty and dedicated poor person who fights their way up the ladder to riches. Alger's rags-to-riches stories fed the imaginations of America's first consumer generation.

Some scholars equate the American Dream with the Alger myth; however, the success myth dates from much later than the phrase's origin, and the American Dream includes many versions beyond the success myth. Nevertheless, the success myth represents one translation of the American Dream. This version relies upon a model of *communication as labour*. Social change occurs for the upwardly-aimed individual via hard work. One of the early definitions of communication is communication as transportation; 'a train communicates down the tracks', or 'a road is a primary vein of communication' because, prior to the emergence of disseminatable electronic media like the telegraph and radio, in order to send messages, space had to be traversed.[31] This is close to the notion of communication underwriting the success myth. In order to transport oneself up the social ladder, one had to labour to manœuvre one's way up the rungs.

Given this stress on transportation and labour, it is hardly surprising that one of the most popular icons of the success myth is Henry Ford. Narratives of Ford told via the American Dream template typically unfold according to the Algeresque model, emphasising hard work as the means to climb the social ladder. Indeed, discussions of Ford cannot seem to resist the dream metaphor. To take just one of innumerable examples, Charles Murphy depicts Ford as 'the businessman, source of the new economic dispensation, the embodiment of the American Dream – the farm boy who became a billionaire'.[32] Ford contributed significantly to the public perception of his life through interviews and self-published books. Importantly, this perception was quite distant from the persona of a typical dreamer. Ford preferred the populist, Alger-esque persona of Progressive era America, including its worldly pragmatism and dedication to hard work. If Ford subscribed to the metaphor at all, then his explanation certainly minimised the import of dreams. For him, *work*, much more than dreams, drove progress. He so frequently repeated Thomas Edison's saying, 'Success is one-tenth inspiration and nine-tenths perspiration,' that Ginny Olson catalogues it as a 'Fordism'.[33]

In short, Ford and the automobile are frequently translated into a version of the American Dream emphasising work. A model of communication as labour underwrites the Ford and Alger versions of the American Dream; those who work hard can change their fortunes, can communicate their way up the social ladder. This success myth version of the American Dream was common and popular at the time of Hollywood's maturation. Many classical movies employ the same narrative template, telling rags-to-riches stories about those who exercise the right effort. Yet there is something different in many Hollywood versions of the American Dream, a different translation making sense of a different mode. As Joss Marsh notes, 'It is important to understand how very much Hollywood helped recast that dream for the twentieth century . . . The movies have loomed large in the ongoing production of the twentieth-century American Dream.'[34]

Analysing these changes requires recognising how the rags-to-riches theme, underwritten by a model of communication as labour, does not quite describe the Hollywood version of the American Dream. Indeed, as Larry May calculates, only 1.5 per cent of the movies shown in the 1920s feature the rags-to-riches theme.[35] The classical mode's focus on the comportment of stars, on lifestyle, on standing out, on individuality, led to a tendency to prefer different narrative themes. More common themes included social change via right consumption or by changed personality. In other words, crafting the right lifestyle was portrayed as the means to achieve the dream. May states, 'In the age of cooperation, personality is a commodity that will advance one up the ladder.'[36] As such, these Hollywood versions structure an economy between standing out and fitting in, or between behaviour and milieu – the two poles of the Hollywood American Dream, according to Deleuze. The Hollywood version is an action-image, moving from situation to action to transformed situation (SAS'); only those whose behaviour appropriately responds – we might say 'comports' or 'transposes' – to the milieu will achieve social change.

Of course, these two poles include a wide variety of narratives and genre, grouping many otherwise dissimilar movies. Yet what they share is a particular model of communication as comportment. Social change comes via correct behaviour; those who comport themselves to the situation can ensure the Hollywood ending. Characters who appropriately transpose themselves to the milieu, who adeptly translocate their attentions, can achieve the happy ending, the transformed situation, the American Dream. The appropriate comportments vary widely across movies and genres, yet the classical cinema remains tied to this behaviourist version of the American Dream. Deleuze, in fact, links the Hollywood American Dream to most classical genres and most famed directors. We see the poles of behaviour and milieu in documentaries, psychosocial films, westerns, 'birth of civilisation' movies, and in the monumental history genre (gladiators, war films, and the battle of good and evil). On a more clichéd note, we have already seen how the Hollywood American Dream shapes Disney's *20,000 Leagues*, as it does their other live-action offerings, including *Treasure Island* (1950), *The Story of Robin Hood and His Merrie Men* (1952) and *The Sword and the Rose* (1953).

The poles of the Hollywood version are similar to the two 'myths' of the American Dream that Fisher outlines, the materialistic myth of individual success and the moralistic myth of egalitarian brotherhood.[37] Rather than, with Fisher, envisioning these as competing myths, however, a modal perspective understands them as the terms of a shared economy. In the classical mode, there is no tension between individual and community, materialistic and moralistic success, or, in our terms, standing out and fitting in. For classical Hollywood, the individual star's behavioural successes save the community; their material comportments lead to moral achievement. The transformed milieu requires individual action but this action is socially oriented, concerned, as with the lifestyle mode, with the appropriate fit into the social picture. The classical mode sparks the translation of American Dream narratives into a model of communication as comportment; the individual must adapt their behaviour to the milieu. These narratives might contain affection-images but achieving the Dream requires action in the context of a community-milieu, not just self-affection. Disney, while maintaining action-images and the SAS' pattern, shifts the emphasis to affection; social change becomes about individual transformation, like the transformation of child into adult, and communication becomes about the transfer of imagination and feeling to another surface.

From the Hollywood to the Disney Version of the American Dream

The association between Disney and the American Dream is widespread, almost taken for granted. Walt's life story, the art of animation, and the themes of Disney features are all tagged with the metaphor. As Kathy Jackson says, introducing a collection of interviews, 'Disney seemed to be the personification of this American moment and the American Dream.'[38] The connection between Disney and the Dream is no surprise because animation is often linked to dreams. The linkage dates to the earliest animated movies. McCay, who drew Gertie the dinosaur, called his debut series *Dreams of Rarebit Fiend*, and another early pioneer, John Bray, released his first work in 1913, entitled *The Artist's Dream*. These cartoons used the dream as a framing device to demarcate between fantasy and reality, and Disney's first series, based on *Alice in Wonderland*, also used a dream sequence.

Yet the Disney version translates the Hollywood version, transforming the American Dream. The Disney version suggests that social change results from dreaming, that all it takes is a dream to make one's dreams come true. This theory of social change, a magical theory of social change, underwrites Disney's animated films. This interpretation relies upon a model of *communication as transfer* that is, like animistic mimesis, a dual transfer, both a surface and an affective transfer. As an ideological expression, the movies' narratives suggest that characters transform through mutual affection, that transfers of affect can create surface transformations.

Of course, as a hybrid translation, elements of both the success myth and the Hollywood version remain in Disney. Most of the stories, for instance, follow the SAS' pattern, rely on action-images, and demand a negotiation of the milieu to achieve the happy ending. Yet these Disney movies are more about transforming the self rather than the milieu. For instance, Snow White does not act to save the day; the Prince saves her by the simple acts of showing up and kissing her. At the end of *Bambi*, the forest has not noticeably transformed. Pinocchio returns home to live with his father, and Dumbo continues to work for a circus. The transformation that occurs is not of the situation but of characters. As we saw previously, these are stories of animistic becomings, the metamorphosis of maid into princess, of toy into boy, of elephant into bird, of child into adult. The milieu changes too – the danger is replaced by the happily-ever-after – but the bright future stems primarily from the transformation of character rather than the alteration of situation.

Additionally, the beliefs, emotions and imaginations of the characters matter more than their behaviours; comportment is secondary to mindset altered by affection. Each story relies on a model of communication as dual transfer, as mutual affection. Snow White dreams of falling in love (affective transfer) and is saved by a kiss (surface transfer). Dumbo's actions are crucial to his becoming-star, but he has the ability to fly all along. Dumbo simply has to believe in order for his ears to become wings; through an imaginative affection (represented by the 'magic' feather) his surfaces transform. In fact, Timothy continually encourages Dumbo, instilling in him the goal of being a star and a belief that he can fly, demonstrating again that the relationship of these two epitomises Disney's mutual affection.

Similarly, Pinocchio rarely engages in the right actions. Throughout the movie, he gets into trouble due to his naïveté about how 'good boys' are supposed to comport themselves. He is conned into serving Stromboli, lies to the Blue Fairy, is enslaved by the Coachman, and is nearly turned into a donkey before he does something right. It is affection that spurs him to this right action; Pinocchio is so saddened by Geppetto's disappearance that he embarks on a mission to find him. This affection results in his surface transformation, the becoming-boy of Pinocchio. He helps them escape the belly of the whale and then his body magically transmutes from wood to flesh. In fact, the entire movie emphasises that the becoming-boy is about mindset rather than action. The Blue Fairy tells Pinocchio that he must be 'truthful and unselfish', and appoints Jiminy to teach him to have a conscience. Certain actions demonstrate that Pinocchio has learned the lesson, but his actions represent the coming-to-surface of deeper affections. By being mutually affected, Pinocchio becomes boy.

Even if actions still play a role in Disney's hybrid movement-time images, the emphasis on hard work is certainly jettisoned. The movies stress, instead, that the right dream leads to transformation, not the right effort. The characters simply must adjust their minds and hearts, not roll up their sleeves. The characters 'Whistle while they work', singing that 'One day my Prince will come,' that 'When you wish upon a star, your dreams come true,' that when you wish into a well, 'Your wish will soon come true,' that 'With the healing of just one heart / Stars align in heaven / Love lights the Dark.'[39] These are all individual dreams and wishes, about *just one* heart and its affected transformation. Actions matter to a degree but they are not socially oriented. The stories are about individual-becomings, like the child becoming an adult. They are not stories of heroes saving the day for the community but of individuals changing themselves so they can live happily ever after. This is why I call this a magical theory of social change; the magical dual transfer transforms the individual, allowing them to achieve the reality of their fantasy, the American Dream.

Interestingly, the story of Walt Disney is also told through this version of the American Dream. The biographies emphasise that Walt had a humble Midwestern upbringing, priming his story for an Alger-like treatment. By 1934, the *New York Times Magazine* would call Walt the 'Horatio Alger of the cinema ... who through industry, courage, and all the other Algerian virtues achieved international recognition'.[40] That same year, *Fortune Magazine* would proclaim, 'Enough has been written about Disney's life and hard times already to stamp the bald, Algeresque outlines of his career as familiarly on the minds of many Americans as the career of Henry Ford or Abraham Lincoln.'[41] Through the repeated corporate and popular portrayals, Walt is perceived as 'the archetypal American rags-to-riches story'.[42] Gregory Waller notes the persistent linkage: 'Seen through the rose-tinted prism of popular journalism,

Disney's life story became a homespun mythic saga and a reassuring affirmation of the American Dream.'[43]

What is Walt Disney's dream, according to popular accounts? The short answer is to make animation into a respected art form. Biographers and journalists frequently trace this dream to his pre-Hollywood days in Kansas City. They retell Disney's story of the train ride he took from Kansas City to Hollywood to get a fresh start in animation. A man on the train asked him what was his business in Hollywood, and Walt replied 'I make animated cartoons.' Apparently, the gentleman looked at him as if he was crazy. Disney put it this way, 'It was like saying, "I sweep up the latrines."' The incident angered him, and he later recounted that he thought of that man on the night *Snow White* premiered to record-breaking success in 1937.[44] Many friends and co-workers also report that Disney believed animation would become a new art form. As artist Millard Sheets reported after a conversation, 'Walt felt that a new art would be born, a new concept of motion pictures. This was his whole dream.'[45]

So far, Disney's connection to the American Dream seems typical, following the Alger mould and composing a story of fantasy become reality. Yet the Disney version departs and diverges from the typical 'success myth' and the Hollywood versions alike. First, the accounts emphasise Walt Disney's dreaming, downplaying Alger's insistence on labour. Walt summarised the interpretation, 'Everybody can make their dreams come true. It takes . . . a dream – faith in it – and hard work. But that's not quite true because it's so much fun you hardly realise it's work.'[46] Although the Disney Studio employed over one thousand workers and hence required a Fordist division of labour, observers emphasise that the fun atmosphere and creative freedom were starkly different from the mind–numbing and spirit-sapping repetition of a Ford factory. Employees and the press frequently lauded the Studio for its open, democratic and fun environment.[47] *Fantasia* star and esteemed critic Taylor exclaimed, 'How can you grow up in this atmosphere, for God's sake? It's like living in Santa Claus's workshop.'[48] The inkers, painters, secretaries and janitors at Disney probably did not share Taylor's pleasure. Undeniably, producing Disney animation requires the tedious and often joyless labour of thousands. Yet in the accounts of Disney's rise, having a dream is often stressed as the most important element because, in Walt's dream, the dream and the medium of its realisation were the same thing. Disney dreamed of making animation into an art and achieved this dream by making animation. The doing *was* the dream. This theory of social change still requires labour, but a labouring to dream.

In Disney's corporate rhetoric, this 'all it takes is a dream' motif was a common vehicle as well. The idea that 'if you can dream it, you can do it,' that 'all your dreams can come true if you have the courage to pursue them,' that 'when you wish upon a star your dreams come true,' and that there are not 'any heights that can't be scaled by a man who knows the secrets of making dreams come true' became popular slogans and the common interpretation of Disney's accomplishments.[49] Journalists and scholars often advance this version as well. Scholar Luca Raffaelli marvels at this new articulation of the American dream:

> It is truly remarkable how Disneyan discourse manages to merge with the American model . . . Cinderella's dream is an ambitious one: but everything is possible in America so long as you hold onto your dreams, as long as you don't throw away the opportunity when it comes.[50]

Shortly after Walt Disney's death in 1966, this version of the American Dream was still circulating. Journalist Norman Vincent Peale hailed Disney as proof of the power of positive thinking: 'In America motivated dreams can come true . . . When you get discouraged and feel like throwing in the sponge, just remember Walt Disney and Mickey Mouse.'[51]

Dreaming, rather than behaviour or labour, underwrites the Disney version's take on social change. This version of the American Dream is based upon a model of communication as transfer. The biographies emphasise that Walt Disney was a poor drawer, did not direct, and did not write the screenplays. Instead, they portray his unique talent as a talent of the imagination, the ability to transfer his ideas to others, by acting it out for the animators. Capodagli and Lynn describe *transfer* as the unique feature of Disney's talent: 'It is no easy matter to convey a dream. Dreams are, by nature, deeply personal experiences. But true to his imaginative genius, Walt Disney was able to transform his dreams into stories that effectively articulated his vision to others.'[52] Eisenstein also saw Disney's genius as one of transfer. He marvelled at how Disney 'transports into one world what he has seen in another, into the spiritual world, what he has seen in the physical world'.[53]

Such an interpretation of social change is nothing if not ideological. A more perfect message for consumerist interests can hardly be imagined. The idea that dreams come true simply by wishing them, as if by magic, is denied by nearly every socioeconomic reality. The suggestion that anyone can simply transform themselves serves the interests of those already at the top, not least because consumer capitalism thrives when people pursue individualised transformation rather than collective effort. Thus Disney's numerous critics indict the movies on similar grounds, faulting such sugary-sweet messages for promoting a patriarchal, racist, national-ist, capitalist and consumerist ideology. Disney's movies deny or ignore more fundamental socioeconomic realities, interpellating subjects into a delusional, imaginary relationship with the social world. The volume of such criticism could fill a small library.[54]

To take an example from the previous chapter, Schickel, one of Disney's first and harshest critics, was also one of the first to critique the Disney version of the American Dream, concluding, 'They are huckster words.'[55] Schickel's contempt proceeds from his belief that Disney perverts the American Dream. In the Disney version, success only takes a dream; it is a magical theory of social change. The translation of the American Dream drops Ford's hard work and Hollywood's call for the correct behaviours. Rather than 90 per cent perspiration and 10 per cent inspiration, the Disney version reverses the formula, placing the emphasis on dreams rather than the work. Rather than an individual negotiating a milieu, the individual mediates themselves and their imagination. Rather than work or comportment, dreams require magic – the magic of dreaming.

These abundant, similar criticisms share a common thread stringing back to the model of communication underwriting Disney's version of the American Dream. With different inflections, each criticism denounces Disney for elevating the individual over the social, for putting personal happiness over collective justice, for suggesting the milieu need not change, and for downplaying the necessity of effort and struggle. The cri-tiques read: Disney suggests that individuals have the agency to transform themselves, however the realities of race, class, gender, power and nation deny such prospects. Disney implies that the current situation promotes happily-ever-afters when most experience misery and oppression. Disney promotes escapism rather than active resistance, individualism over col-lective struggle. Despite their differences, then, these criticisms all fault Disney due to the primary features of the Disney version of the American Dream. The criticisms represent another attempt, like the attempts of the biographers, the marketers and the moviemakers, to make sense of the mode of animistic mimesis.

Implications for Ideology Theory

Recognising the differences in ideological expression, such as the transla-tion into the Disney version of the American Dream, has implications not only for the shape of consumer culture but also for one of its most commonly practised analytical tools, ideological criticism. Ideological critics like Schickel, Adorno and many others correctly acknowledge that the Disney version overemphasises the possibilities and downplays the obstacles. For Schickel, this distortion results because 'hucksters' perpetuate the Disney version of the American dream for selfish gains. For Adorno, the commodity form imprints hidden messages onto every media experience. The role of ideology and power should not be dismissed and specific interests (including the Disney Corporation) certainly benefit from American Dream ideology. Yet seeing the corporate speaker or huckster as origin precludes answering many questions relevant to the constitution of rhetoric like different versions of the American Dream. This is because this interpretation relies on an instrumentalist model that ignores the constitutive import of media and modes. In contrast, the perspective advanced throughout this book understands the Disney version of the American Dream as a translation, the social capture or molarisation (to use a Deleuzian concept) of new virtual bodies and affects.

What are some limitations of the interest-based, ideological explanation? First, how can a collective phenomenon such as the American Dream metaphor be attributed to some speakers and not others? Which ones? Why did they choose the terms magic and dream? If the choices are arbitrary, why are dream, magic, child, innocence and other terms so persistently connected to Disney, by proponents and opponents alike? Also, if such words are obviously the fare of hucksters, easily seen through and only able to evoke a 'faint queasiness', as Schickel contends, why does the Disney version continue to circulate? Must the critic assume that the audience is composed of suckers susceptible to the manipulations of hucksters? Further, what determines the speaker's perspective? Why do these speakers, especially ones not employed by the corporation, choose to defend Disney?

These questions reveal the inadequacy of an instrumental model of communication portraying ideology as simply a tool of previously positioned interests. In these takes, rhetoric instrumentally conveys the chosen meanings, either hiding or exposing the speaker's 'real' interests. Discourse mediates between the speaker and the audience, seen as two stable, separate and pre-existing entities. Discourse only transmits the meanings based on previously existing interests and perceptions. Schickel and many Disney critics rely on this instrumental model of communication. Discourse remains ancillary, a means of transmitting meanings whose basis rests elsewhere, either in the exigence or in the speakers.

Special Affects challenges such a typical explanation. A modal perspective envisions ideology as the result of attention, habit and affect, the 'making sense' of various sociocultural practices. The widespread existence of the Disney version of the American Dream, evident in the movies and the corporate rhetoric but also in the discourse of scholars, historians and other social commentators, indicates that there is something more occurring than the simple imposition of ideology. There has always been active and far-flung criticism of and resistance to the Disney hucksters. Yet the linkage between animation, the Disney version of the American Dream, and the associated constellation of metaphors such as the child, imagination, wonder, genius and innocence persists among advocates and critics alike. Instead of conceiving that a controlling exigence or a dominant interest constitutes the rhetoric about Disney and consumerism, a modal theory conceives rhetorical situations such as the Disney version of the American Dream as collectively constituted, the result of a certain perceivability of new consumers and commodities due to the emergence of new modes. Ideology emerges via the making sense of common practices of communication; the American Dream is a rhetorical translation of various modes, translations that vary and even contradict, yet that share a similar process of making sense of our new, virtual bodies and the concomitant affections experienced.

History also confirms that such emergence is the production of difference, rather than sameness. Contrary to Adorno's insistence that all consumer media promote the same modes and infuse the same hidden messages, the major lesson of post-1950s American capitalism seems to be that counter- and resistant messages sell, too.[56] In more recent history, hate for the American Dream makes more dough than the old mould, as *Wall-E* will illustrate in the concluding chapter. Anti-consumerism, green consumerism and ethical consumerism are all new commodity fads. The hidden messages Adorno points to have been recognised and resisted, met with contempt and boredom alike, and corporations have learned that diversity and rebellion can also grease the wheels. Consumer desires, as well as the media of commodification, have changed, in turn sparking adaptations by the culture industry. What Adorno's analysis cannot decipher is why these changes take place, what makes new consumers and commodities perceivable. What forces motivate these changes? The commodity has existed for centuries, so why does the commodity and fetishism take a particular shape in the early twentieth century? If the commodity is the dominant medium whose effects are tragically predictable, why, then, has the commodity form and consumer practice altered over time? How did these new consumers become perceivable?

Paying specific attention to the various consumer modes offers a superior explanation for the spread of fetishism and modern consumer ideology. Rather than contending that commodification imprints all media in a similar manner, modes point to diversity of interfaces between consumers and media, and their differences in affect/effect. An analysis of modes allows that cinema and animation, translated through the commodity, often favour ideological messages similar to the American Dream, as Adorno contends. Producers can transfer hidden ideological cues to the surface yet, as we have seen here, these messages are not uniform. Different versions of the American Dream change in relation to the substance of the medium and the perceptions and affections of audiences. Modes depend on engagement; modes even illustrate that the perceptual experience has become the commodity, that consumers achieve pleasure from affecting and being affected. Understanding these modal affections and the subsequent desires requires going beyond ideology theory to an analysis of the modes, those emergent bodies of different, virtual consumers.

In stark contrast to Adorno, Douglas Brode goes against the grain to celebrate the liberatory potential of Disney, arguing that Disney galvanised the 1960s counterculture. He exhaustively illustrates the persistence of themes such as anti-conformity, pro-rebellion, pro-environment and anti-religion throughout the Disney corpus. Brode contends that such themes fed the dissatisfaction with reality that fuelled the 1960s social movements. Disney movies so affected audiences that, rather than seeking more escape, they were stirred to change their realities. Thus Brode concludes that Disney 'may now be considered and viewed as something of a radical'.[57]

Yet Brode also relies on an instrumental notion of communication, simply inverting Adorno's priority. Instead of being imprinted like a surface, the audience's affective investments generate creative, even resistant, agency. Such a view places the emphasis on the second transfer and praises Disney for innervating powerful desires. Such a view also ends with a case of debilitating rhetoric that praises consumer media because audiences interpret resistive and liberatory values from the content. Ending with such praise leaves the waste, oppression and destruction of consumer capitalism in place. It celebrates the affective transfer while ignoring or downplaying the surface transfer, specifically the monopolistic control of cultural surfaces. While Disney's content might, at times, promote resistance, there is still a significant need to counter many of their corporate practices. The corporation recognises that transfer is the name of their game, and they seek to transfer their images to every possible surface. Furthermore, Disney's reliance on transferable images presents them with a problem, one they must seek to control. The very plasmatic nature of their characters allows for their easy reproducibility, often in locations or manners that Disney does not approve. Disney responds by stamping their products with the Disney trademark and vigorously pursuing copyright protection. 'Disney has always employed what his daughter termed a "regular corps of attorneys" whose business it is to pursue and punish any person or organisation, however small, which dares to borrow a character, a technique, an idea patented by Disney.'[58]

This copyright stance is a result of animation's transferability and indicates one of the major ways that Disney represents a precursor to the digital economy and, especially, the control society, as further outlined in the final chapter. In fact, transfer has a third definition taken from the legal sphere that reads 'to make over the possession or control of'. This third form of transfer is a form of legal magic, seeking to protect the semblances of Disney images from the play of cultural appropriation. Thus Disney reins in the liberatory potentials of affective transfer by subjecting the surfaces to legal sanction enforced through copyright law and armies of lawyers, whose threats alone deter even most fair use of their images. Furthermore, transferability drives Disney to become a multinational media conglomerate with control over a vertically integrated entertainment empire. If Disney controls all the surfaces, then it can control the transfers. Ownership of the television and radio waves, the video rentals and cinemas, the comic books and children's stories, the toys and clothes, we might say *the paper and plastic screens*, leaves publics with few spaces for their own creative and resistive appropriations of the common stock of images. As a result, we can transfer our images to screens but only for a price. Unfortunately, the price is too high for most. Disney's oligopolistic control creates a major impediment to competition and diversity in culture. Worse yet, given the spatial and temporal dominance of these media empires, they dominate public discourse, posing a serious threat to public space, discourse and hence democracy by refusing to air or by outright belittling alternative perspectives.

In sum, ideological analysis of Disney relies on an instrumental model of communication, rather than understanding ideology as the collective expression of modes and their affections. Disney's proponents celebrate the affective transfers, praising Disney's artistic genius and the child-like wonder. The opponents condemn the surface transfers, fearing a spread of childishness and the control of art by giant corporations. Each side bears some truth, yet each presents an incomplete case and a limited understanding of change, of ideological emergence. In contrast, a perspective focused on modes and affects envisions Disney animation as a complex translation resulting in some distinct cultural and rhetorical 'messages', in McLuhan's sense. Outlining such 'messages', as has occurred throughout *Special Affects*, aids in understanding the history of consumer culture as well as the changes that the emergence of digital media is causing to cinema, animation and consumerism. Analysis of the classical Hollywood and animistic mimesis modes, as well as the daydreaming and lifestyle consumer, has provided a historical basis for comparison and a picture of the materials that these new, digital translations modulate. It is thus to an analysis of the digitalisation of animation and consumerism that the final chapter turns.

CHAPTER 8

Walt and Wall-E in Control Society

Today, with the proliferation of digital devices and the computer's remediation of nearly every prior medium, the connection between media and consumerism may seem apparent, even obvious, a given part of the social environment. Just as consumption of digital devices and products such as games, websites and apps continues to expand into multi-billion dollar industries, so too does much consumption of more materialised commodities like toys and clothes occur via digital networks. *Special Affects* began with the recognition that consumer booms seem to accompany the emergence of every new medium, extending this connection between media and consumerism into the early and middle twentieth century, and has illustrated why such a fundamental connection exists. The virtual-abilities of media enable new relations with human folding capacities, constituting new modes – newly virtualised bodies. These modes facilitate the generation of creases, splits or fusions in the folds, allowing different parts of the body–mind to rub against one another, producing friction that, when reaching a heightened intensity, creates affective sparks. Those sparks, as they are habituated, become sources of value and are translated into consumer ideology and practice, making newly visible consumers and articulable commodities as well as new templates for the American Dream. That is, people seek to 'make sense' of these modal experiences and affects, in turn producing the cultural practices of consumerism as well as rhetorical understandings of that culture.

Special Affects demonstrates this conclusion through the oft-told case of classical Hollywood cinema and Disney's full-length features of the late 1930s and early 1940s. Disney and classical Hollywood translate the marvellous spark of early animation and the astonishing spark of early cinema, producing modes for the innervation of the fantastical spark of classical cinema and the wondrous spark of Disney. Although cinema and animation evoke other affections, the novelty of the marvellous, astonishing, fantastic and wondrous sparks helps explain the great attraction (and distress) of these media, an attraction responsible for the consumer booms that accompany their emergence. As people feel the astonishment of early cinema, the marvel of early animation, the fantastic spark of classical cinema, and the wonder of Disney animation, they make sense of those affections, translating them into regimes of consumer value and ideologies of consumerism. Doing so, the perceived consumers and commodities along with American Dream narratives become transformed. Affect becomes captured, personalised into emotion and molarised into institutions of the consumer economy, thus explaining the fundamental connection between consumerism and media so evident today.

In contrast to much previous history and theory that tend to conflate different modes of media and consumption, beginning with modes and affects retells the mid-twentieth-century emergence of Disney's full-length features as the unfolding of difference rather than sameness. Rather than simply a part of cinema, as Benjamin, Deleuze and many others maintain, Disney animation presents a unique mode of animistic mimesis, one translated from prior modes such as graphic narrative and classical cinema. Yet rather than being distinct from the visual space of live-action cinema, as McLuhan contends, classical Disney animation translates cinematic techniques, creating a hybrid mode that draws upon cinema's creation of Renaissance space through transposability and trans-locatability, as well as animation's transformability and transferability. Rather than, as Benjamin implies, simply one of the reproducible media responsible for the decline of aura, animistic mimesis translates auratic modes, relying on the viewer's endowment of life (the ability to look back) on to the image-object via an affective transfer. Rather than assimilating animation to cinema's movement-image regime, then, as Deleuze does, this retelling uncovers the mutual affection-images of animistic mimesis, which constitute hybrid movement- and time-images.

When turning to the impacts of Disney animation on twentieth-century consumer culture, this series of 'rathers' expands. Rather than furthering the success myth or Hollywood versions of the American Dream, animistic mimesis becomes translated into the Disney version of the American Dream, a narrative stressing self-transformation through the magical power of dreaming. Rather than exclusively a contributor to a generally cinematic, post-Fordist regime of consumerism, Disney animation illustrates the diversity of modes, affects and desires fuelling consumer culture. Rather than a part of a consumer culture bent on selling commodities for lifestyle consumers, animistic mimesis makes visible a daydreaming consumer who generates affect and hence desire directly through image-objects. Rather than teaching consumers a form of narcissism based in a self-image that either stands out from or fits into a socius full of camera-eyes, animistic mimesis makes visible a daydreaming consumer who fetishistically imagines life in commodities. Thus rather than articulating and selling commodities for distinction, Disney seeks to produce commodities for affection and transfer its icons of affection from surface to surface. Rather than selling material goods for the management of self-image, Disney, and soon many others, begin proffering modal experiences for the generation and capture of affect.

In short, by translating the classical Hollywood mode, Disney helps instruct culture industries in a primary lesson that today dominates the affect economy and control society – *that the mode is the message*. Since there are many modes of the moving image, Disney is far from alone in teaching this lesson, yet its hybrid time- and movement-images and its reliance on generating a pleasurable affective experience mark animistic mimesis as an important contributor to this message. With Disney and other translations of the classical cinematic mode, the culture industries learn the central conclusion illustrated throughout *Special Affects* – that there is a fundamental connection between media and consumerism. Such a conclusion may seem obvious today, yet we should remember how astonishing, wondrous, marvellous and fantastic were the emergent media of the time, how people had never before experienced such splits and fusions to their selves, and thus how these new modes ruptured the sense of self that accompanied prior modes, thereby provoking new conceptualisations of subjectivity. Indeed, for the culture industries, learning this lesson demanded a new understanding of their audiences. The culture industries had to learn that media were not just a new attraction for individuals with pre-constituted bodies but also the opportunity for new bodies, new modes, whose special affective experiences can vary greatly and thereby constitute new consumer subjects who prefer different commodities.

Today, the proliferation of media has made apparent both the connection between media and consumerism as well as the diversity of modes, illustrating McLuhan's thesis that the emergence of new media exposes previously taken-for-granted grounds of the social. These exposed grounds are why scholars have recently stressed concepts such as affect, the cyborg, the posthuman and the interface as crucial to understanding the present sociocultural condition. *Special Affects* has demonstrated that such concepts can assist in re-evaluating media history as well, while arguing that performing an ethology of modes can contribute significantly to both projects. As a concept, modes add to this ongoing scholarship by providing a way of understanding bodies as distributed in time and space, as an interfacing of relational, virtual capacities. Doing so, the concept not only escapes the division between subject and object dogging many prior theories, a division that other concepts such as affect, cyborgs and the interface also critique, but modes also provide a means of performing critical analysis that avoids the historical, technological and social conflations critiqued throughout this book. Conflation erases change and difference, and thereby erases history and the series of translations through which cultural forms, practices and habits emerge. Conflation thereby works against an understanding of the motivations and operations driving cultural becomings. Conflating the rhetoric of consumerism dampens a deeper understanding of motivation by downplaying the distinct affections of consumer modes; the attraction of early and classical cinema, of graphic narrative and animistic mimesis, cannot be encapsulated by categories such as 'postmodern' or cinematic consumerism, nor by the same metaphors of dreaming and childishness, of escapism and innocence. Conflating modes also precludes a more robust analysis of the operations of desiring-machines; people learn to interface with different consumer media in different ways not reducible to the general platitudes of technological determinism, ideological analysis or the modernity thesis.

For scholars, conflation's limitations point to the need to continue attending to cultural emergence from the perspective of affect. Affect directs focus on the differing dynamics of molecular experience, both to the level of the interactions and orientations that generate affections as well as to the animations of affect – the movement, life and differing that occur in transition from one moment to the next. Thus, hopefully, *Special Affects* has made a theoretical contribution to affect studies as well, illustrating the need to append any exploration of affect with an exposition of modes. As argued in the introductory chapter, affect and affection flow forth from (and feed back into) particular manners of relating or orienting toward the world. Modes allow us to conceive and describe bodies as in motion, in duration, as distributed in an environment, as always engaged in relations, and thus as continually affecting and being affected. Performing an ethology of modes thereby helps explain how and why particular affections are generated, and a recognition of different modes helps preclude the conflations that media-, ideological or era-focused analyses tend to produce.

Since *Special Affects* repeatedly argues against conflating media, contending that media and consumerism are fundamentally connected and that the culture industry learns a central lesson may seem to be a contradiction because it conflates Disney animation and many other media. Yet contending that history is an unfolding of difference from the angle of affect and modes does not preclude recognising shared trends from a different angle. Indeed, the molarisation of these special affects is precisely their sedimentation into habit, their institutionalisation into consumer capitalism, and the provision of resources for their regularised repetition. Molarisation produces sameness from difference, and this production of sameness from difference is our lesson from a media history based in a theory of translation, modes and affect. Translation, due to its economy between freedom and fidelity or the non-translatable and translatable, illustrates both the kinship between modes and the transformation that occurs in their evolving growth and renewal. Translation reveals a shared heritage and a transformed life because it operates through an economy of fidelity to its past and creative licence with respect to the future. Translation is a process of generating difference *and* repetition. Therefore, although attending to differences in affect, approaching media history from the perspective of modes does not preclude recognising kinship in translation. In fact, a careful analysis of the differences in mode helps more precisely illuminate what those media share as well. Thus *Special Affects* has prepared the ground for outlining, as a way of concluding, what today's digital translations of cinema and animation share with the classical cinematic mode and animistic mimesis. In what ways does the digital remediation of cinema and animation share a kinship with these previous modes and, more importantly, in what ways do they differ? As a result of these differences, what impacts on consumer culture can we expect to emerge as people begin to make sense of the changes?

The Digital Translation of Animation and the Future of Consumer Culture

To begin, we should first ask what kinship the digital translation of animation shares with animistic mimesis. The answer is, in short, that Disney's translation into animistic mimesis constitutes a predecessor of the affect economy and a precursor of control society. Disney is a precursor of control society in two ways. First, Disney's animistic mimesis signals a new perceivability of the consumer, away from the individuals of the lifestyle mode targeted and understood according to demographic categories (masses) into a consumer understood as a conglomeration of affections, what Deleuze calls dividuals. Dividuals are subjects conceived not as indivisible individuals, who are moulded into pre-determined forms by disciplinary techniques, but as divisible bundles of affects that emerge in the transition from one modulation to another. Whereas cinema's lifestyle consumers sought to become an individual who stood out from the crowd, the dividual continually modulates himself or herself to produce different affections, affections that demarcate the subject as belonging to a population defined according to those affections, rather than a mass defined by demographic categories. As Deleuze states, '(C)ontrols are a *modulation*, like a self-transmuting molding continually changing from one moment to the next . . . Individuals become "*dividuals*", and masses become samples, data, markets, or "*banks*".'[1]

Computers enable and enhance both aspects of control society. Computers proliferate modes, enabling the production of a wide variety of affects and thereby enticing the perception of subjects as dividuals, and they also facilitate the data-tracking of those dividuals into populations known as markets or banks. Yet animistic mimesis can nevertheless be called a precursor of control society since it flags the emergence of the dividual. Animistic mimesis illustrates that media can differently divide – split or fuse – elements of the embodied self, creating new creases in human folds that can become sources of affection. Via animistic mimesis, subjects become differently divisible, split or folded into relations of self-to-self that innervate affects. Of course, this potential to divide, split or crease the subject differently comes with every medium, yet Disney signalled the emergence of an understanding of the dividual via its difference with classical cinema, which relied upon a notion of the individual and the mass rather than the dividual. Indeed, Walt Disney advanced this understanding of the consumer as a dividual, and the shared kinship with digital animation specifically and digital media more generally, in his conceptualisation of his audience as 'The Mickey audience'. Disney explicitly rejected the idea that his audience was made up of children, a demographic grouping based on age, and instead advanced an understanding of his audience as dividuals, based upon certain capacities for affection:

> Everybody in the world was once a child. We grow up. Our personalities change, but in every one of us something remains of our childhood . . . It's where all of us are simple and naïve without prejudice and bias. We're friendly and trusting and it just seems that if your picture hits that spot in one person, it's going to hit that same spot in almost everybody. So, in planning a new picture, we don't think of grownups and we don't think of children, but just of that fine, clean, unspoiled spot down deep in every one of us that maybe the world has made us forget and that maybe our picture can help recall.[2]

Second, Disney also signals the coming tactics of control society: namely, control. Control society generates markets not by specialising or improving production but by controlling access to the interfaces for affective experience. 'The digital language of control is made up of codes indicating whether access to some information should be allowed or denied.'[3] As noted previously, the plastic, reproducible nature of Disney's icons motivated a stringent copyright stance, which seeks to deny access to anyone who does not pay the piper. Digital media today, especially due to their easy sharability, have greatly enhanced the battles over copyright and the attempts by corporations to control access to their products, with Disney's ferocious prosecution being the common response, at least initially, as the many copyright suits and controversies around file-sharing in the music industry demonstrate. Disney's control tactics also extend beyond copyright. Disney uses its movies as the opportunity for a synergistic, multimedia marketing campaign, controlling access to these offerings by gobbling up ownership of all types of mediated surfaces. Today, such cross-media integration and marketing have become common practices, resulting in the extreme concentration of media empires through corporate consolidation. Indeed, the 'culture industry' seems an extremely prophetic moniker, with each of the five major conglomerates selling culture writ large, dominating output in all sundry media.

Such battles over access and control make Deleuze's remarks on control society seem equally prescient. Yet since Disney constitutes a precursor of control society long operating according to its logics, his prescience turns out to be, instead, insightful analysis of conditions that were already foreshadowed during Deleuze's day. In addition, Disney represents a predecessor of the affect economy by instructing in the profitability of selling affections via modes. Disney exemplifies the shift, also occurring with the time-image, from the attractions that beckon audiences to 'look here', which dominated earlier entertainment culture, to a 'feel here', or a 'come here and experience' directly the possible affections of a new virtual body. Different attractable contents simply provide new avenues for the renewal of modal experience, and it is this renewability that addresses the dilemmas of boredom, fatigue and scarcity faced by consumer capitalism reliant on selling material goods instead of immaterial experiences. The special affective pleasures of a mode can be returned to again and again, enticing further consumption as the affections become habitual, anticipated and pursued. Selling affect thus helps fuel the brisk pace and seeming insatiability of modern consumerism. Affect's renewability makes it a perfect source of value for capitalism, as long as culture industries can continue to produce and control new modes. Media prove to be powerful allies in the task.

Manovich has attended to this shared kinship, noting how digital cinema is becoming more like animation.[4] I concur that a shared kinship can be traced between digital cinema and earlier animation, especially since digital cinema relies on compositing computer-generated imagery (CGI) with live-action film, thus enhancing the role of transferability and increasing the amount of frame-by-frame construction. Yet when Manovich turns to the differences, to what makes digital media 'new', his comparative example is primarily live-action cinema. Indeed, much live-action cinema now relies more on transferability since the live action is composited into scenes with CG bodies and into digitally constructed, three-dimensional spaces. Yet while live-action cinema may be becoming more like animation, animation is also transforming, moving away from the frame-by-frame construction and the reliance on transferability. Thus our proceeding analysis enables us to recognise the differences between animation and digital cinema as well. So, as a way to conclude, I will turn briefly to the Disney–Pixar CG animated movie, *Wall-E* (2008), with the caveat that a more thorough investigation than one movie remains necessary. *Wall-E* reveals some significant differences in -abilities and perceivable consumers from Disney's initial feature movies, differences that beckon a more complete analysis of the modes of digital animation in future work.

Specifically, how Pixar constructed *Wall-E* with computer graphic technology reveals some significant differences in -abilities from hand-drawn animation. Computer animation typically proceeds through three major steps known as modelling, animating and rendering.[5] First, animators create a model of the space, objects and characters, detailing their size and other capacities such as movement. We can call this *modelability*. Then, animators place these models into space by rendering (*renderability*): that is, by telling the computer where the 'camera', 'lights' and models are located, as well as detailing how shading and shadows interact with the models and their various surfaces (since light bounces differently off skin or glass or rock surfaces). Finally, animators instruct the computer on the models' movements, including the effects (affections) resultant from their interactions. The computer then fills in the movements from point A to point B, based on the capacities of the models (*animatability*). A final, post-processing step includes such processes as image compositing (combining a live-action clip within the animated scene), blending and retouching.

Modelability, renderability and animatability mean that the transferability between layers becomes much less important if not irrelevant (only occurring at the post-processing stage). Instead, each object constitutes a model, and the models interact through their rendering and animation, not through the transfer of the figure on to the background. The rendering stage imitates many of these transfers, and the animating stage produces the movements that were constructed via the in-between drawings in Disney's earlier animation. These -abilities make for a few important differences. The bodies on the screen are not figures placed on a layered stack but are placed into a three-dimensional environment composed via digital code. Since the models and environment share digital substance, transferability does not adequately describe the capacity relating the models and the environment. These are not separate layers but separate objects, which must, through programming, be instructed how to relate to one another. In other words, the computer animation directs the relation of environment and model by programming certain capacities for affect and affection, telling the models how they react and relate to the environment and vice versa, both visually at the rendering stage and physically at the modelling and animation stages. In other words, the models and environments have built-in capacities for movement and affection, capacities that were only drawn in animistic mimesis rather than inherent to the model, wherever and whenever it moves in the three-dimensional environment.

Second, the movement is not so much a transformability from pose to pose, which is filled in by in-between drawings and the viewer's sense of movement. Instead, the computer generates the movement; it actualises the capacities for movement and affection of the virtual body (model). Thus while the computer may operate frame by frame, the animator operates instead with a model, programmed with capacities for animation. The artist does not directly transform the figure frame by frame and the images are not placed in a stack, requiring the management of the various layers. In short, the animation becomes automatable, rather than generated by the tedious work of in-between drawers, with automatability being one of the characteristics of digital media according to Manovich.

In sum, then, the capacities of three-dimensional computer animation necessitate conceiving of bodies as *modes*, as certain relations of capacities or potentials for affection and movement. The modelability and animatability of computer animation constitute a field of potential for the bodies. Such bodies are modes, bundles of virtual capacities, actualised in movement and related to one another via rendering. Such a view correlates closely with the theoretical perspective advanced in *Special Affects*, which has taken the socioecological changes of digital media as an opportunity to retell an episode of media history. Such a perspective results, via translation, in a newly perceivable consumer as well – the consumer as mode-switcher or dividual – which is evident throughout and critiqued in *Wall-E*. *Wall-E* tells the futuristic story of a rubbish-compacting robot left behind on an abandoned, trashed Planet Earth. Wall-E assiduously compacts trash under orders from humans, who now live on a giant spaceship called the *Axiom*, far from the uninhabitable Earth. The humans have been floating for 700 years, yet they periodically send probes (represented by EVE, Wall-E's love interest and co-star) to search for signs of life in the form of plants. EVE (an extraterrestrial vegetation evaluator) finds a plant and ships come to return her to the space cruiser. Wall-E hitches a ride, not wanting to lose his love, and the two proceed to try to save the plant, awaken the humans from their pleasure-induced stupor, and persuade them to return home.

Wall-E evinces much kinship with previous Disney animation, especially in some particularly moving mutual affection-images featuring Wall-E and Eve, and John and Mary (the main 'human' characters). These mutual affection-images feature the same blinks and opening mouths (intensive micromovements) contrasted with the reflective surface of the other character's face, done with even more precision due to the technological capacities of digital animation. Gone, however, is animistic mimesis, especially since the synchronisation of sound and movement is basically non-existent. *Wall-E* is not a musical and seems much closer to classical cinema rather than stressing a mimetic communication between character and viewer. Furthermore, *Wall-E* demonstrates some differences in the 'making sense' of digital media expressed at the level of content. Unlike classical cinema and Disney animation that sought to hide the technological production of the films, *Wall-E* makes digital technology an explicit part of the content, issuing a dire warning about the connection between media and consumerism, about the consequences for humanity and the environment of rampant, continual mode-switching. Indeed, *Wall-E* begins by portraying the American Dream in ruins. Not only has consumerism wreaked planetary ecological havoc, but long gone are the individuals of American Dream tales, whether of the Disney or Hollywood versions, replaced by mode-switching dividuals whose everyday activities are controlled by the *Axiom*'s mainframe computer. The humans on the *Axiom* float in hover chairs along controlled pathways, communicating to the world via screens that can switch modes (from games, to video, to phone and so on) at the push of the button. Not only has such mode-switching led to a trashed planet and turned humans into lazy, nearly immobile blobs, but the people on the *Axiom* also seem to have lost many of the personal connections and affections of human relationships. The last remnants of human individuality persist in an old VHS tape of *Hello, Dolly* and the lonely robot it has inspired to stand out, Wall-E, whose task is to free the humans from their control and awaken them to the benefits of individuality.

In short, *Wall-E* is, as Sobchack has recognised, a media ecological allegory, one that cautions against the rise of digital media and mode-switching dividuals while singing the praises of the motion picture, animated and live action alike, and mourning their decline due to the competition resultant from the proliferation of computer-based media.[6] This warning attests to the mode-switching consumer perceived by the moviemakers. When Wall-E reaches the space cruiser, we are introduced to the humans, who all look like oversized babies. These humans move around on luminous blue tracks via hovering recliners with attached screens, through which they communicate and interact with the world. One scene shows John floating along, talking through the screen to his friend, who floats right next to him. They discuss what to do today; John proposes golf but his friend expresses his boredom, saying they did that yesterday. The camera pans out to reveal thousands of humans floating along, talking through and interacting with the multi-windowed screens as robots serve their every consumer whim. Shout out for a parasol or a drink, and a robot comes immediately. Other scenes show robots cutting hair, doing makeup, playing tennis, cleaning and feeding. The advertisements for the monopolistic, corporate overlord 'Buy-N-Large' instruct consumers that blue is the new style, and with the switch of a button, clothing changes from red to blue. John tries to hand Wall-E his finished cup, which Wall-E refuses to take, causing John to spill out of his lounger. Robots immediately come to reroute traffic around John and instruct him that service bots will be there shortly to assist him into his chair. Here we learn that the humans are so overweight and atrophied that they can barely walk on their own. Wall-E then sees EVE being taken away; he chases after her and jumps into a train compartment with EVE and some humans, including Mary. Wall-E tries to get by Mary, who is so distracted by her screen that she does not notice him. Wall-E breaks the screen, causing Mary to awaken and stare in awe at all of the thousands of billboard screens covering the inside of the ship and beckoning further consumption. She exhales, 'Woah,' then exclaims, 'I didn't know we had a pool.'

In *Wall-E*, humans interface with the world via computer screens, and their interaction is almost exclusively directed towards leisure-based consumption. With the flick of a button, they immediately switch from one mode of consumption to another. Robots are programmed with singular 'directives' (compacting rubbish, cutting hair), and humans are controlled via the tracks along which they move and through the screens and buttons they push to have their consumer whims fulfilled. Access to consumption is facilitated but moving outside the prescribed channels and tracks is forbidden. Life has become a pleasure cruise, and, importantly, even the captain has to be told by the mainframe computer about things like gardening that used to occur on Earth. These scenes provide an explanation for why Earth has become uninhabitable. Humans engage the world solely through mediated consumer channels and have thus so lost touch with each other and nature as not even to be aware that they have trashed the entire planet. The mode-switching consumer has resulted in the ultimate form of control, an entire socius whose access is regulated by computers programmed by a single corporation, Buy-N-Large.

The movie suggests that the solution to such a situation is to break out of control, to become individuals, to cease mode-switching in order to tend to one another and to plants, especially via love and gardening. Robots and humans alike become affected to become individuals by Wall-E, who follows his heart, not his directives. These humans and robots then begin to act differently, noticing one another, awakening to the immediacy of their bodies and environment, pursuing a greater good by not attending to consumerist desires. The movie claims that access to so many modes has led to the atrophy of human and natural bodies, and only the concentrated attention to one another (via love) and to plants (via gardening) can save us. Those who break out of the control via their continual mode-switching begin to tend to one another rather than attend to various consumer products and experiences. Eventually, Wall-E and the newly awakened EVE, John, Mary and the Captain save the plant from the robots programmed by Buy-N-Large to extinguish it and return the cruiser to Earth, with the Captain instructing children in the basics of gardening and Wall-E and EVE finally figuring out how to hold hands (since their hands are so different). Love and gardening will renew the Earth, or so we are led to believe through the typical happily-ever-after ending.

Wall-E thus constitutes a translation of the American Dream for the digital age, even if its translation is fundamentally nostalgic for a prior era in which motion pictures held the premier position in the media landscape. As expected, this ideological translation has garnered much attraction and distress, with *Wall-E* promoting a necessary environmental consciousness for some and with others lambasting the movie for promoting leftist propaganda. How can we describe the affections sparking such translations? Here, much more research into this movie and other computer animation needs to be done. However, reviewers repeatedly describe the film as wonderful, astonishing, marvellous and numerous other synonyms, especially stunning and amazing. Most find the first half of the film, the part on Earth without any human presence, as the most remarkable. In this half, the computer animation is so realistically rendered that one cannot see the artifice of form, as we can with Disney's earlier, more cartoonish characters. The trashed Earth and the moving robots appear as if they have been shot with a live-action camera (Figure

Figure 8.1 Computer-animated photorealism in *Wall-E*.
(Screenshot from *Wall-E* DVD)

8.1). Indeed, in a couple of scenes there are composited live-action images of the CEO of Buy-N-Large talking on a billboard, yet those live-action images appear old, faded and less lifelike than the astonishing animated images. As one reviewer, Ryan Cracknell, states:

> (I)t's easy to marvel at the film's computerized beauty … Like all Pixar films, *Wall-E* strives to push the technical boundaries of computer animation. This time out the focus is on the smallest of details: dirt, grime, dust storms, fire extinguisher foam floating in space. The line between live-action and animation is further blurred with the inclusion of *Hello Dolly* and the speech snippets from the always funny Fred Willard. Foreground or background, the details are everywhere with vivid clarity.[7]

We can call this special affection the marvellous astonishment. The wonder remains in the mutual affection-images, yet something else tickles or strikes. Viewers know this is computer animation (marvel) yet are stunned or amazed by the astonishing, lifelike movement. This astonishing marvel over the computer generation of lifelike scenes also stuns and attracts many videogame players, as evidenced by the constant push for more hyper-realistic graphics and their celebration and admiration by players with every new advance. This special affection, like the movie itself, its version of the American Dream and digital media more generally, is a hybrid one, combining aspects of pre-digital animation's marvel and live-action film's astonishment. Hybridity thus seems to be a difference between earlier film and the digital. The computer mixes all previous art forms, translating them into a digital code that enables their entering into hybrid relations much easier than was possible before. This hybridity represents a major difference between hand-drawn animation and computer animation, and is on display throughout *Wall-E*, with its seamless combination of live-action and computer-animated worlds. Hybridity is also represented throughout *Wall-E* in the characters, with robots who behave like humans and humans who behave like computers (as mode-switchers).

Such hybridity offers some unique insights into the changing landscape of the contemporary media ecology due to digital media, especially explaining why *Wall-E* constitutes an ode to cinema as a whole despite the fact that it offers a seemingly new and different iteration of (animated) cinema. *Wall-E* sings the praises of cinema throughout, portraying an old movie (*Hello, Dolly!*) as the inspiration that teaches Wall-E human affection, modelling Wall-E on Buster Keaton and Charlie Chaplin, and paying tribute to the silent cinema, with the first half of the movie containing very little dialogue and instead relying upon non-verbal forms of communication.[8] Rather than being concerned with the distinction between live action and animation or the digital and the analogue, as some scholars maintain, *Wall-E* suggests that the hybridity of digital media pushes live action and animation closer together. The hybridity of digital media troubles many of these prior distinctions, creating a media environment where cinema and animation, whether digital or analogue, share much more in common – such as their centralised distribution, their status as an experiential attraction, and their projection on the big screen in a darkened cinema – than they do with the mobile, miniaturised, wireless media that dominate the contemporary media ecology.

If digital media's hybridity makes animation and live-action cinema more similar, as Manovich and *Wall-E* both suggest, how do digital media also alter the media ecology in ways that make cinema (animated and live action alike) fundamentally differ from other, common digital media? Primarily, *Wall-E* contends that the difference is a difference in the direction of movement and the degree of interactivity and immersion. Whereas live-action and animated cinema were both attractions, requiring the viewer to come to the cinema, mobile, digital media go to their audiences, enabling mediated consumption to occur in any-space-whatsoever. Whereas cinema relied on the passivity of the viewer and their immersion in the cinema and film, mobile, digital media profit from the interactivity of the consumer and their ability to switch rapidly between modes in any-space-whatsoever. Such a distinction is not purely fictional but, at least in part, adequately describes the contemporary media ecology. Indeed, mode-switching constitutes one of the primary -abilities of the computer, especially with its windowed interfaces. As Steven Johnson notes:

In an average day working at a computer, chances are you switch back and forth between dozens of different modes without thinking twice about it . . . You have a mode for creating a new text document; a mode for editing an existing spreadsheet; a mode for rearranging a file directory; and a mode for changing your system preferences . . . [Windows] were a way of representing *modes* – and, more important, a way of switching back and forth between modes.[9]

The proliferation of media enables such an environment of mode-switching, with Disney's translation being one of the predecessors. As these modes, these virtual bodies, become captured by corporate regimes, with their access limited via mechanisms of control, media and consumerism prove powerful allies indeed. Despite the hypocrisy of a major player in the consumer economy critiquing consumerism, *Wall-E*'s warning against such an environment of consumerist mode-switching resonates with many of the critical concerns underwriting this book: namely, concerns that consumer culture pillages the environment and exploits labour, with devastating consequences for both found in species extinction, disease, global warming, resource wars, oppression, sweat shops, slavery, hunger, and racial and gender oppression. As Deleuze remarks, in control society,

A man is no longer a man confined but a man in debt. One thing, it's true, hasn't changed – capitalism still keeps three quarters of humanity in extreme poverty, too poor to have debts and too numerous to be confined: control will have to deal not only with vanishing frontiers, but with mushrooming shantytowns and ghettos.[10]

Such horrible conditions, fuelled by a consumerism aided and abetted by the media, makes *Wall-E*'s message desperately needed. Perhaps the solution of more love and gardening may seem simplistic, yet both represent modes quite different from the mode-switching marking the current media ecology. Love and gardening require the patient investment of time, a tending rather than a continually shifting a-ttending, tending to the affects and affections, the bodies and manners, of an other, rather than seeking self-affection via consumer mediation. Gardening constitutes a mode, a virtual body related to plants that requires tending, hearing the requests of another life form, watering when they need watering, feeding when they need feeding, pruning, picking, weeding and staking. Likewise, love is not expressed in *Wall-E* by name nor conceived as a blissful state of perfect union but is portrayed as a mode, a manner of affection accomplished through such acts as holding hands with another. Interestingly, love and gardening are two modes that, according to many philosophers and historians, make humans most human. Perhaps the solution remains too simple, since much more is needed, including organised activism and resistance, yet any solution will demand a healthy dose of both modes. Care for nature and others remains an essential ingredient for any progressive change.

Yet *Wall-E* falls short because this message only operates at the level of ideology, not at the level of affect. Indeed, *Wall-E* presents such a wonderful, marvellous, astonishing experience of the pleasures of mode-switching, of the self-affected joys of consumer media, that it undermines its own message. Why give up on mediated modes and pursue gardening or love when *Wall-E* feels so good? *Wall-E*, in fact, is not just a movie with a positive message but also a multimedia, consumerist campaign selling a multitude of consumer goods, especially toys. Given their interest in furthering regimes of consumerism, we cannot rely on Disney to make sense of these changes in affect and mode. Their efforts are likely to translate those affections into molarised ideologies and institutions designed for their continued control, massive profits, and further ecological and human ruin. There is a dramatic need not just to think ourselves as controlled, not just to conceive of the harms of consumerist mode-switching, but to *feel* those controls and harms, to be affected by them. Only then will people be able to make sense of the ongoing sociocultural changes and dilemmas in ways necessary for ethical, healthy social change. Affect remains a crucial motivating force for generating the energy necessary for any sustained, meaningful social change, without which battles at the level of rhetoric and ideology will continue to fall short.

Thus, politically and critically, the primary focus should not be directed at the content of those positions, or even the (radical? reactionary?) themes in Disney movies. As I illustrated, animistic mimesis encourages commodity fetishism. The two seem so intrinsically connected that even a few anti-consumerist animated movies are unlikely to change it, as the example of *Wall-E* makes all too clear. The better questions are: how can we establish new sources of pleasure? How can we direct cinematic and mimetic modes of seeing into critical resistance producing social change? Or better yet, how can we see, through cinematic and animatic modes, the monopolisation of communication media in control society and the subsequent destitution of the planet and its people due to affect's capture in regimes of consumerism? By proliferating modes, digital media create a crisis in attention for the individual, transforming them into dividuals: that is, mode-switching consumers controlled by capitalist regimes. Yet such proliferation and crisis also create an opportunity, an opportunity to reshape our virtual bodies, to perform the hybrid mixing of modes enabled by the computer, perhaps in ways that work against rather than for consumerist ends. Indeed, *Wall-E*'s portrayal of a consumerist American

Dream in ruins illustrates that many have begun to sense the far-reaching changes in affect and affection sparked by the transition to digital media, that the 'making sense' of these new modes and their affections proceeds apace. Such moments of transition are also moments of opportunity, the chance for making a new sense, one, we can hope, that exposes rather than hides the devastating consequences of a consumer lifestyle.

In fact, the proliferation of modes due to the spread of digital media necessarily creates a larger field of potential in which the possibility for anti- or extra-consumerist modes expands as well. Some of that potential can be seen in the use of digital media to create communities of free file-sharing and crowd-sourced creative productions, in the emergence of a copy-left movement that seeks to share intellectual productions collectively rather than profit individually from them, in the emergence of hacker groups such as Anonymous and Wikileaks that perform watchdog functions, and in the spread of 'culture jamming', originally pioneered by Debord and today continued by the Adbusters group, with what have been called Internet 'memes' that frequently comment on the sociopolitical condition.[11] Yet in exploring these possibilities, the central role of control – particularly access – must be kept in mind. File-sharing, creative commons copyrights and Internet memes can only go so far to resist corporate control if access to such content remains managed and profits continue to accrue to those who own the platforms. As Jaron Lanier argues, the control of access by giant media corporations tends to shrink the middle class and creative, artistic output alike by creating rewarding 'network effects' for those who control access to the platforms and punishing 'network effects' for those on the outside.[12] In sum, changes in content will matter little as long as access to it is restricted and control over networks and software remains profitable. The medium remains the message.

In the struggle to make sense of digital media and control society, both proponents and opponents have intuited this central importance of access. For instance, the Occupy movement expresses a sense that two societies exist, one with unlimited access (the 1%) and another (the 99%) whose access is restricted and who is exploited by those who control access, as signified through the reference to Wall Street. Similarly, yet reaching the opposite conclusion, proponents of the digital revolution and the Internet repeatedly express the benefits in the language of freedom and choice, portraying the computer as launching a revolution in liberties against claims that digital media have narrowed freedom by expanding control and limiting access.[13] Such attempts to make sense of the contemporary changes in media, mode and affect are in their infancy today but, as *Special Affects* has maintained and demonstrated, will continue to proceed apace.

Seizing the opportunity to make new sense of these changes requires a careful understanding of the modes and affections behind them. *Special Affects* has demonstrated the fundamental connection between media and consumerism, tracing it to the emergence of cinema and animation. Such a conclusion begs that we ask how the two allies of consumerism and media may be divorced, divested, separated, made into enemies via some new translations? The answer is beyond the scope of this book, yet understanding how the two became allies is the first step in helping begin the process of making another sense, one desperately needed as the American Dream continues to reveal itself to be a worldwide nightmare.

Movies Referenced in *Special Affects*

Bambi (*two-disc diamond edition*), DVD, David Hand. Burbank: Disney, 2011 (originally 1942).

Dumbo, DVD, Ben Sharpsteen. Burbank: Disney, 2011 (originally 1941).

Fantasia/Fantasia 2000 (*two-disc special edition*), DVD, Ben Sharpsteen. Burbank: Disney, 2010 (originally 1940).

All Felix shorts from *Felix the Cat: 8 Full-Length Episodes*, DVD, Pat Sullivan. Golden Movie Classics (New York: Genius Products, Inc., 2004).

Pinocchio 70th Anniversary, DVD, Norman Ferguson. Burbank: Disney, 2009 (originally 1940).

Snow White and the Seven Dwarfs (*Disney special platinum edition*), DVD, David Hand. Burbank: Disney, 2001 (originally 1937).

'Steamboat Willie' and 'Plane Crazy' in *Mickey Mouse in Black and White: The Classic Collection*, DVD. Burbank: Disney, 2002 (originally 1928 and 1929).

20,000 Leagues Under the Sea (*special edition*), DVD, Richard Fleischer. Burbank: Disney, 2003 (originally 1954).

Wall-E, DVD, Andrew Stanton. Burbank: Disney/Pixar, 2008.

Notes

Chapter 1

1. See Manuel Castells, *The Information Age: Economy, Society and Culture. Volume 1. The Rise of Network Society* (Oxford: Blackwell, 1996).
2. See Chapter 7.
3. This turn to affect typically finds predecessors in Baruch Spinoza, Henri Bergson and their adaptation by Deleuze and Guattari. See Baruch Spinoza, *Ethics, Treatise on the Emendation of the Intellect and Selected Letters* (Indianapolis: Hackett, 1992); Henri Bergson, *Matter and Memory* (New York: Zone, 1988); Henri Bergson, *Creative Evolution* (Mineola, NY: Dover, 1998); Gilles Deleuze and Félix Guattari, *Anti-Oedipus: Capitalism and Schizophrenia* (Minneapolis: University of Minnesota Press, 1983). Another theory of affect recently finding uptake comes from Silvan S. Tomkins, *Affect, Imagery, Consciousness: The Complete Edition* (New York: Springer, 2008).
4. For a few representative examples of the ideological critique of Disney, see Mike Budd and Max H. Kirsch, eds, *Rethinking Disney: Private Control, Public Dimensions* (Middletown, CT: Wesleyan University Press, 2005); Ariel Dorfman and Armand Mattelart, *How to Read Donald Duck : Imperialist Ideology in the Disney Comic* (New York: International General, 1975); Henry A. Giroux, *The Mouse That Roared: Disney and the End of Innocence* (Lanham, MD: Rowman & Littlefield, 1999); Richard Schickel, *The Disney Version: The Life, Times, Art and Commerce of Walt Disney* (New York: Simon & Schuster, 1968).
5. Theodor W. Adorno, 'On the Fetish Character of Music and the Regression of Listening', in *The Culture Industry: Selected Essays on Mass Culture* (London: Routledge, 2001).
6. Nigel Thrift, 'Understanding the Material Practices of Glamour', in *The Affect Theory Reader*, ed. Melissa Gregg and Gregory J. Seigworth (Durham, NC: Duke University Press, 2010), 290.
7. Gilles Deleuze, 'Postscript on Control Societies', in *Negotiations: 1972–1990* (New York: Columbia University Press, 1995), 177–82. For affect economy, see Michael Hardt, 'Affective Labour', *Boundary 2*, 26, no. 2 (1999), 89–100; Antonio Negri, 'Value and Affect', *Boundary 2*, 26, no. 2 (1999), 77–88; Michael Hardt and Antonio Negri, *Empire* (Cambridge, MA: Harvard University Press, 2000). Also see many of the essays in the following col-

lection: Patricia Ticineto Clough and Jean Halley, eds, *The Affective Turn: Theorizing the Social* (Durham, NC: Duke University Press, 2007).

8. See, for instance, Jonathan Beller, *The Cinematic Mode of Production: Attention Economy and the Society of the Spectacle* (Hanover, NH: Dartmouth College Press, 2006).

9. Patricia Clough notes that control society unleashes flows of affect and aims 'at the never-ending modulation of moods, capacities, affects, and potentialities' because 'value is produced through modulating affect', through 'the expansion or contraction of affective capacity'. Patricia Clough, 'Introduction', in Clough and Halley, *The Affective Turn*, 19, 20, 25.

10. Deleuze, 'Postscript on Control Societies', 181.

11. For the term 'dividual', see Deleuze, 'Postscript on Control Societies'. For cyborg and posthuman, see among others Donna J. Haraway, *Simians, Cyborgs, and Women: The Reinvention of Nature* (New York: Routledge, 1990); N. Katherine Hayles, *How We Became Posthuman: Virtual Bodies in Cybernetics, Literature, and Informatics* (Chicago: University of Chicago Press, 1999). For interface, see Steven A. Johnson, *Interface Culture* (New York: Basic, 1997); Alexander R. Galloway, *The Interface Effect* (Cambridge: Polity, 2012). For desiring-machines and assemblages, see Deleuze and Guattari, *Anti-Oedipus*.

12. Marshall McLuhan, *Understanding Media: The Extensions of Man* (New York: New American Library, 1964), 63.

13. See John Durham Peters, *Speaking into the Air: A History of the Idea of Communication* (Chicago: University of Chicago Press, 2001); Carolyn Marvin, *When Old Technologies Were New: Thinking about Electric Communication in the Late Nineteenth Century* (New York: Oxford University Press, 1988).

14. Jay David Bolter and Richard Grusin, *Remediation: Understanding New Media* (Cambridge, MA: MIT Press, 2000).

15. Lev Manovich, *The Language of New Media* (Cambridge, MA: MIT Press, 2001), 9.

16. Ibid., 302.

17. Ibid., 298.

18. Ibid., 302.

19. Paul Wells, *Animation – Genre and Authorship*, illustrated edition (London: Wallflower, 2002), 1.

20. See Paul Wells, *Understanding Animation* (London: Routledge, 1998); J. P. Telotte, *The Mouse Machine: Disney and Technology* (Urbana: University of Illinois Press, 2008); J. P. Telotte, *Animating Space: From Mickey to WALL-E* (Lexington: University Press of Kentucky, 2010); Donald Crafton, *Shadow of a Mouse: Performance, Belief, and World-Making in Animation* (Berkeley: University of California Press, 2013); Thomas Lamarre, *The Anime Machine: A Media Theory of Animation* (Minneapolis: University of Minnesota Press, 2009); Scott Bukatman, *The Poetics of Slumberland: Animated Spirits and the Animating Spirit* (Berkeley: University of California Press, 2012).

21. For a cataloguing of the various scholarly traditions of affect, see Gregory J. Seigworth and Melissa Gregg, 'An Inventory of Shimmers', in *The Affect Theory Reader*, ed. Melissa Gregg and Gregory J. Seigworth (Durham, NC: Duke University Press, 2010).

22. Deleuze's most extensive definition of affect comes in one of his two books on Spinoza. See Gilles Deleuze, *Spinoza: Practical Philosophy*, trans. Robert Hurley (San Francisco: City Light, 1988), 48–51; Spinoza, *Ethics, Treatise on the Emendation of the Intellect and Selected Letters*, 77, 103–7.

23. Gilles Deleuze, 'Deleuze/Spinoza' (Cours Vincennes, 24 January 1978), http://www.webdeleuze.com/php/texte.php?cle=14&groupe=Spinoza&langue=2 (accessed 16 January 2014).

24. Silvan Tomkins offers an account of affect that contends that there are eight primary affects, which he puts in pairs to designate their lower and heightened intensities: interest–excitement, enjoyment–joy, surprise–startle, distress–anguish, fear–terror, shame–humiliation, contempt–disgust and anger–rage. Tomkins, *Affect, Imagery, Consciousness*.

25. Damasio is one of the neuroscientists to distinguish between affect and consciousness. Antonio Damasio, *Looking for Spinoza: Joy, Sorrow, and the Feeling Brain* (Orlando: Harcourt, 2003).

26. Brian Massumi, *Parables for the Virtual: Movement, Affect, Sensation* (Durham, NC: Duke University Press, 2002), 28.

27. Teresa Brennan, *The Transmission of Affect* (Ithaca, NY: Cornell University Press, 2004).

28. Roland Barthes, *Camera Lucida: Reflections on Photography* (New York: Hill & Wang, 1982).

29. Gregory J. Seigworth, 'Fashioning a Stave, or, Singing Life', in *Animations of Deleuze and Guattari*, ed. Jennifer Daryl (New York: Peter Lang, 2003), 88.

30. Barthes, *Camera Lucida*.

31. Ibid., 26.

32. Ibid., 115.

33. See Jay Ruby, *Secure the Shadow: Death and Photography in America* (Cambridge, MA: MIT Press, 1999).

34. See Henry Jenkins, *Convergence Culture: Where Old and New Media Collide* (New York: New York University Press, 2006). Bolter and Grusin, *Remediation*.

35. Spinoza, *Ethics, Treatise on the Emendation of the Intellect and Selected Letters*, 134.

36. Tomkins, *Affect, Imagery, Consciousness*.

37. Neal Gabler, *Walt Disney: The Triumph of the American Imagination* (New York: Alfred A. Knopf, 2006), 276–8.

38. Ibid., xii.

39. Gabler, *Walt Disney*, xii.

40. Janet Wasko, *Understanding Disney: The Manufacture of Fantasy*, reprinted

edn (Cambridge: Polity, 2005), 48–68. Giroux, *The Mouse That Roared*, 2.

41. Benjamin discusses this second fetish, which is typically called 'culture'. Walter Benjamin, 'Marx', in *The Arcades Project*, ed. Rolf Tiedemann (Cambridge, MA: Belknap Press of Harvard University Press, 2002), 669. [X13a].

42. Most historians credit the first use of 'American Dream' to James Truslow Adams, *The Epic of America* (Boston: Little, Brown, 1931).

43. Paul Wells, *Animation and America* (New Brunswick, NJ: Rutgers University Press, 2002), 16.

44. Lawrence Grossberg, *We Gotta Get Out of This Place: Popular Conservatism and Postmodern Culture* (New York: Routledge, 1992), 82–3.

45. As Brian Massumi writes, 'Affect *is* the whole world: from the precise angle of its differential emergence.' Massumi, *Parables for the Virtual*, 43.

46. Massumi contends that only the affect theory can comprehend ideology because affect allows thinkers 'to connect ideology to its real conditions of emergence'. Ibid., 42.

47. For the associations provided by Disney audiences, see Eileen R. Meehan, Mark Phillips and Janet Wasko, eds, *Dazzled by Disney? The Global Disney Audiences Project* (London: Leicester University Press, 2001).

48. Seigworth, 'Fashioning a Stave, or, Singing Life', 89.

49. Gilles Deleuze, 'The Actual and the Virtual', in *Dialogues II*, trans. Eliot Ross Albert (London: Continuum, 2002), 112–15; Massumi, *Parables for the Virtual*; Pierre Levy, *Becoming Virtual: Reality in the Digital Age* (New York: Plenum Trade, 1998).

50. Bergson, *Creative Evolution*, 147.

51. Deleuze, 'The Actual and the Virtual', 115.

52. Massumi, *Parables for the Virtual*, 16.

53. Gilles Deleuze, *Difference and Repetition* (New York: Columbia University Press, 1994), 208–9.

54. Sara Ahmed, *The Cultural Politics of Emotion* (New York: Routledge, 2004).

55. Ibid., 8.

56. Deleuze, *Spinoza*, 48.

57. Ibid., 123–4.

58. Ibid., 125–6.

59. See Jacques Derrida, *Limited Inc* (Chicago: Northwestern University Press, 1988), 7.

60. See Samuel Weber, *Benjamin's -abilities* (Cambridge, MA: Harvard University Press, 2010).

61. Ibid., 42.

62. Gilles Deleuze, *Foucault* (Minneapolis: University of Minnesota Press, 1988).

63. Ibid., 104–5.

64. Ibid., 100.

65. The concept of economy is borrowed from Derrida. Jacques Derrida, *Of*

Grammatology, corrected edn (Baltimore: Johns Hopkins University Press, 1997).

66. Gayatri Chakravorty Spivak, 'Translator's Preface', in *Of Grammatology*, corrected edn (Baltimore: Johns Hopkins University Press, 1997), xlii.

67. This notion of metaphor is closest to Ricœur, who explains metaphor as a 'seeing as'. Paul Ricœur, *The Rule of Metaphor: Multi-disciplinary Studies of the Creation of Meaning in Language* (Toronto: University of Toronto Press, 1975), 212.

68. Deleuze, 'Deleuze/Spinoza'.

69. The bear example comes first from William James, whose theories of emotion are one forebear to the affective turn. William James, 'Discussion: The Physical Basis of Emotion', *Psychological Review*, 1, no. 5 (September 1894), 516–29. John Dewey also takes up the bear example, arguing for the import of 'modes of behaviour'. John Dewey, 'The Theory of Emotion. (1) Emotional Attitudes', *Psychological Review*, 1, no. 6 (November 1894), 553–69; John Dewey, 'The Theory of Emotion. (2) The Significance of Emotions', *Psychological Review*, 2, no. 1 (January 1895), 13–32.

70. Ahmed, *The Cultural Politics of Emotion*, 7.

71. Lawrence Grossberg, 'Affect's Future: Rediscovering the Virtual in the Actual', in *The Affect Theory Reader*, ed. Melissa Gregg and Gregory J. Seigworth (Durham, NC: Duke University Press, 2010), 316.

72. Ibid., 315–16.

73. McLuhan, *Understanding Media*.

74. Walter Benjamin, *The Arcades Project*, ed. Rolf Tiedemann (Cambridge, MA: Belknap Press of Harvard University Press, 1999).

75. Walter Benjamin, 'Dream City and Dream House, Dreams of the Future, Anthropological Nihilism, Jung', in *The Arcades Project* (Cambridge, MA: Belknap Press of Harvard University Press, 2002), 392 [K2,5].

76. The phrase 'making sense' dovetails nicely with Deleuze's work, *The Logic of Sense*, where he describes sense as an entity with one side turned towards affective experience and another side turned towards the proposition and language. He also depicts the social as the struggle to make 'good' or 'common' sense, ousting what is feared to be nonsense. Ideology can be seen as the making of common sense. Gilles Deleuze, *The Logic of Sense* (New York: Columbia University Press, 1990).

Chapter 2

1. Eric Smoodin contends that animation played a prominent role on the film bill. Eric Smoodin, *Animating Culture: Hollywood Cartoons from the Sound Era* (New Brunswick, NJ: Rutgers University Press, 1993), 45.

2. Tom Gunning, 'The "Cinema of Attractions": Early Film, its Spectator, and the Avant-Garde', *Wide Angle*, 8, no. 3–4 (1986), 63–70.

3. Eisenstein describes an attraction as calculated to produce 'certain emotional

shocks'. Sergei Eisenstein, 'Montage of Attractions: *For Enough Stupidity in Every Wiseman*', trans. Daniel Gerould, *Drama Review: TDR*, 18, no. 1 (March 1974), 78. Gunning describes these shocks as 'astonishment' and Gaudreault depicts them as the 'peak' and 'aggressive moments'. Tom Gunning, 'An Aesthetic of Astonishment: Early Film and the (In)Credulous Spectator', in *Film Theory and Criticism*, ed. Leo Braudy and Marshall Cohen (Oxford: Oxford University Press, 1999). André Gaudreault, 'From "Primitive Cinema" to "Kine-Attractography"', in *The Cinema of Attractions Reloaded*, ed. Wanda Strauven (Amsterdam: Amsterdam University Press, 2006), 96.

4. Lizabeth Cohen, *Making a New Deal: Industrial Workers in Chicago, 1919–1939* (New York: Cambridge University Press, 1990), 125.

5. See Stephen Kern, *The Culture of Time and Space, 1880–1918*, 2nd edn (Cambridge, MA: Harvard University Press, 2003).

6. This period has been labelled the classical Hollywood mode, with parameters mostly shared between filmmakers and audiences by 1917. See David Bordwell, Janet Staiger and Kristin Thompson, *The Classical Hollywood Cinema: Film Style & Mode of Production to 1960* (New York: Columbia University Press, 1985).

7. Walter Benjamin, 'The Task of the Translator: An Introduction to the Translation of Baudelaire's Tableaux Parisiens', in *Illuminations: Walter Benjamin Essays and Reflection*, ed. Hannah Arendt (New York: Schocken, 1968), 70.

8. Ibid., 78.

9. Ibid., 75.

10. Walter Benjamin, 'The Work of Art in the Age of its Technological Reproducibility: Second Version', in *Walter Benjamin: Selected Writings, Volume 3: 1935–1938*, ed. Howard Eiland and Michael W. Jennings (Cambridge, MA: Belknap Press of Harvard University Press, 2006), 101–33.

11. Gunning, 'An Aesthetic of Astonishment'.

12. Quoted in Charles Musser, *The Emergence of Cinema: The American Screen to 1907* (New York: Charles Scribner's Sons, 1990), 15. Henry V. Hopwood, *Living Pictures: Their History, Photo-production, and Practical Working* (New York: Arno, 1970). Originally published 1899.

13. Quoted in Charles Musser, *Before the Nickelodeon: Edwin S. Porter and the Edison Manufacturing Company* (Berkeley: University of California Press, 1991), 62.

14. *Los Angeles Times*, 5 July 1896, 8.

15. *New York Herald*, 24 April 1896, 11.

16. Musser, *Before the Nickelodeon*, 63.

17. See Stephen Bottomore, 'The Panicking Audience: Early Cinema and the "Train Effect"', *Historical Journal of Film, Radio and Television*, 19, no. 2 (1999), 177–216.

18. Ibid., 186.

19. Ibid.
20. Quoted in Gunning, 'An Aesthetic of Astonishment', 832.
21. Ibid.
22. Livio Belloi, 'Lumière and His View: The Cameraman's Eye in Early Cinema', *Historical Journal of Film, Radio and Television*, 15, no. 4 (October 1995), 461–74.
23. Benjamin, 'The Work of Art in the Age of its Technological Reproducibility: Second Version'.
24. Ibid., 113.
25. Ibid., 104–5.
26. Ibid., 104.
27. Musser reports that local views 'drew huge crowds'. Musser, *The Emergence of Cinema*, 405.
28. Ibid.
29. Musser, *Before the Nickelodeon*, 66.
30. Musser, *The Emergence of Cinema*, 298.
31. André Gaudreault, *Film and Attraction: From Kinematography to Cinema* (Urbana: University of Illinois Press, 2011), 96–7.
32. Gaudreault, 'From "Primitive Cinema" to "Kine-Attractography"', 94.
33. Eisenstein, 'Montage of Attractions', 79. Originally 1923.
34. Tom Gunning, 'The Whole Town's Gawking: Early Cinema and the Visual Experience of Modernity', *Yale Journal of Criticism*, 7, no. 2 (1994), 189–201.
35. Ibid., 94.
36. Ibid.
37. David Bordwell, *On the History of Film Style* (Cambridge, MA: Harvard University Press, 1997). One excellent work that spells out the modernity thesis for nineteenth-century visual culture is Jonathan Crary, *Suspensions of Perception: Attention, Spectacle, and Modern Culture* (Cambridge, MA: MIT Press, 2001).
38. Esther Leslie, *Hollywood Flatlands: Animation, Critical Theory and the Avant-Garde* (New York: Verso, 2004).
39. For a critique of the idea of modernism as a well-defined historical period, see Bruno Latour, *We Have Never Been Modern*, trans. Catherine Porter (Cambridge, MA: Harvard University Press, 1993).
40. Musser frequently mentions using the film as a visual newspaper, and his work provides evidence for all of these other modes as well. See Musser, *The Emergence of Cinema*.
41. Quoted in Friedrich Kittler, *Gramophone, Film, Typewriter* (Palo Alto: Stanford University Press, 1999), 145.
42. Quoted in ibid., 167.
43. Hugo Münsterberg and Richard Griffith, *The Film: A Psychological Study* (Mineola, NY: Dover, 1970), 95.
44. Viva Paci, 'The Attraction of the Intelligent Eye: Obsessions with the Vision

Machine in Early Film Theories', in *The Cinema of Attractions Reloaded* (Amsterdam: Amsterdam University Press, 2006), 125.

45. Benjamin, 'The Work of Art in the Age of its Technological Reproducibility: Second Version', 117–18.

46. Ibid., 117.

47. Ibid., 30.

48. Rudolph Arnheim, *Film as Art* (Berkeley: University of California Press, 1957), 65.

49. Ibid., 75.

50. André Bazin, *What Is Cinema?*, vol. 1 (Berkeley: University of California Press, 2004), 21.

51. Siegfried Kracauer, *Theory of Film: The Redemption of Physical Reality* (Princeton: Princeton University Press, 1997), 12.

52. Ibid., 37, 77.

53. See Miriam Hansen, *Babel and Babylon: Spectatorship in American Silent Film* (Cambridge, MA: Harvard University Press, 1991), 33.

54. Ibid., 79.

55. Gaudreault, *Film and Attraction*, 50.

56. Gilles Deleuze, *Cinema 1: The Movement-Image* (Minneapolis: University of Minnesota Press, 1986), 19–20.

57. Sergei Eisenstein reports that D. W. Griffith carried around a copy of a Dickens novel that inspired him to develop parallel montage. Sergei Eisenstein, 'Dickens, Griffith, and the Film Today', in *Film Form; Essays in Film Theory*, ed. Jay Leyda (New York: Harcourt, 1949).

58. Nick Browne, 'The Spectator-in-the-text: The Rhetoric of *Stagecoach*', in *Film Theory and Criticism: Introductory Readings*, ed. Leo Braudy and Marshall Cohen, 4th edn (New York: Oxford University Press, 1992), 210–16.

59. Deleuze, *Cinema 1*, 96.

60. Christian Metz, *The Imaginary Signifier: Psychoanalysis and the Cinema* (Bloomington: Indiana University Press, 1977), 51.

61. Barker produces an excellent examination of the tactility of cinematic experience based on a similar observation that the film also has a body, also 'sees' in ways that are different yet similar to viewers. Jennifer M. Barker, *The Tactile Eye: Touch and the Cinematic Experience* (Berkeley: University of California Press, 2009).

62. Marshall McLuhan, 'Guttenberg Galaxy', in *Essential McLuhan*, ed. Eric McLuhan and Frank Zingrone (New York: Basic, 1995), 131–3.

63. Deleuze, *Cinema 1*, 12.

64. Walter Benjamin, 'The Work of Art in the Age of its Technological Reproducibility: Third Version', in *Walter Benjamin: Selected Writings, Volume 4: 1938–1940*, ed. Howard Eiland and Michael W. Jennings (Cambridge, MA: Belknap Press of Harvard University Press, 2006).

65. This analysis is based on Benjamin's description. Ibid., 259.

66. Ibid.

67. Ibid., 260.

68. Ibid.

69. Ibid.

70. Ibid., 120.

71. See Barbara Kennedy, *Deleuze and Cinema: The Aesthetics of Sensation* (Edinburgh: Edinburgh University Press, 2003); Patricia Pisters, *The Matrix of Visual Culture: Working with Deleuze in Film Theory* (Palo Alto: Stanford University Press, 2003); Steven Shaviro, *The Cinematic Body* (Minneapolis: University of Minnesota Press, 1993), 45–6; and Elena del Río, *Deleuze and the Cinemas of Performance: Powers of Affection* (Edinburgh: Edinburgh University Press, 2008).

72. Benjamin, 'The Work of Art in the Age of its Technological Reproducibility: Second Version', 119.

73. Noël Carroll, *Mystifying Movies: Fads and Fallacies in Contemporary Film Theory* (New York: Columbia University Press, 1988), 102.

74. Metz, *The Imaginary Signifier*, 45.

75. Ibid.

76. Ibid., 64.

77. Carroll, *Mystifying Movies*, 38.

78. Ron Burnett describes a kind of reverie. Ron Burnett, *Cultures of Vision: Images, Media, and the Imaginary* (Bloomington: Indiana University Press, 1995). Steven Shaviro insists he rarely identifies with the characters, instead preferring to be struck by the visceral qualities. Shaviro, *The Cinematic Body*, 255. Mary Ann Doane describes what she sees as a typically female form of viewer reception, glancing at the surface of the image for peripheral details. Mary Ann Doane, *The Desire to Desire: The Woman's Film of the 1940's* (Bloomington: Indiana University Press, 1987), 31.

79. David Bordwell, 'Space in the Classical Film', in *The Classical Hollywood Cinema: Film Style & Mode of Production to 1960*, ed. David Bordwell, Janet Staiger and Kristin Thompson (New York: Columbia University Press, 1985), 54.

80. Kristin Thompson, 'Classical Narrative Space and the Spectator's Attention', in *The Classical Hollywood Cinema: Film Style & Mode of Production to 1960*, ed. David Bordwell, Janet Staiger and Kristin Thompson (New York: Columbia University Press, 1985), 227.

81. As one of the best interpreters of Deleuze's film theory, D. N. Rodowick, states, 'What the cinema presents is not photograms or the series of individual frames on the film strip . . . In other words, what counts for Deleuze is the brute empiricism of an image in movement, the immediate evidence of our eyes.' D. N. Rodowick, *Gilles Deleuze's Time Machine* (Durham, NC: Duke University Press, 1997), 22.

82. Deleuze, *Cinema 1*, 8.

83. David Bordwell, 'Classical Narration', in *The Classical Hollywood Cinema: Film Style & Mode of Production to 1960*, ed. David Bordwell, Janet Staiger

and Kristin Thompson (New York: Columbia University Press, 1985).

84. Ibid., 39.
85. Deleuze, *Cinema 1*, 141–2.
86. Bordwell, 'Space in the Classical Film', 58.
87. Thompson, 'Classical Narrative Space and the Spectator's Attention', 214–15.
88. Deleuze, *Cinema 1*, 30.
89. Ibid., 141.
90. Ibid., 144.
91. Ibid., 141.
92. Ibid., 148.

Chapter 3

1. Marshall McLuhan, *Understanding Media: The Extensions of Man* (New York: New American Library, 1964), 254–5.
2. Guy Debord, *Society of the Spectacle* (Detroit: Black & Red, 2000); Max Horkheimer and Theodor W. Adorno, *Dialectic of Enlightenment* (New York: Continuum, 1972); Jonathan Beller, *The Cinematic Mode of Production: Attention Economy and the Society of the Spectacle* (Hanover, NH: Dartmouth College Press, 2006).
3. Grant David McCracken, *Culture and Consumption: New Approaches to the Symbolic Character of Consumer Goods and Activities* (Bloomington: Indiana University Press, 1988), 3.
4. Chandra Mukerji, *From Graven Images: Patterns of Modern Materialism* (New York: Columbia University Press, 1983).
5. Neil McKendrick, John H. Plumb and John Brewer, *The Birth of a Consumer Society: The Commercialization of Eighteenth-Century England* (Bloomington: Indiana University Press, 1982).
6. Rosalind H. Williams, *Dream Worlds: Mass Consumption in Late Nineteenth Century France* (Berkeley: University of California Press, 1991).
7. Mary Anne Doane, *The Desire to Desire: The Woman's Film of the 1940s* (Bloomington: Indiana University Press, 1987), 30.
8. Gilles Deleuze and Félix Guattari, *Anti-Oedipus: Capitalism and Schizophrenia* (Minneapolis: University of Minnesota Press, 1983), 29.
9. Ibid., 5.
10. Ibid., 109.
11. Ibid., 38.
12. Thorstein Veblen, *The Theory of the Leisure Class* (New York: Oxford University Press, 2008).
13. Mary Douglas and Baron Isherwood, *The World of Goods*, 2nd edn (New York: Routledge, 1996), 62; Pierre Bourdieu, *Distinction: A Social Critique of the Judgement of Taste* (Cambridge, MA: Harvard University Press, 1987); Dick Hebdige, *Hiding in the Light: On Images and Things*, Comedia (London,

New York: Routledge, 1988); Mike Featherstone, *Consumer Culture and Postmodernism*, 2nd edn (London: Sage, 1991).

14. The label 'emulationist' comes from Colin Campbell, *The Romantic Ethic and the Spirit of Modern Consumerism* (New York: Basil Blackwell, 1989), 55.
15. Veblen, *The Theory of the Leisure Class*, 49–52.
16. Douglas and Isherwood, *The World of Goods*, 38.
17. Campbell, *The Romantic Ethic and the Spirit of Modern Consumerism*.
18. Ibid., 89–90.
19. Ibid., 87.
20. Walter Benjamin, 'The Collector', in *The Arcades Project*, ed. Rolf Tiedemann (Cambridge, MA: Belknap Press, 1999). McCracken's curatorial consumer acts as a museum curator, preserving family history. Grant David McCracken, *Culture and Consumption: New Approaches to the Symbolic Character of Consumer Goods and Activities* (Bloomington: Indiana University Press, 1988).
21. See April Lane Benson, *I Shop, Therefore I Am: Compulsive Buying and the Search for Self* (Northvale, NJ: Jason Aronson, 2000).
22. Campbell, *The Romantic Ethic and the Spirit of Modern Consumerism*, 56.
23. Gilles Deleuze, *Foucault* (Minneapolis: University of Minnesota Press, 1988).
24. Ibid., 51–2.
25. Campbell, *The Romantic Ethic and the Spirit of Modern Consumerism*, 88.
26. Richard Fleischer, *Disney's 20,000 Leagues Under the Sea* (Walt Disney Video, 2003).
27. John M. Miller, '20,000 Leagues Under the Sea', *Turner Classic Movies*, http://www.tcm.com/this-month/article/152601|0/20-000-Leagues-Under-the-Sea.html (accessed 1 April 2011).
28. Bosley Crowther, 'Movie Review. 20,000 Leagues Under the Sea. The Screen in Review. "20,000 Leagues" in 128 Fantastic Minutes', *New York Times.com*, 24 December 1954, http://movies.nytimes.com/movie/review?res=9D05E6DD1F3EE03BBC4C51DFB467838F649EDE (accessed 17 January 2014); Steve Biodrowski, 'Captain Nemo Double Bill', *Cinefantastique Online*, 25 August 2007, http://cinefantastiqueonline.com/2007/08/hollywood-gothique-captain-nemo-double-bill/ (accessed 17 January 2014).
29. As stated on 'The Making of 20,000 Leagues Under the Sea'. Miller, '20,000 Leagues Under the Sea'.
30. Sianne Ngai, *Our Aesthetic Categories: Zany, Cute, Interesting* (Cambridge, MA: Harvard University Press, 2012), 149.
31. Ibid., 134.
32. Ibid., 25.
33. Ibid., 23.
34. Gregory Bateson, *Steps to an Ecology of Mind* (New York: Ballantine, 1972), 381.

35. Ngai, *Our Aesthetic Categories*, 143.

36. Ibid., 170.

37. John Berger, *Ways of Seeing: Based on the BBC Television Series* (London: Penguin (Non-Classics), 1990), 46.

38. Ibid.

39. Vivian Sobchack, *Carnal Thoughts: Embodiment and Moving Image Culture* (Berkeley: University of California Press, 2004), 152.

40. Ibid., 49.

41. Benjamin elucidates: 'The direction of this change is the same for the film actor and the politician . . . It tends toward the exhibition of controllable, transferable skills.' Walter Benjamin, 'The Work of Art in the Age of its Technological Reproducibility: Second Version', in *Walter Benjamin: Selected Writings, Volume 3: 1935–1938*, ed. Howard Eiland and Michael W. Jennings (Belknap Press of Harvard University Press, 2006), 128.

42. Leo Braudy, *The World in a Frame: What We See in Films* (Garden City, NY: Anchor, 1976).

43. See Kristin Thompson, 'The Formulation of the Classical Narrative', in *The Classical Hollywood Cinema: Film Style & Mode of Production to 1960*, ed. David Bordwell, Janet Staiger and Kristin Thompson (New York: Columbia University Press, 1985), 189–92.

44. Braudy, *The World in a Frame*, 197.

45. Ibid., 198.

46. Quoted in Larry May, *Screening Out the Past: The Birth of Mass Culture and the Motion Picture Industry* (New York: Oxford University Press, 1980), 230–1.

47. Richard Dyer, *Heavenly Bodies: Film Stars and Society*, 2nd edn (New York: Routledge, 2003), 7.

48. Braudy, *The World in a Frame*.

49. Dyer, *Heavenly Bodies*, 12.

50. John Ellis, *Visible Fictions: Cinema, Television, Video*, revised edn (New York: Routledge, 1992), 97.

51. Ibid.

52. May, *Screening Out the Past*, 237.

53. See Jackie Stacey, *Star Gazing: Hollywood Cinema and Female Spectatorship* (London: Routledge, 1994).

54. A recent volume entitled *Hollywood Goes Shopping*, exploring the link between classical cinema and consumerism, provides evidence for the connection between cinema and lifestyle modes, since each essay features examples primarily geared toward lifestyle construction David Desser and Garth S. Jowett, eds, *Hollywood Goes Shopping* (Minneapolis: University of Minnesota Press, 2000).

55. Charles Eckert, 'The Carole Lombard in Macy's Window', in *Movies and Mass Culture*, ed. John Belton (New Brunswick, NJ: Rutgers University Press, 1995), 95–118.

56. Quoted in ibid., 100.
57. Thomas Frank, *The Conquest of Cool: Business Culture, Counterculture, and the Rise of Hip Consumerism* (Chicago: University of Chicago Press, 1997). Frederic Jameson, *Postmodernism or, the Cultural Logic of Late Capitalism* (Durham, NC: Duke University Press, 1991). Jean Baudrillard, *For a Critique of the Political Economy of the Sign* (St Louis: Telos, 1981).
58. Kalle Lasn, *Culture Jam: The Uncooling of America* (New York: Eagle Brook, 1999).
59. Stacey, *Star Gazing*.
60. Anne Friedberg, *Window Shopping: Cinema and the Postmodern* (Berkeley: University of California Press, 1993). Eckert, 'The Carole Lombard in Macy's Window', 98.
61. Beller, *The Cinematic Mode of Production*, 9.
62. Mary Anne Doane, 'The Economy of Desire: The Commodity Form in/of the Cinema', *Quarterly Review of Film and Video*, 11, no. 1 (May 1989), 31.
63. Beller, *The Cinematic Mode of Production*, 244, 232.
64. Doane, 'The Economy of Desire', 30.
65. Friedberg, *Window Shopping*.

Chapter 4

1. Joseph Anderson and Barbara Anderson, 'The Myth of the Persistence of Vision Revisited', *Journal of Film and Video*, 45, no. 1 (Spring 1993), 3–12.
2. Charles Musser, *The Emergence of Cinema: The American Screen to 1907* (New York: Charles Scribner's Sons, 1990), 43.
3. Nicolas Dulac and André Gaudreault, 'Circularity and Repetition at the Heart of the Attraction: Optical Toys and the Emergence of a New Cultural Series', in *The Cinema of Attractions Reloaded*, ed. Wanda Strauven (Amsterdam: Amsterdam University Press, 2006), 228.
4. *New York World*, 28 May 1895, 30.
5. Quoted in Musser, *The Emergence of Cinema*, 31–2.
6. Sergei Eisenstein, *Eisenstein on Disney*, ed. Jay Leyda (Calcutta: Seagull, 1986), 55.
7. Buchan concurs on this condition of animated spectatorship: '(W)e are constantly aware of the animator's creation of the "world" we see.' Suzanne Buchan, 'The Animated Spectator: Watching the Quay Brothers' "Worlds"', in *Animated Worlds*, ed. Suzanne Buchan (New Barnet: John Libbey, 2006), 23.
8. Musser, *The Emergence of Cinema*, 18.
9. Ashton Stevens, 'McCay on Stage', *Chicago Examiner*, 9 February 1914.
10. Roland Barthes, *Camera Lucida: Reflections on Photography* (New York: Hill & Wang, 1982), 115.
11. Ibid.
12. Eisenstein, *Eisenstein on Disney*, 3.

13. Baudrillard's comments on Disneyland also reflect the metaphysical questioning of animation's *spark*, grappling with the changing parameters of the real. Jean Baudrillard, *Simulacra and Simulation* (Ann Arbor: University of Michigan Press, 1994).

14. Quoted in Steven Watts, *The Magic Kingdom: Walt Disney and the American Way of Life* (Boston: Houghton Mifflin, 1997), 122.

15. William Kozlenko, 'The Animated Cartoon and Walt Disney', in *The Emergence of Film Art: The Evolution and Development of the Motion Picture as an Art, from 1900 to the Present*, ed. Lewis Jacobs, first published 1936 (New York: Hopkinson & Blake, 1969), 246.

16. Walter Benjamin, 'Mickey Mouse', in *Walter Benjamin: Selected Writings, Volume 2: Part 2: 1931–1934*, ed. Howard Eiland and Michael W. Jennings (Cambridge, MA: Belknap Press of Harvard University Press, 2005), 545. Benjamin, 'The Work of Art in the Age of its Technological Reproducibility: Second Version', in *Walter Benjamin: Selected Writings, Volume 3: 1935–1938*, ed. Howard Eiland and Michael W. Jennings (Cambridge, MA: Belknap Press of Harvard University Press, 2006), 117.

17. Robert D. Feild, *The Art of Walt Disney* (New York: Macmillan, 1942).

18. Ibid., 62.

19. Donald Crafton, *Before Mickey: The Animated Film 1898–1928* (Chicago: University of Chicago Press, 1993), 4, 6.

20. Erwin Panofsky even excludes animation from his definition of film. Erwin Panofsky, 'Style and Medium in the Motion Pictures', in *Film Theory & Criticism: Introductory Readings*, ed. Gerald Mast, Marshall Cohen and Leo Braudy (New York: Oxford University Press, 1992), 247. Cavell and Mast both contend that most film theory is flawed because the emphasis on cinema's reality effect cannot account for the genre of animation. Stanley Cavell, *The World Viewed*, enlarged edn (Cambridge, MA: Harvard University Press, 1979), 168. Gerald Mast, *Film/Cinema/Movie: A Theory of Experience* (New York: Harper & Row, 1977), 4.

21. Crafton, *Before Mickey*, 4, 5.

22. Alan Cholodenko, 'Introduction', in *The Illusion of Life 2: More Essays on Animation*, ed. Alan Cholodenko (Sydney: Power, 2007), 36.

23. Ibid.

24. Paul Watson, 'True Lye's: (Re)Animating Film Studies', *Art & Design Magazine*, no. 53 (1997), 46.

25. Deleuze, *Cinema 1: The Movement-Image* (Minneapolis: University of Minnesota Press, 1986), 5.

26. Panofsky, 'Style and Medium in the Motion Pictures', 235.

27. Quoted in Wells, *Understanding Animation* (London: Routledge, 1998), 7.

28. Philip Brophy, *The Illusion of Life: Essays on Animation*, ed. Alan Cholodenko (Sydney: Power, 1991), 71.

29. Quoted in Wells, *Understanding Animation*, 10.

30. William Schaffer, 'Animation 1: The Control-Image', in *The Illusion of Life*

      2: More Essays on Animation, ed. Alan Cholodenko (Sydney: Power, 2007),
      461.
31. Ibid., 38.
32. Eisenstein, *Eisenstein on Disney*, 21.
33. Panofsky, 'Style and Medium in the Motion Pictures', 239.
34. Walter Benjamin, 'Painting, or Signs and Marks', in *Walter Benjamin:
    Selected Writings Volume 1, 1913–1926*, ed. Marcus Bullock and Michael
    W. Jennings (Cambridge. MA: Belknap Press of Harvard University Press,
    1996), 83.
35. Vivian Sobchack, 'The Line and the Animorph or "Travel is More Than
    Just A to B"', *Animation: An Interdisciplinary Journal*, 3, no. 3 (2008),
    251–65.
36. Norman Klein, *Seven Minutes: The Life and Death of the American Animated
    Cartoon* (London: Verso, 1996), 39.
37. Crafton, *Before Mickey*, 301.
38. Ibid., 66.
39. Klein remarks that such early animation was not really narrative: 'It was not
    a story in three acts; it was a singular event, like an implausible trapeze act
    flying through an unlikely ceiling.' Klein, *Seven Minutes*, 22.
40. Crafton, *Before Mickey*, 10.
41. Ibid., 297.
42. See Donald Crafton, 'Pie and Chase: Gag, Narrative, and Spectacle in
    Slapstick Comedy', in *The Cinema of Attractions Reloaded*, ed. Wanda
    Strauven (Amsterdam: Amsterdam University Press, 2007), 355–64.
43. *Feline Follies* was viewed on Youtube at http://www.youtube.com/
    watch?v=ZbX-BeSY_18 on 4 March 2012. The other examples all come
    from different episodes on the same DVD. See Pat Sullivan, *Felix the Cat: 8
    Full-Length Episodes*, DVD, Golden Movie Classics (Genius Products, Inc.,
    2004).
44. Crafton, *Before Mickey*, 12.
45. For Felix, see ibid., 342. For Disney, see Michael Barrier, *The Animated
    Man: A Life of Walt Disney* (Berkeley: University of California Press, 2008),
    33.
46. 'Steamboat Willie', *Variety*, 21 November 1928.
47. Quoted in Leonard Maltin and Jerry Beck, *Of Mice and Magic: A History of
    American Animated Cartoons*, revised and updated edn (New York: Plume,
    1987), 35.
48. Quoted in ibid.
49. *Exhibitor's Herald*, November 1928.
50. J. P. Telotte, *Animating Space: From Mickey to WALL-E* (Lexington:
    University Press of Kentucky, 2010), 64.
51. J. P. Telotte, *Mouse Machine: Disney and Technology* (Urbana: University of
    Illinois Press, 2008), 28.
52. Crafton, *Before Mickey*, 297.

53. For an excellent article on *Looney Tunes* that describes a 'control image', similar to the motion-image, see Schaffer, 'Animation 1'.

54. Telotte, *Mouse Machine*, 24.

55. Deleuze, *Cinema 1*, 77.

56. Quoted in Maltin and Beck, *Of Mice and Magic*, 33.

Chapter 5

1. For an extended examination of the connection between animals, animation, animism and anthropomorphism, see Paul Wells, *The Animated Bestiary: Animals, Cartoons, and Culture* (New Brunswick, NJ: Rutgers University Press, 2009).

2. Richard Schickel, *The Disney Version: The Life, Times, Art and Commerce of Walt Disney* (New York: Simon & Schuster, 1968), 10.

3. The idea that wonder leads to reflection is a major claim of Philip Fisher, *Wonder, the Rainbow, and the Aesthetics of Rare Experiences* (Cambridge, MA: Harvard University Press, 1998).

4. Mark Phillips, 'The Global Disney Audiences Project: Disney Across Cultures', in *Dazzled by Disney? The Global Disney Audiences Project*, ed. Janet Wasko (London: Leicester University Press, 2001), 46.

5. Chuck Jones, 'What's Up, Down Under? Chuck Jones Talks at the Illusion of Life Conference', in *The Illusion of Life: Essays on Animation*, ed. Alan Cholodenko (Sydney: Power, 1991), 59.

6. John C. Flinn Sr, 'Snow White and the Seven Dwarfs', *Variety*, 29 December 1937, http://www.variety.com/review/VE1117794991/ (accessed 16 January 2014).

7. Ibid.

8. Frank Nugent, 'The Music Hall Presents Walt Disney's Delightful Fantasy, "Snow White and the Seven Dwarfs"', *The New York Times*, 14 January 1938.

9. 'Snow White and the Seven Dwarfs', *BoxOffice Magazine*, 4 February 1938, http://www.boxoffice.com/reviews/theatrical/2008–08-snow-white-and-the-seven-dwarf (accessed 16 January 2014).

10. 'Cinema: Mouse & Man', *Time Magazine*, 27 December 1937, http://www.time.com/time/subscriber/article/0,33009,758747-1,00.html (accessed 16 January 2014).

11. 'Pinocchio', *Variety*, 31 December 1939, http://variety.com/1939/film/reviews/pinocchio-2-1200413016/ (accessed 16 January 2014).

12. Frank S. Nugent, '"Pinocchio", Walt Disney's Long-Awaited Successor to "Snow White", Has its Premiere at the Center Theatre', *The New York Times*, 8 February 1940.

13. 'Music: Disney's Cinesymphony', *Time*, 18 November 1940, http://www.time.com/time/subscriber/article/0,33009,777534-2,00.html (accessed 16 January 2014).

14. Bosley Crowther, 'Walt Disney's "Fantasia", an Exciting New Departure in Film Entertainment, Opened Last Night at the Broadway', *The New York Times*, 14 November 1940, 'Amusements' section.

15. Bosley Crowther, 'Walt Disney's Cartoon, "Dumbo", A Fanciful Delight, Opens at the Broadway', *The New York Times*, 24 October 1941, http://query.nytimes.com/mem/archive/pdf?res=F00F14FD385F1A7A93C6AB178BD95F458485F9 (accessed 16 January 2014).

16. Ibid.

17. 'The New Pictures, Oct. 27, 1941', *Time Magazine*, 27 October 1941, http://www.time.com/time/subscriber/article/0,33009,849603-2,00.html (accessed 16 January 2014).

18. For an account of these criticisms, see Steven Watts, *The Magic Kingdom: Walt Disney and the American Way of Life* (Boston: Houghton Mifflin, 1997).

19. Quoted in John Canemaker, 'Vlad Tytla: Animation's Michaelangelo', in *The American Animated Cartoon: A Critical Anthology*, ed. Gerald Peary and Danny Peary (New York: E. P. Dutton, 1980), 86.

20. Leonard Maltin and Jerry Beck, *Of Mice and Magic: A History of American Animated Cartoons*, revised and updated edn (New York: Plume, 1987), 57.

21. Anna Gibbs, 'After Affect: Sympathy, Synchrony, and Mimetic Communication', in *The Affect Theory Reader*, ed. Melissa Gregg and Gregory J. Seigworth (Durham, NC: Duke University Press, 2010), 186.

22. Teresa Brennan, *The Transmission of Affect* (Ithaca, NY: Cornell University Press, 2004); Silvan S. Tomkins, *Affect, Imagery, Consciousness: The Complete Edition* (New York: Springer, 2008).

23. For the baby example, see Daniel N. Stern, *The Interpersonal World of the Infant* (New York: Basic, 1985).

24. Walter Benjamin, 'Doctrine of the Similar', in *Walter Benjamin: Selected Writings Volume 2, Part 2, 1931–1934*, ed. Marcus Paul Bullock, et al. (Cambridge, MA: Belknap Press of Harvard University Press, 1996), 694.

25. Walter Benjamin, 'A Child's View of Colour', in *Walter Benjamin: Selected Writings Volume 1, 1913–1926*, ed. Marcus Paul Bullock and Howard Eiland (Cambridge, MA: Belknap Press of Harvard University Press, 1996), 51.

26. Michael Taussig, *Mimesis and Alterity: A Particular History of the Senses* (New York: Routledge, 1993), xiii.

27. Anna Gibbs, 'After Affect: Sympathy, Synchrony, and Mimetic Communication', in *The Affect Theory Reader*, ed. Melissa Gregg and Gregory J. Seigworth (Durham, NC: Duke University Press, 2010), 193.

28. Marshall McLuhan, *Understanding Media: The Extensions of Man* (New York: New American Library, 1964), 67.

29. Ibid., 105.

30. Taussig, *Mimesis and Alterity*, 57–8.

31. Walter Benjamin, 'The Work of Art in the Age of its Technological Reproducibility: Second Version', in *Walter Benjamin: Selected Writings*

Volume 3: 1935–1938, ed. Howard Eiland and Michael W. Jennings (Belknap Press of Harvard University Press, 2006), 127.

32. Walter Benjamin, 'A Glimpse into the World of Children's Books', in *Walter Benjamin: Selected Writings Volume 1, 1913–1926*, ed. Marcus Paul Bullock, et al. (Cambridge, MA: Belknap Press of Harvard University Press, 1996), 435.

33. Walter Benjamin, 'Old, Forgotten Children's Books', in *Walter Benjamin: Selected Writings Volume 1, 1913–1926*, ed. Marcus Paul Bullock, et al. (Cambridge, MA: Belknap Press of Harvard University Press, 1996), 411.

34. Scott Mccloud, *Understanding Comics: The Invisible Art* (New York: Harper Paperbacks, 1994).

35. Eisenstein reports that Disney animation evoked memories of childhood. Sergei Eisenstein, *Eisenstein on Disney*, ed. Jay Leyda (Calcutta: Seagull, 1986), 7.

36. Crowther, 'Walt Disney's "Fantasia", an Exciting New Departure in Film Entertainment, Opened Last Night at the Broadway'.

37. Frank Thomas and Ollie Johnston, *The Illusion of Life: Disney Animation* (New York: Hyperion, 1981), 34–5.

38. Quoted in Canemaker, 'Vlad Tytla: Animation's Michaelangelo', 82.

39. Clampett quoted in Jeff Lenburg, *The Great Cartoon Directors* (Cambridge, MA: Da Capo, 1993), 57.

40. Quoted in Michael Barrier, *The Animated Man: A Life of Walt Disney* (Berkeley: University of California Press, 2008), 99.

41. Thomas and Johnston, *The Illusion of Life*, 100.

42. Eisenstein deplores the later Disney: Eisenstein, *Eisenstein on Disney*, 99. Panofsky critiques *Fantasia* and other Disney features, first published in 1934: Erwin Panofsky, 'Style and Medium in the Motion Pictures', in *Film Theory & Criticism: Introductory Readings*, ed. Gerald Mast, Marshall Cohen and Leo Braudy (New York: Oxford University Press, 1992), 239.

43. Siegfried Kracauer, 'Dumbo', *The Nation*, 8 November 1941, 463.

44. Ibid.

45. See Paul Wells, *Animation – Genre and Authorship*, illustrated edition (Wallflower, 2002); Esther Leslie, *Hollywood Flatlands: Animation, Critical Theory and the Avant-Garde* (New York: Verso, 2004).

46. Leslie, *Hollywood Flatlands*, 147–8.

47. Kracauer, 'Dumbo', 463.

48. Quoted in Barrier, *The Animated Man*, 132.

49. See J. P. Telotte, *Animating Space: From Mickey to WALL-E* (Lexington: University Press of Kentucky, 2010). See also J. P. Telotte, *Mouse Machine: Disney and Technology* (Urbana: University of Illinois Press, 2008).

50. Thomas and Johnston, *The Illusion of Life*, 47.

51. David Abram, *The Spell of the Sensuous: Perception and Language in a More-Than-Human World* (New York: Vintage, 1997), 58.

52. Bertolt Brecht, *Brecht on Theatre: The Development of an Aesthetic*, trans. John Willett (New York: Hill & Wang, 1964), 136–7.
53. Quoted in Maltin and Beck, *Of Mice and Magic*, 40.
54. Richard Neupert, 'Painting a Plausible World: Disney's Colour Prototypes', in *Disney Discourse: Producing the Magic Kingdom*, ed. Eric Smoodin (New York: Routledge, 1994), 112.
55. Walter Benjamin, 'A Child's View of Colour'.
56. Neupert, 'Painting a Plausible World'. J. P. Telotte, *Mouse Machine*.
57. Robert Edmond Jones, 'The Problem of Colour', in *The Emergence of Film Art: The Evolution and Development of the Motion Picture as an Art, from 1900 to the Present*, ed. Lewis Jacobs (New York: Hopkinson & Blake, 1969), 206.
58. Ibid.
59. Ibid., 269.
60. Ibid., 208.
61. Neupert, 'Painting a Plausible World', 116.
62. Quoted in Walt Disney, 'The Making of Fantasia' (USA: Buena Vista Home Entertainment, 2000 (1940)).
63. Brennan, *The Transmission of Affect*, 68–73.
64. Max Horkheimer and Theodor W. Adorno, *Dialectic of Enlightenment* (New York: Continuum, 1972), 184.
65. Quoted in the audio commentary. Disney, 'Fantasia'.
66. I quote Donald Crafton here because it is from his research that I draw the information on shadows. Donald Crafton, *Shadow of a Mouse: Performance, Belief, and World-Making in Animation* (Berkeley: University of California Press, 2013), 288, 290.
67. Ibid., 191.
68. Ibid., 191–2.
69. As reported in Disney, 'The Making of Fantasia'.
70. Quoted in Eisenstein, *Eisenstein on Disney*, 53.
71. Ibid., 52.
72. Ibid., 56.

Chapter 6

1. Frank Thomas and Ollie Johnston, *The Illusion of Life: Disney Animation* (New York: Hyperion, 1981), 287.
2. Gilles Deleuze, *Cinema 2: The Time-Image* (Minneapolis: University of Minnesota Press, 1989), 62.
3. Thomas and Johnston, *The Illusion of Life*, 285.
4. Ibid., 15, 23.
5. Quoted in Neal Gabler, *Walt Disney: The Triumph of the American Imagination* (New York: Alfred A. Knopf, 2006), 272.
6. Thomas and Johnston, *The Illusion of Life*, 473.
7. Ibid., 172.

8. Gilles Deleuze, *Cinema 1: The Movement-Image* (Minneapolis: University of Minnesota Press, 1986), 88.

9. Ibid.

10. Ibid., 87.

11. Ibid., 96.

12. Ibid., 97.

13. This anecdote is recounted in numerous places, including the 'Making of' section of the DVD.

14. Thomas and Johnston, *The Illusion of Life*, 477–8.

15. Sianne Ngai, *Ugly Feelings* (Cambridge, MA: Harvard University Press, 2005).

16. Thomas and Johnston, *The Illusion of Life*, 477.

17. Ibid., 478.

18. Leonard Maltin and Jerry Beck, *Of Mice and Magic: A History of American Animated Cartoons*, revised and updated edn (New York: Plume, 1987), 59.

19. Deleuze, *Cinema 2*, 189.

20. Deleuze, *Cinema 1*, 5.

21. Keith Broadfoot and Rex Butler, 'The Illusion of Illusion', in *The Illusion of Life: Essays on Animation*, ed. Alan Cholodenko (Sydney: Power, 1991), 263–98.

22. Deleuze, *Cinema 2*, 83.

23. Jean Baudrillard, 'Disneyworld Company', *Liberation* (4 March 1996): para 3, http://www.egs.edu/faculty/jean-baudrillard/articles/disneyworld-company/ (accessed 16 January 2014). Jean Baudrillard, *Simulacra and Simulation* (Ann Arbor: University of Michigan Press, 1994).

24. Alan Bryman, *The Disneyization of Society* (London: Sage, 2004), 159.

25. Henry A. Giroux, *The Mouse That Roared: Disney and the End of Innocence* (Lanham, MD: Rowman & Littlefield, 1999).

26. Bryman, *The Disneyization of Society*, 160.

27. Colin Campbell, *The Romantic Ethic and the Spirit of Modern Consumerism* (New York: Basil Blackwell, 1989), 83–4.

28. Ibid., 78.

29. Walter Benjamin, 'Little History of Photography', in *Walter Benjamin: Selected Writings, Volume 2: Part 2: 1931–1934*, ed. Michael W. Jennings, Howard Eiland and Gary Smith (Cambridge, MA: Belknap Press of Harvard University Press, 2005), 507–30.

30. Walter Benjamin, 'On Some Motifs in Baudelaire', in *Walter Benjamin: Selected Writings, Volume 4: 1938–1940*, ed. Howard Eiland and Michael W. Jennings (Cambridge, MA: Belknap Press of Harvard University Press, 2006), 338.

31. Ibid.

32. The comparison is made through the words of Valéry. Ibid., 339.

33. Karl Marx, *Capital: A Critique of Political Economy*, trans. Ben Fowkes, 3 vols, vol. 1 (London: Penguin, 1976).

34. Marx, *Capital*, 164.
35. Ibid.
36. Ibid., 165.
37. Ibid., 165.
38. Ibid., 209.
39. Ibid., 165.
40. Ibid.
41. Max Horkheimer and Theodor W. Adorno, *Dialectic of Enlightenment* (New York: Continuum, 1972).
42. Sean Cubitt, *The Cinema Effect* (Cambridge, MA: MIT Press, 2004), 12.
43. Ben Crawford, 'Intertextual Personae: Character Licensing in Practice and Theory', in *The Illusion of Life 2: More Essays on Animation*, ed. Alan Cholodenko (Sydney: Power, 2007), 404.
44. Ibid., 407.
45. For the connection between Disney and childhood, see Nicholas Sammond, *Babes in Tomorrowland: Walt Disney and the Making of the American Child, 1930–1960* (Durham, NC: Duke University Press, 2005); Gary Cross, *The Cute and the Cool: Wondrous Innocence and Modern American Children's Culture* (New York: Oxford University Press, 2004).
46. Maurya Wickstrom, 'Commodities, Mimesis, and the Lion King: Retail Theatre for the 1990s', *Theatre Journal*, 51, no. 3 (1999), 284, 91.

Chapter 7

1. Interestingly, this idea of emergence as translation is also similar to Derrida's notion of rhetorical constitution as a process based in metaphor. See Jacques Derrida, 'White Mythology: Metaphor in the Text of Philosophy', *New Literary History*, 6, no. 1 (Autumn 1974), 5–74.
2. Walter Benjamin, 'Dream City and Dream House, Dreams of the Future, Anthropological Nihilism, Jung', in *The Arcades Project* (Cambridge, MA: Belknap Press of Harvard University Press, 2002), 392[K2,5].
3. Brian Massumi, 'Introduction: Like a Thought', in *A Shock to Thought: Expression after Deleuze and Guattari*, ed. Brian Massumi (New York: Routledge, 2002), xxv.
4. For other examples of the ideological criticism of Disney, see Brenda Ayres, 'Introduction: (H)egemony Cricket! Why in the World Are We Still Watching Disney?', in *The Emperor's Old Groove: Decolonizing Disney's Magic Kingdom*, ed. Brenda Ayres (New York: Peter Lang, 2003); Eric Smoodin, ed., *Disney Discourse: Producing the Magic Kingdom* (New York: Routledge, 1994); David Kunzle, 'Introduction to the English Edition', in *How to Read Donald Duck: Imperialist Ideology in the Disney Comic*, ed. Ariel Dorfman and Armand Mattelart (New York: International General, 1975); Janet Wasko, *Understanding Disney: The Manufacture of Fantasy*, repr. edn (Cambridge: Polity, 2005); Henry A. Giroux, *The Mouse That Roared: Disney and the End of*

Innocence (Lanham, MD: Rowman & Littlefield Publishers, 1999). Although in a more historical than ideological register, Chris Pallant shares the concern with demystifying Disney myths: Chris Pallant, *Demystifying Disney: A History of Disney Feature Animation* (New York: Continuum, 2011).

5. Theodor W. Adorno, 'On the Fetish Character of Music and the Regression of Listening', in *The Culture Industry: Selected Essays on Mass Culture* (London: Routledge, 2001), 37.

6. In his critique of childishness, Disney is a preferred target. See Max Horkheimer and Theodor W. Adorno, *Dialectic of Enlightenment* (New York: Continuum, 1972), 138.

7. Theodor W. Adorno, *The Stars Down to Earth and Other Essays in Irrational Culture*, ed. Stephen Cook (London: Routledge, 1994), 59. For more on the hidden messages, see Theodor W. Adorno, 'How to Look at Television', in *The Culture Industry: Selected Essays on Mass Culture*, ed. J. M. Bernstein (London, New York: Routledge, 2001). And Theodor W. Adorno, 'Transparencies on Film', in *The Culture Industry: Selected Essays on Mass Culture*, ed. J. M. Bernstein (London, New York: Routledge, 2001).

8. Massumi, 'Introduction: Like a Thought', xxxiii.

9. The term ideograph stands for an ideologically loaded word or phrase. Michael Calvin McGee, 'The "Ideograph": A Link Between Rhetoric and Ideology', *Quarterly Journal of Speech*, 66, no. 1 (February 1980), 1–16.

10. John Durham Peters, *Speaking into the Air: A History of the Idea of Communication* (Chicago: University of Chicago Press, 2001).

11. James W. Carey, *Communication as Culture: Essays on Media and Society* (New York: Routledge, 1989), 203. Daniel Czitrom makes a similar point: Daniel J. Czitrom, *Media and the American Mind: From Morse to McLuhan* (Chapel Hill, NC: University of North Carolina Press, 1983), 8–14.

12. Massumi, 'Introduction: Like a Thought', xxxix.

13. Fisher discusses the use of American Dream rhetoric by Nixon and other presidents: Walter R. Fisher, 'Reaffirmation and Subversion of the American Dream', *Quarterly Journal of Speech*, 59, no. 2 (April 1973), 160–8. See also Dana L. Cloud, 'Hegemony or Concordance? The Rhetoric of Tokenism in "Oprah" Winfrey's Rags-to-riches Biography', *Critical Studies in Mass Communication*, 13, no. 2 (June 1996), 115–27; Robert C. Rowland and John M. Jones, 'Recasting the American Dream and American Politics: Barack Obama's Keynote Address to the 2004 Democratic National Convention', *Quarterly Journal of Speech*, 93, no. 4 (n.d.), 425–48; Vanessa Bowles Beasley, 'The Logic of Power in the Hill-Thomas Hearings: A Rhetorical Analysis', *Political Communication*, 11, no. 3 (September 1994), 287–97; Kristen Hoerl, 'Cinematic Jujitsu: Resisting White Hegemony through the American Dream in Spike Lee's *Malcolm X*', *Communication Studies*, 59, no. 4 (December 2008), 355–70; Joss Lutz Marsh, 'Fitzgerald, Gatsby, and The Last Tycoon: The "American Dream" and the Hollywood Dream Factory – Part One', *Literature Film Quarterly*, 20, no. 1 (1992), 3–13.

14. Gentles concludes, 'The Dream is a mixture of economic, religious, demo-cratic, national, and social elements woven together in a complex fabric': Frederick Gentles, 'It's Only a Dream', in *Dream On, America: A History of Faith and Practice*, ed. Frederick Gentles and Melvin Steinfield (San Francisco: Canefield, 1971), 3.

15. Jim Cullen, *The American Dream: A Short History of an Idea that Shaped a Nation* (New York: Oxford University Press, 2004).

16. Fisher, 'Reaffirmation and Subversion of the American Dream'.

17. See Robert Fossum and John K. Roth, *The American Dream* (Durham: British Association for American Studies, 1981), http://www.baas.ac.uk/index.php?option=com_content&view=article&id=216%3Arobert-h-fossum-a-john-k-roth-the-american-dream&catid=18&Itemid=11 (accessed 16 January 2014); Gentles, 'It's Only a Dream'; Cullen, *The American Dream*; Charles R. Hearn, *The American Dream in the Great Depression* (Westport, CT: Greenwood, 1977); Stewart Holbrook, *Dreamers of the American Dream* (Garden City, NY: Doubleday, 1957); Kenneth S. Lynn, *Dream of Success: A Study of the Modern American Imagination* (Boston: Little, Brown, 1955); Ernest G. Bormann, *The Force of Fantasy: Restoring the American Dream* (Carbondale: Southern Illinois University Press, 1985).

18. James Truslow Adams, *The Epic of America* (Boston: Little, Brown, 1931).

19. Ibid., viii.

20. Ibid., 410–11. The Ford references occur a few pages earlier.

21. Ibid.

22. Daniel J. Boorstin, *The Image or, What Happened to the American Dream* (New York: Atheneum, 1962), 240.

23. McGee, 'The "Ideograph": A Link Between Rhetoric and Ideology'. See also Celeste Michelle Condit and John Louis Lucaites, *Crafting Equality: America's Anglo-African Word* (Chicago: University of Chicago Press, 1993).

24. Horace M. Kallen, *The Decline and Rise of the Consumer: A Philosophy of Consumer Cooperation* (New York: D. Appleton Century, 1936), 198.

25. Sigmund Freud, *The Interpretation of Dreams* (New York: Avon, 1998).

26. Quoted in Fossum and Roth, *The American Dream*, para. 34.

27. Cullen, *The American Dream*, 184.

28. Lloyd F. Bitzer, 'The Rhetorical Situation', *Philosophy & Rhetoric*, 1, no. 1 (1968), 6.

29. Lynn, *Dream of Success*; John William Tebbel, *From Rags to Riches: Horatio Alger, Jr. and the American Dream* (New York: MacMillan, 1963).

30. Lynn, *Dream of Success*, 9.

31. See Raymond Williams, *Keywords: A Vocabulary of Culture and Society* (New York: Oxford University Press, 1985).

32. Charles J. V. Murphy, 'Mr. Ford's Legacy', in *The Best of Ford: A Collection of Short Stories and Essays*, ed. Mary Moline (Van Nuys, CA: Rumbleseat, 1973), 334; William Adams Simonds, *Henry Ford: His Life, His Work, His Genius* (Los Angeles: F. Clymer, 1946), 107, 4, 279.

33. Ginny Olson, 'Fordisms: A Collection', in *The Best of Ford: A Collection of Short Stories and Essays*, ed. Mary Moline (Van Nuys, CA: Rumbleseat, 1973), 343.

34. Marsh, 'Fitzgerald, Gatsby, and The Last Tycoon', 9.

35. Larry May, *Screening Out the Past: The Birth of Mass Culture and the Motion Picture Industry* (New York: Oxford University Press, 1980), 216.

36. Ibid., 217.

37. Fisher, 'Reaffirmation and Subversion of the American Dream'.

38. Frank Nugent, 'That Million-Dollar Mouse', in *Walt Disney: Conversations*, ed. Kathy Merlock Jackson (Jackson: University Press of Mississippi, 2006), xii.

39. These are all choruses to popular songs from Disney's features.

40. Quoted in Steven Watts, *The Magic Kingdom: Walt Disney and the American Way of Life* (Boston: Houghton Mifflin, 1997), 47.

41. Ibid.

42. Ibid., 30.

43. Gregory A. Waller, 'Mickey, Walt, and Film Criticism from Steamboat to Bambi', in *The American Animated Cartoon: A Critical Anthology*, ed. Danny Peary and Gerald Peary (New York: Dutton, 1980), 53.

44. Stefan Kanfer, *Serious Business: The Art and Commerce of Animation in America from* Betty Boop *to* Toy Story (New York: Scribner, 1997), 108.

45. Quoted in Michael Barrier, *The Animated Man: A Life of Walt Disney* (Berkeley: University of California Press, 2008), 297.

46. Quoted in Watts, *The Magic Kingdom*, 397.

47. Robert D. Feild, *The Art of Walt Disney* (New York: Macmillan, 1942), 80, 75.

48. Quoted in Bob Thomas, *Walt Disney: An American Original* (New York: Simon & Schuster, 1976), 153.

49. All of the quotations come from Walt Disney, 'Walt Disney Quotations', Thinkexist.com, http://thinkexist.com/quotes/walt_disney/ (accessed 16 January 2014).

50. Luca Raffaelli, 'Disney, Warner Brothers, and Japanese Animation: Three World Views', in *A Reader in Animation Studies*, ed. Jayne Pilling (London: J. Libbey, 1997), 117.

51. Norman Vincent Peale, 'The American Dream Still Bursts Forth', *Spokesman Review Sunday Magazine*, 2 July 1972.

52. Bill Capodagli and Lynn Jackson, *The Disney Way: Harnessing the Management Secrets of Disney in Your Company* (New York: McGraw-Hill, 1999), 15.

53. Sergei Eisenstein, *Eisenstein on Disney*, ed. Jay Leyda (Calcutta: Seagull, 1986), 39.

54. Critics continually target Disney, bemoaning the association with wonder, magic and innocence, portraying such feelings as the tasty but unhealthy bait that traps unsuspecting viewers in a nationalist, sexist, heterosexist, racist and especially consumerist ideology. Stacy Warren wonders if anything is 'more universally reviled': Stacey Warren, 'Saying No to Disney: Disney's

Demise in Four American Cities', in *Rethinking Disney: Private Control, Public Dimensions*, ed. Mike Budd and Max H. Kirsch (Middletown, CT: Wesleyan University Press, 2005), 16.

55. Richard Schickel, *The Disney Version: The Life, Times, Art and Commerce of Walt Disney* (New York: Simon & Schuster, 1968), 10.

56. See Thomas Frank, *The Conquest of Cool: Business Culture, Counterculture, and the Rise of Hip Consumerism* (Chicago: University of Chicago Press, 1998).

57. Douglas Brode, *From Walt to Woodstock: How Disney Created the Counterculture* (Austin: University of Texas Press, 2004), 233.

58. Kunzle, 'Introduction to the English Edition', 18.

Chapter 8

1. Gilles Deleuze, 'Postscript on Control Societies', in *Negotiations: 1972–1990* (New York: Columbia University Press, 1995), 178–9, 180.

2. Quoted in Steven Watts, *The Magic Kingdom: Walt Disney and the American Way of Life* (Boston: Houghton Mifflin, 1997), 160.

3. Deleuze, 'Postscript on Control Societies', 180.

4. Lev Manovich, *The Language of New Media* (Cambridge, MA: MIT Press, 2001).

5. Isaac Victor Kerlow, *The Art of 3D Computer Animation and Effects* (Hoboken, NJ: John Wiley, 2009).

6. Vivian Sobchack, 'Animation and Automation, Or, The Incredible Effortfulness of Being', *Screen*, 50, no. 4 (Winter 2009), 375–91.

7. Ryan Cracknell, 'Wall-E', *Movie Views*, 7 November 2008, http://movie views.ca/wall-e (accessed 16 January 2014).

8. See Tim Hauser, *The Art of Wall-E* (San Francisco: Chronicle, 2008).

9. Steven A. Johnson, *Interface Culture* (New York: Basic, 1997), 81–2.

10. Deleuze, 'Postscript on Control Societies', 181.

11. For an examination of the potential and limitations of many of these anti-consumerist and anti-corporate movements, see Christine Harold, *OurSpace: Resisting the Corporate Control of Culture* (Minneapolis: University of Minnesota Press, 2007).

12. Jaron Lanier, *Who Owns the Future?* (New York: Simon & Schuster, 2013), 169–74.

13. Castells has outlined this 'libertarian' culture of digital media. See Manuel Castells, *The Internet Galaxy: Reflections on the Internet, Business, and Society* (New York: Oxford University Press, 2001), 36–63. Evgeny Morozov has critiqued this 'freedom'-centred ideology: Evgeny Morozov, *The Net Delusion: The Dark Side of Internet Freedom* (New York: PublicAffairs, 2011).

Index